Mindfulness-Based Cognitive Therapy *for* Anxious Children

A Manual for Treating Childhood Anxiety

RANDYE J. SEMPLE, PhD
JENNIFER LEE, PhD

New Harbinger Publications, Inc.

"Anxiety Got the Best of Me" by Denis Kucharski, copyright © 2008 by Denis Kucharski. Used with permission.

"So Just Be" copyright © 2007, "No Man's Land" copyright © 2002, "Magic Show" copyright © 2005, "I Don't Take Criticism Well" copyright © 2007, and "River of Feelings" copyright © 2005 by William Menza. Used with permission.

Excerpt from MINDFULNESS-BASED COGNITIVE THERAPY FOR DEPRESSION by Zindel V. Segal, J. Mark Williams, and John D. Teasdale, copyright © 2002 by Guilford Press. Used by permission of Guilford Press.

Distributed in Canada by Raincoast Books

Copyright © 2011 by Randye J. Semple and Jennifer Lee
New Harbinger Publications, Inc.
5674 Shattuck Avenue
Oakland, CA 94609
www.newharbinger.com

FSC
Mixed Sources
Product group from well-managed
forests and other controlled sources
Cert no. SW-COC-002283
www.fsc.org
© 1996 Forest Stewardship Council

Illustrations copyright © Denise McMorrow Mahone, 2011

Cover design by Amy Shoup; Acquired by Catharine Meyers, Edited by Jean Blomquist

Library of Congress Cataloging in Publication Data on file

Semple, Randye J.
Mindfulness-based cognitive therapy for anxious children : a manual for treating childhood anxiety / Randye J. Semple and Jennifer Lee.
  p. ; cm.
Includes bibliographical references.
ISBN 978-1-57224-719-2 (pbk.) -- ISBN 978-1-57224-720-8 (PDF e-book)
1. Anxiety in children. 2. Cognitive therapy for children. I. Lee, Jennifer, 1972- II. Title.
[DNLM: 1. Anxiety Disorders--therapy. 2. Adolescent. 3. Child. 4. Cognitive Therapy--methods. 5. Psychotherapy, Group. WM 172]
  RJ506.A58S46 2011
  618.92'8522--dc23

                                    2011012685

13   12   11

10   9   8   7   6   5   4   3   2   1   First printing

To the children

Contents

Part 3
MBCT-C in Perspective

Foreword

A man was talking to his three-year-old grandson. The little boy was pleased because his dad had been showing him the rudiments of how to play chess. His grandfather asked which of the pieces he liked best. He pointed to the knight. "The horse," he said. "Why the horse?" asked his grandfather. "Because it can go both down and across."

Randye Semple and Jennifer Lee have made, in this book, the knight's move. They have gone both down and across. After much time and thought, they have taken a mindfulness-based intervention developed for adults with recurrent depression and skillfully taken it "down" a generation from adults to children, and then "across" from depression to anxiety. Then they waited until they had carefully evaluated the efficacy of their approach, and the book you hold in your hands is the result.

To make such a knight's move takes enormous skill, perseverance, and clinical wisdom. Not only did they need to understand the core intentions of the original MBSR (mindfulness-based stress reduction) and MBCT (mindfulness-based cognitive therapy) programs, but they also needed to find a way to address the very specific mechanisms that both clinical experience and research tell us are the factors that maintain and exacerbate anxiety in children.

This is our task in treatment development. We cannot assume that an intervention that is helpful for one community, one age group, or one diagnosis will be helpful for another. If we learn one thing from the cumulative research findings of psychological treatments over the past thirty years, it is that the vulnerability factors and triggering factors—especially the *maintaining* factors—for different types of psychological problems are different, and need to be specifically addressed to offer the most freedom from suffering to those who come to us for help.

Unless we are teaching a class for people who have a wide range of problems and diagnoses, we need to keep the fundaments of the curriculum intact and yet also adapt the way they are offered. So, if we are offering a class for people who come with specific issues, such as recurrent depression, general anxiety, social phobia, eating disorders, cancer, addiction, or psychosis, or for those with no "diagnosis" but who wish to prepare for an event such as childbirth, in these different situations there are core issues that all share, but there are also differences in the way that suffering is maintained—different "vortices" into which they can be drawn. When we see these differences clearly, offering a generic "cognitive" approach or a generic "mindfulness" approach that does not address these differences is to offer less than the best.

With this in mind, Randye Semple and Jennifer Lee have developed a twelve-session, ninety-minute-per-week program (sixty minutes a week if offered to individual children rather than a class). It is a program specifically for children whose lives are dominated by their worries, anxieties, and daily stressors. In this book you will find help in both the practices and the way they are expressed, because they can be understood, in heart and mind, by children, their parents, and the clinicians themselves: "Listening to the Sounds of Silence," "Mindfully Moooving Slooowly," or knowing "What the Nose Knows." These classes are fun to do.

Of course, we know the dangers of having such specific instruction in a manual: it looks like an invitation to start to teach the program before understanding it from the inside. From the outset, therefore, this book assumes that clinicians have their own mindfulness practice. Without an on-going practice, a clinician is sending young and vulnerable participants on a journey they themselves are not on. The practices used in MBCT-C, as in MBSR and MBCT, are introducing participants to a completely different mode of being: it is a different landscape of the mind, and requires a different (experiential) understanding from the one we are accustomed to in therapy. It is like venturing up a high mountain range for the first time: better with a guide, but we need to find a reliable guide who actually walks the terrain regularly, not one who just loves to study maps.

Making the knight's move in treatment development, and knowing where to adapt and where to stay with an existing practice are hard to do. Clinicians and those who seek their help will have reason to be glad that these authors had a passion for this work and stayed with it until they had a scientifically proven approach. It will bring benefit to many, many children and their families.

Mark Williams
John Teasdale
Zindel Segal

November 2010

Acknowledgments

This book came into being with the encouragement and caring support of a great many people. I would like to offer my deep appreciation to Richard H. Lathrop, a very special friend, who offered his many insightful and constructive suggestions with great loving-kindness. In addition, Rick's meticulous editing of the initial drafts was invaluable to us. The fourteen thousand words he removed now sit in a large jar on my desk as a reminder to be more concise next time. We have learned that publishing a book is more complex than we ever imagined. I would like to express my gratitude to Ann Lathrop for her wise advice about all those small publishing details that authors really do need to know. Many thanks to Beatrice L. Wood for her encouragement and thoughtful critique of earlier drafts. My very special thanks to Tenzin Robert A. F. Thurman. His good humor, directness, and talent for cutting through confusion were tremendously helpful. Lastly, I offer my wholehearted appreciation to my spiritual teachers, Ken McLeod and Thanissaro Bhikkhu (Ajaan Geoff), for their scholarship and skillfulness at translating the dharma, and especially for two decades of patience with my incessant questions about Buddhism. In part, our treatment model emerged from their profound dharma wisdom.

—RJS

I express my deepest gratitude to my parents, Moon Jung and Won Jay Lee, who, through their example and devotion, taught me the value of pursuing work that I love. I am evermore grateful for my sisters, Lisa Lee and Julie Lewe, for their loving counsel and support throughout each step of the process. To my family, thank you for being the first inspiration. I express my heartfelt appreciation to my mentors, including David A. Crenshaw, Richmond Greene, Roni Beth Tower, and Suzanne Button. With their compassionate wisdom, they have graciously pointed the way to true north. I'd like to offer a special acknowledgment to the memory of John Moseley, my beloved teacher, who taught me all that I know about writing and what it means to write from the heart. I am especially indebted to Scott Jeffrey for his countless hours of encouragement, for generously sharing his intimate knowledge of publishing, and for his uncanny, elvish ability to see what lies ahead. Thank you for your caring presence on this journey.

—JL

Adapting many of the concepts and approaches from mindfulness-based cognitive therapy (MBCT), we were fortunate to have received long-standing support and encouragement from the developers of that program. We would like to express our gratitude and offer many thanks to Zindel V. Segal, John D. Teasdale, and J. Mark G. Williams, whose insights and experiences have been invaluable to the evolution of this program. We are honored that Jon Kabat-Zinn, developer of mindfulness-based stress reduction (MBSR), shared with us some of the profound understandings gained over his many years of practice and teaching. We offer our deep appreciation to Jon for his generous review of earlier drafts of the manuscript and for helping us write about complex concepts with clarity and attention to each word. We express our sincere gratitude to Lisa Miller for her devoted mentoring over the years and for inspiring us to follow our hearts. We thank Dinelia Rosa for supporting our work with her astute clinical wisdom and expertise. And to the loving memory of the late Barbara Principe, who graciously introduced us to the children and their families. The program and its development were wholly inspired by the wisdom of these esteemed teachers.

Our illustrator, Denise McMorrow Mahone, deserves a very special acknowledgment. At what may well have been the busiest time of her life, Denise generously contributed her remarkable artistic talents and many thousands of her precious moments to prepare the original, creative, and beautifully integrated drawings you see throughout the handouts.

Many other people enthusiastically donated their time, talents, and knowledge to the development of mindfulness-based cognitive therapy for children (MBCT-C). We offer our thanks and gratitude to Marla R. Brassard, Sarah Brazaitis, Marisol Cunnington, Daphne D. Edwards, Barry A. Farber, Mirna E. Gonzales, Christy Ann Hall, Bruce Hubbard, Robert E. Kelly Jr., Lisa Kentgen, Robert L. Leahy, Patrecia Lenore, Mark Lukowitsky, Susan Masullo, David Mellins, MaryAnn Mustac, Xavier Naranjo, Carol Nasr, Dolores Perin, Beatriz Plaza, Migdalia Rodriguez-DelValle, Brigid Shogan, Ferris Urbanowski, Helena Verdeli, Polly Wheat, Mary M. Whelley, Bettina Wolf, and Justyna Zapolska. We thank the Center for Integrative Studies and Teachers College, Columbia University, for providing research funding for the project.

We are especially grateful to the staff at New Harbinger Publications for their mindful attention to each step in the creation of this book. We extend our sincere gratitude to Matthew McKay for believing in this project. We'd like to thank the editorial manager, Jess Beebe, for providing valuable feedback in the early stages of the process. We appreciate all of the time Heather Garnos, the prepublication director, and Jean M. Blomquist, the copyeditor, put into this book and their meticulous attention to every detail. We greatly appreciate the help of Michele Waters, Jesse Burson, Jeannette Mann, Julia Kent, Amy Shoup, and Nelda Street for their coordinated efforts in bringing the book into being. We particularly wish to recognize Catharine Meyers, our acquisitions director. Catharine gave us cheerful support and wholehearted encouragement from start to finish. The team at New Harbinger has been simply wonderful to work with.

Lastly, we extend our warmest appreciation to the families for their enthusiastic involvement in MBCT-C. We are forever grateful to the children who took part in the program, gave their devoted attention to bringing mindfulness into their own lives, and in the process, inspired us and touched our hearts.

—RJS & JL

Introduction

In our work as clinical psychologists, we see the suffering experienced by many children with anxiety disorders. Suffering may be intensified when thoughts and feelings *about* the experiences are not differentiated from direct perceptions *of* the experiences. For many children, anxious thoughts and feelings can feel more real than the actual anxiety-provoking situation. When we taught mindful awareness practices to children, we found that some changed how they related to their own thoughts and feelings. Some children realized that what they infer is not necessarily true, what they fear is not necessarily real, and thoughts are just thoughts.

We wrote this book to share with you a psychotherapy that may help children with anxiety experience less suffering. Mindfulness-based cognitive therapy for children (MBCT-C) is a twelve-session therapy developed for children between the ages of nine and twelve. With age-appropriate modifications, MBCT-C may be useful with children a few years older or younger. Initially developed as a group intervention, we also offer suggestions for conducting MBCT-C with a single child. This book, with its accompanying CD-ROM, provides detailed instructions for conducting each session and includes reproducible written materials and handouts. The session summaries and home practices found in appendix C should be read in conjunction with the instructions for each session. The structured program presented here is intended to help children become more aware, moment by moment, of their multifaceted journey through life.

A few important points are foundational for the material that follows. First, MBCT-C is not a spiritual practice. Second, it is not a conventional cognitive therapy. Third, MBCT-C integrates psychological models that may seem contradictory—because mindfulness promotes accepting things as they are, while cognitive therapy promotes changing things we don't like. Fourth, it challenges us as therapists to abandon the desire for change in our clients, even though change is a time-honored goal of therapy. Finally, MBCT-C offers us opportunities to incorporate mindfulness into our own lives. Let's look briefly now at each point.

MBCT-C is not a spiritual practice. Mindfulness-based therapies have grown quickly in acceptance and popularity. Several, including MBCT-C, integrate Buddhist meditative practices. Buddhist psychology describes a perspective about the world that is quite different from Western thought. It expresses clear ideas about how to be happy in the world, of which practicing mindful awareness is but one component. Mindfulness means paying careful, nonjudgmental attention—in the present moment—to our rich and complex inner and outer worlds. As therapists, we do not teach Buddhist religious precepts to children, but we adopt a mindfulness-based approach and encourage children to cultivate greater awareness because it is often helpful.

MBCT-C is not a conventional cognitive therapy. Cognitive therapy is effective in treating anxiety for many, but not for all. Many children (one-third to one-half) respond to it only partially or not at all. Cognitive therapy assumes that distorted thoughts can increase anxiety, so changing those thoughts can decrease anxiety. In short, cognitive therapy teaches children to change what they think. In contrast, MBCT-C assumes that how we relate to our thoughts, feelings, and body sensations can increase anxiety, so finding a different way to relate to these experiences can reduce anxiety. In other words, MBCT-C teaches children greater awareness and acceptance of the thoughts, feelings, and body sensations that contribute to their felt experiences.

MBCT-C and cognitive therapy are paradoxical models of acceptance and change. MBCT-C integrates successful elements of cognitive therapy into a complementary mindfulness-based paradigm. In many ways, these models work very well together. In other ways, they are paradoxical, because cognitive therapy is focused on change while mindfulness is focused on acceptance. As children cultivate greater awareness of their experiences, they can also cultivate compassionate acceptance of those experiences. In practice, as acceptance grows, profound changes may occur in thoughts and behaviors.

MBCT-C challenges us to abandon the desire for change. As therapists, our work involves offering interventions to help children. Because of the focus in MBCT-C on acceptance instead of change, the way its "interventions" are used may seem incongruous. Paradoxically, we seek to create change by accepting things just as they are. MBCT-C seeks to change not thoughts but how children relate to thoughts. In other words, we hope to cultivate acceptance from nonacceptance.

In practicing mindful awareness and acceptance, children can learn to apprehend the world in different and perhaps more adaptive ways—and then intentionally choose to make changes. By enabling the child to accept herself and her life exactly as they are, we fertilize the ground from which changes can emerge spontaneously. The most difficult component of MBCT-C for a conventionally trained therapist may be to abandon the desire for change. In some ways, we offer instructions in how *not* to change. Letting go of the desire to change may in itself catalyze significant changes.

MBCT-C offers us opportunities to incorporate mindfulness into our own lives. You may be reading this book with a personal interest in incorporating mindfulness into your own life. The traditional way is to sit on a cushion and watch the breath. How can this simple activity effect meaningful life changes?

Mindful awareness, in part, is simply paying attention to life as it is. This may sound easy, but it is not. For most, the practices themselves are not difficult. Remembering to practice can be more challenging. We believe that the only way to understand mindfulness is to practice bringing mindful awareness to your life. Your teachings must be grounded in an experiential understanding. We hope that your personal commitment to practice will bring about transformations as profound as those you hope to see in the children you serve.

PART 1

A Mindfulness-Based Approach to Treating Childhood Anxiety

CHAPTER 1

Dancing Between Two Worlds: Buddhist Psychology and Cognitive Psychology

All that we are arises with our thoughts. With our thoughts, we create the world.

>The Buddha (*Dhammapada*, classic Buddhist text, circa 5th century BCE)

Individuals are often emotionally affected by the way they cognitively distort interpretations of their world, their future, and their self.

>Aaron T. Beck (*Cognitive Therapy of Depression*, 1979)

This is a book about conducting mindfulness-based cognitive therapy with children. Mindfulness-based psychotherapies are neither religious nor spiritual practices, and religious or spiritual practices are not integral to psychotherapy—so you may wonder why we begin by discussing Buddhist psychology and meditation practices.

The psychotherapy described in this book incorporates Buddhist meditation practices into a conventional Western cognitive therapy. This blend creates an interesting dialectic, in part because cognitive therapy aims for remediation of specific deficits while Buddhist practices cultivate spiritual transformation. Nevertheless, as Alan Watts (1961) suggested, "If we look deeply into such ways of life as Buddhism,…we do not find either philosophy or religion…we find something more nearly resembling psychotherapy… The main resemblance between Eastern ways of life and Western psychotherapy is in the concern of both with bringing about changes of consciousness, changes in our ways of feeling our own existence and our relation to human society and the natural world" (pp. 3–4).

Spiritual teachers and psychotherapists both seek to reduce human suffering, but their approaches and methods derive from quite different worldviews. We do not seek to map one onto the other. Ken McLeod, a Buddhist teacher and scholar knowledgeable about both perspectives, observed (perhaps tongue-in-cheek) that Western psychology assumes that most of us are sane and only a few of us are crazy, while Buddhist psychology is based on the understanding that most of us are crazy and only a few of us are sane.

Notwithstanding their considerable differences, a number of next-generation Western psychotherapies incorporate approaches and techniques from Eastern contemplative traditions. Collectively these are becoming known as the "third wave" of behavioral and cognitive therapies (Hayes, 2004). Some interventions may look like Buddhist meditation practices. Nevertheless, we are therapists, and this book is about psychotherapy, not religious or spiritual practices.

WHAT IS MINDFULNESS ANYWAY?

No single English word precisely captures the Buddhist concept of mindfulness. It has been treated inconsistently as a state of consciousness, an active process, and a set of techniques (D. A. Shapiro, 1987). The Pali word *sati* (*smrti* in Sanskrit) is generally translated as "mindfulness." *Sati* literally means "that which is remembered" (Pio, 1988), but also means attention, awareness, consciousness, alertness, recognition, remembering, intentness, wakefulness or lucidity of mind, self-possession, presence of mind, self-consciousness, and insight. *Sati* can be an activity; a state of mind; a non-conceptual awareness; or a moment-by-moment, nonjudgmental watchful-ness—sometimes described as the direct apprehension of reality. Gunaratana (1993) suggested that mindfulness is that brief instant of pure awareness just before conceptualization arises—the moment *before* we say, "Oh yes, that is a cat." Mindfulness is easily understood as an experiential practice, yet extremely difficult to describe in words.

Enhancement of attention is a defining characteristic of mindfulness (Bishop et al., 2004; Washburn, 1978). S. R. Bishop and colleagues (2004) proposed that "[m]indfulness is a process of regulating attention in order to bring a quality of nonelaborative awareness to current experience and a quality of relating to one's experience within an orientation of curiosity, experiential openness, and acceptance" (p. 234). Hendricks (1975) described it as the moment-by-moment practice of discriminating thoughts and emotions from external events. Jon Kabat-Zinn (1994) defined mindfulness as "paying attention in a particular way: on purpose, in the present moment, and nonjudgmentally" (p. 4). At its most basic level, mindful awareness is the cultivation of attention.

Mindful awareness can be learned and seems to enhance components of attention (Baer, 2003; Chambers, Lo, & Allen, 2008; Jha, Krompinger, & Baime, 2007; Semple, 2010; Tang et al., 2007). To cultivate mindfulness is to refine the capacity for awareness—of whatever occurs in each moment as it occurs. Mindful awareness helps us see that idiosyncratic thoughts and feelings may relate to, but are different from, external events. With mindful-ness, we practice *looking* so that we may learn to *see*, rather than distorting events with cognitive elaborations or emotional filters. By cultivating mindful attention, we learn simply to observe anxious thoughts and feelings, which enhances the ability to respond consciously to events (Deikman, 1996).

DIFFERENT FRAMEWORKS FOR UNDERSTANDING

Contemporary psychotherapists seek to understand and relieve psychological suffering. "How might I help this child feel better?" is a question that guides most therapists. In one of Buddhism's core teachings, known as the "four noble truths," mindfulness is a means to wisdom (or enlightenment), which is the state of perfect mental health. The four noble truths might be interpreted as diagnosing a distressing psychological symptom, describing its etiology, offering a prognosis, and outlining a treatment plan. The first noble truth describes the universality of *dukkha*, which is often translated as "suffering." Dukkha refers to the unhappiness that arises from pushing away unwanted experiences, clinging to desired experiences, and the general sense of dis-ease or unsatisfactoriness that is so pervasive in life. The etiology of the problem of dukkha is described in the second truth. The third truth offers a prognosis, and the fourth describes in detail the appropriate treatments (Dhammananada, 1993).

The seminal book *Anxiety Disorders and Phobias: A Cognitive Perspective* (Beck & Emery, 1985) discusses cognitive psychology's perspective on anxiety. Beck and Emery list the symptoms associated with anxiety disorders, identify factors that contribute to its etiology and maintenance, offer a prognosis for those who suffer from it, and describe specific treatments believed to reduce it. Table 1 lists some of the basic precepts of Buddhist and cognitive psychologies of anxiety. Although both aim to reduce suffering, their assumptions, strategies, processes, and mechanisms are different.

Table 1. Perspectives from Buddhist and Cognitive Psychologies

The Problem	Buddhist Psychology	Cognitive Psychology
1. Nature	The world is perfect exactly as it is (including its imperfections), but is not always exactly as we would like it to be. For most of us, therefore, life inevitably includes suffering.	Anxiety is a normal human experience. Some anxiety is adaptive. A minority of people experience excessive or unwarranted anxiety, which is distressing, impairing, and pathological.

The Problem	Buddhist Psychology	Cognitive Psychology
2. Etiology	Suffering is caused by attachment to things that are intrinsically impermanent. Everything is impermanent.	Cognitive distortions can create and maintain the emotional and behavioral symptoms associated with anxiety disorders.
	Attachments arise from false beliefs and expectations that are incongruent with reality.	Maladaptive schemas and distorted cognitions represent a mismatch between perceptual interpretations and the environment.
3. Prognosis	The cessation of suffering is attainable.	Anxiety disorders are treatable.
4. Treatment	The noble eightfold path leads to the cessation of suffering.	Cognitive therapy (CT) leads to the reduction or elimination of anxiety symptoms.
	The eightfold path describes a lifetime cultivation of disciplined practices and behaviors.	CT is a short-term therapy that focuses on learning specific skills and adaptive behaviors.
	The ultimate aim is to achieve the end of suffering.	The ultimate aim is to alleviate anxiety symptoms.
	The three domains of interest are wisdom, ethical conduct, and mental discipline.	The three domains of interest are thoughts, feelings, and behaviors.

The Problem	Buddhist Psychology	Cognitive Psychology
	Wisdom (*Prajñā*) • Right view • Right intention	Changing distorted or maladaptive thinking leads to changes in emotional states and behaviors.
		Thoughts are examined using Socratic questioning methods.
	Ethical conduct (*Śīla*) • Right speech • Right action • Right livelihood	Examining thoughts is done kindly, not judgmentally nor self-critically.
		Homework and practice are important.
		Client and therapist work collaboratively.
	Mental Discipline (*Samādhi*) • Right effort • Right mindfulness • Right concentration	Specific strategies are practiced to restructure distorted thoughts.
		Observing thoughts is a prerequisite to changing them.
		Treatment goals are clearly defined.

CONTRADICTORY OR COMPLEMENTARY WORLDVIEWS?

Buddhist and cognitive psychologies share a few basic concepts and principles. They are united by the desire to understand the workings of the mind and to apply that understanding to reduce human suffering. Both psychologies share the insight that thoughts do not always reflect reality accurately. In other ways, however, Buddhist and cognitive psychologies hold incompatible worldviews, and reconciling the differences may be a challenge for a conventionally trained therapist. Let's examine how these curious bedfellows might complement each other in a mindfulness-based cognitive therapy framework.

An Apple Is Not an Orange

We begin with a few words of caution about ignoring the subtle and not-so-subtle differences between Buddhist and cognitive psychologies. Modern cognitive psychology began about fifty years ago. A Buddhist theory of mind was clearly defined over two millennia ago. Cognitive psychology focuses on cognitions, cognitive information processing, and the ensuing behaviors. Buddhist psychology enumerates basic functions of the mind in an effort to comprehend phenomenological reality. With differing aims, times, cultures, and worldviews, it's simply not possible to translate some concepts directly from one to the other. For example, they have radically differing perspectives on anxiety. Let's look at the concept of anxiety in Buddhist psychology.

The *Abhidhamma* is an ancient scholarly text that explains the Buddhist psychology of mind. It describes multiple states of mind, provides a detailed compendium of cognitive processes, and defines fifty-two discrete mental factors along with their attributes and interrelationships (Bhikkhu Bodhi, 1993). Unlike cognitive psychology, thoughts and emotions are not clearly differentiated; instead, these mental factors contribute to the quality of experiences. Changes in suffering are the primary construct of interest. The *Abhidhamma* classifies mental factors as being wholesome or unwholesome based on the likelihood of that factor decreasing or increasing suffering. For example, mindfulness, compassion, and empathic joy are wholesome mental factors. Hatred, envy, greed, conceit, and doubt are unwholesome ones. These concepts are broadly consistent with Western psychology.

Among the fifty-two mental factors described in the *Abhidhamma*, anxiety and worry are not represented. No word in Pali or Sanskrit translates precisely to the emotion we know as anxiety or to the cognitive concept of worry. Does this mean that people living in ancient India did not experience anxiety and worry? This seems unlikely. The Pali word closest to worry may be *kukkucca*, which is defined as a restlessness associated with knowledge of taking an action that one knows to be unwholesome (Bhikkhu Bodhi, 1993).

Buddhist psychology advises increasing one's motivation to avoid unwholesome actions in the first place and thereby avoid the suffering associated with *kukkucca* altogether.

In cognitive psychology, by contrast, *kukkucca* seems more closely associated with remorse, generally not considered a harmful emotion. Remorse may not feel pleasant, but it is often evidence of atonement, morality, or a precursor to reparative action (Proeve, 2001). We typically define the absence of remorse as severely psychopathic. Such differences—a list of mental factors that omits anxiety, contradictory beliefs about *kukkucca*—illustrate the pitfalls of trying to map one paradigm to the other.

Cognitive Psychology in a Nutshell: Changing Thoughts

Thoughts influence emotions and behaviors. Cognitive theories attempt to understand thoughts and cognitive processes in order to explain behaviors. From the perspective of cognitive theory, we are quasi-logical creatures who make choices based on (seemingly) sensible reasons. If thoughts are distorted and inaccurate, or assumptions are irrational and maladaptive, then we will make inappropriate choices. Since thoughts affect how we feel and behave, changing thoughts will change feelings and behaviors.

Buddhist Psychology in a Nutshell: Creating Our Own Suffering

Two universal truths are foundational in Buddhist psychology. First, everyone experiences pain. Pain is present in our lives in a multitude of ways. Pain, however, is not the same as suffering. Suffering is a distressing affective experience that arises when events in our lives are not precisely to our liking. Anxiety is a distressing affective experience that is suffering, not pain. Second, we often create our own suffering, and this is the central problem. Getting what we don't want is suffering. Not getting what we do want is suffering. Ultimately, clinging to anything impermanent is suffering (Dumoulin, 1994). The Buddhist understanding of the human condition was nicely captured by Walt Kelly and his cartoon character Pogo, who declared, "We have met the enemy and he is us."

Seeing Clearly

Buddhist psychology accepts that suffering exists, believes it is universal, and focuses on how to alleviate it. The core question is, "Can the mind function in such a way that it does not create more suffering for itself?" The conclusion is that learning to see clearly could enable us to cease creating our own suffering.

If the root of suffering is not seeing clearly, then what is it that prevents us from seeing clearly? Buddhist psychology suggests that one significant obstacle is our own thoughts—inaccurate beliefs, unrealistic expectations, and insatiable desires. Thinking is a cognitive elaboration about reality, not the direct apperception of reality. Thoughts may give rise to fixed beliefs, expectations, or desires, which then reshape our perceptions. Thoughts can be as agile as wild monkeys jumping from branch to branch and as uncontrollable as drunken elephants crashing through the forest. The mind sometimes feels like it has a mind of its own.

Each moment of experience is composed of a multitude of what we might call "moment-dots." Moment-dots consist of perceptions, sensations, thoughts, emotions, and interactions present in the moment. However, we tend to clump present moment-dots with seemingly similar moment-dots remembered from the past or ones that anticipate the future. We often add selected beliefs from the past, unrealistic expectations of the present, or fears and desires about the future. We efficiently connect all these distorted dots, stringing them together in a matrix of time and space, until a picture appears. The picture now feels familiar, cohesive, and satisfying.

The problem is that thoughts, beliefs, desires, and expectations are created in our minds and may be unrelated to the reality of current events. Our perceptions may be distorted. The picture may not accurately mirror reality. Living inside these distorted moment-dot pictures, we may construct inappropriate cognitive interpretations, experience emotional distress, or make unwise choices. From the perspective of Buddhist psychology, it's no wonder that most of us are not considered sane.

⁂ The Pursuit of Happiness

Helen walks into our office and announces that she's not happy because some unfavorable experiences have occurred. Beliefs emerge: "Bad things should never happen to me." Imagining a multitude of things that might go wrong in her life, she is worried and anxious. Anticipatory anxiety impairs her attention, increasing the probability that things will indeed go "wrong." Ruminating over how little control she has over events and people around her, unrealistic expectations emerge: "I expect other people to act the way I want them to." Other unrealistic and unattainable expectations are soon added: "Worrying about everything in advance will prevent bad things from happening." Sometimes she takes it personally and then gets depressed: "Bad things happen, so there must be something wrong with me." Trying to make sense of the world, she has created unrealistic beliefs, unreasonable expectations, and catastrophic anticipations that distort many of her moment-dots.

Inevitably something will go "wrong." This is the nature of life. We are not certain of many things, but we can assume that life will continue to present Helen with unfavorable experiences. Her picture of the world is composed of all her moment-dots distorted by beliefs and expectations that are not accurate to reality. Inside her distorted dot-picture, Helen is anxious and miserable. Her life is unsatisfactory. From any perspective, Helen's beliefs are pathological. Her worried, anxious efforts to avoid suffering are futile and perhaps even self-sabotaging.

Living in the Present

Attention seems to be like a pipeline: it can hold only so much. When we try to attend to too many things, the pipeline gets full, and attention to something else suffers. Thoughts consume attention. We think about what to wear, what to eat, what to do, our tasks, appointments, or upcoming events. We replay in our heads that lovely holiday in San Francisco or things that didn't get done yesterday. Thoughts keep going and going and going.

Attention given to past and future moments detracts from attention available to experience the present moment. We may spend more time replaying past moments or anticipating future ones than we spend living in the present. So we never saw the pale-pink rose blooming outside the window, never smelled its fragrance, never touched its soft velvet petals. We didn't taste the breakfast we hurriedly ate and can barely remember our drive to work. All those moments passed by unnoticed while we were attending to the world of thoughts inside our heads—thinking, thinking, thinking about the past and the future. What a waste of lovely present moments!

Children in general appear to spend less time in past or future ruminations than do adults. Children aged nine to twelve are beginning to develop abstract reasoning skills. Future events may seem distant. The relationship between current and future events may not be clear. Thinking may be concrete and focused on specifics. This is not to say that children are incapable of logical reasoning. Children as young as three or four can follow simple "if-then" (conditional) reasoning: "If I take my friend's cookie, then Mommy will make me go to my room." Nine- or ten-year-old children can extend their reasoning forward in time and increase the number of conditionals, but they still tend to produce direct, concrete relationships: "If I study hard all semester, then I'll get a good grade in math, and my dad will reward me by letting me have a dog."

Children with significant anxiety spend more time engaged in anxious or depressive ruminations and anticipatory worries than do those who are not anxious. An adult may worry about not being successful in life (expressing a long-term, abstract, and complex relationship). A child may worry about striking out during a baseball game (a short-term, specific, and uncomplicated relationship). The simple, immediate, concrete worries of children, however, can be just as distressing as the complex, long-term, abstract worries of an adult. Ruminations are still past oriented, and worries are still future oriented. The intervention for children and adults is the same—practice living in the present.

Life Is Not Always the Way We Want It to Be

Life is perfect exactly as it is, but it will not always be the way we want it to be. We all seem to have a tendency to "should" (or "shouldn't") on life. A child may say, "I should have gotten a better grade on my term paper," or "He should have let me play with his video game." Another favorite is "if only": "If only I were prettier, taller, thinner, richer...then I could be happy." "If only" we could accept the inevitable. When we expect sunny skies and it rains on our picnic, we may become unhappy. We may become anxious just thinking about the possibility of rain. When we stop and consider for a moment, rejecting our experiences seems pretty silly. Rain is just something that happens. There is no direct cause-and-effect relationship between rain and unhappiness. Grass doesn't become unhappy when it rains. Neither does a squirrel or a car. Why do we?

Anxious children often hold onto unrealistic beliefs, include them in their moment-dots, and connect those moment-dots to create pictures that may not resemble reality. To some extent, we all do this. Have you ever felt angry when someone cut in line, anxious about being late for an appointment, or ashamed about the unkind remark you made yesterday? These emotions arise in response to dot-pictures that contain at least one unrealistic belief or expectation. Buddhist and cognitive psychologies substantially agree that many of us are anxious and unhappy, and that false beliefs about reality are a big part of the problem. They differ significantly in their understandings of how many of us suffer these false beliefs and what to do about them.

MORE THINKING IS PROBABLY NOT THE SOLUTION

Cognitive therapy helps a child (1) identify her cognitive biases, (2) recognize that thoughts influence emotions and behaviors, (3) distance herself from her own idiosyncratic perspectives, and (4) develop more realistic self-statements (Beck, 1976). Some have argued that consistent mindfulness practices encourage comparable changes (De Silva, 1985). However, applying differing worldviews to cognitive or mindfulness-based therapies results in different approaches and interventions.

Changing the Contents of Thoughts

Cognitive therapy is based on changing thoughts in order to change emotions and behaviors. Cognitive factors, and particularly distorted interpretations of events and recurrent thoughts about stressful events, are believed to play a key role in the etiology and maintenance of anxiety disorders (Piacentini & Bergman, 2001). The principal intervention in cognitive therapy is cognitive restructuring. As therapists, we observe the content of the thoughts, identify their inaccuracies, and substitute more helpful thoughts.

Accepting the Process of Thinking

In contrast, mindful awareness involves observing the process of thinking. The practice is simply to watch thoughts being thoughts. With non-judgmental awareness, we notice whatever occurs. We may observe that thoughts come and go unbidden; sometimes they seem to be slow and drifting, other times they feel jittery and racing. We may note that sometimes thoughts appear in a logical, linear sequence, while other times they seem jumbled and disorganized. Mindful attention is not solely focused on what the thoughts are saying; it is also focused on the process of thinking—just watching what the thoughts are doing. This content versus process distinction is one fundamental difference between cognitive and mindfulness-based therapies.

Watching the process of thinking may promote four behavior-altering insights (Bhikkhu Bodhi, 1993). First, we may learn—from direct experience—that thoughts can, and sometimes do, distort our perceptions, affect our emotions, and change how we interpret events. Second, it often becomes apparent that some thoughts and associated emotions are habituated, conditioned reactions, which bear little resemblance to current events. Third, we may grow that thoughts are transient; they constantly come and go. Last, we may grow to appreciate how little control we have over them. Theoretically these four insights produce a way of seeing in which thoughts are accepted as just thoughts—as ever-changing, sometimes distorted phantoms. These insights create space between thoughts and the sometimes inappropriate emotions and behaviors that follow (Wenk-Sormaz, 2005), so the power of thoughts to influence our emotions and behaviors may decrease.

MBCT-C teaches acceptance, which means that, unlike cognitive therapy, we do not teach children to change their thoughts in any way. We do suggest that thoughts are "just" thoughts. We practice bringing greater awareness to thoughts—then letting them be. The acceptance we teach means staying present with whatever arises. It does not mean disengaging or adopting a passive, fatalistic attitude toward one's own life. Mindfulness teaches us how to be present and engaged with what Jon Kabat-Zinn (1990) calls the "full catastrophe" of life. Being present gives us more opportunities to take responsibility for our own lives.

EMOTIONS ARE NOT FACTS

Education to identify emotions, and to understand the relationships between thoughts, emotions, and behaviors, forms an essential component of both cognitive and mindfulness-based therapies. Children have a limited ability to recognize or discriminate different emotional states (Southam-Gerow & Kendall, 2000). Anxious children typically show a poor understanding of the variability of emotions (Daleiden & Vasey, 1997). Highly anxious children sometimes have difficulty separating their emotions from reality (Barlow, 2002). Life can be challenging for the anxious child who behaves as if her emotions were an accurate guide to events around her.

⁂ I Feel Anxious, Therefore…

Twelve-year-old Emily has always been a shy and quiet child, timid and usually uncomfortable interacting with other children. She never raises her hand or speaks in class. She fears that she will say something "stupid," and then everyone will laugh at her. Approaching adolescence with severe social anxieties, Emily frequently has harshly negative thoughts about herself. Emily says, "I feel like everyone is watching me and thinking what a loser I am." She began to report frequent headaches and stomach upsets that caused her to miss many days of school. The anxiety escalated until she refused to go to school, and then she was brought in for treatment.

Emily acts as if her emotions provide accurate information about her social interactions. She has a hard time differentiating her thoughts from her feelings. Anxious ruminations occupy much of her attentional "pipeline." She does not really see how the anxious thoughts and feelings contribute to her felt experiences. She can easily miss seeing things that might correct the false beliefs. By cultivating mindful awareness, Emily can learn to identify thoughts as "just thoughts." Thoughts will continue to be a part of her reality, but will no longer define it.

MINDFULNESS-BASED MODELS

Two other interventions provided the theoretical and practical foundations for MBCT-C: the mindfulness-based stress reduction program (MBSR) and mindfulness-based cognitive therapy (MBCT). Both are group interventions developed for adults. Appendix A provides information and training resources for MBSR and MBCT. One important characteristic differentiates these two programs from other interventions with a mindfulness orientation, such as dialectical behavior therapy (DBT) or acceptance and commitment therapy (ACT): the facilitator is expected to maintain a personal mindfulness practice. A core principle of MBSR and MBCT is that in order to effectively teach mindfulness, the facilitator must actively cultivate this awareness in her own life. MBSR instructors and MBCT therapists embody mindfulness as group participants. Such an understanding arises only from personal commitment and experience. This core principle also applies to MBCT-C. We will discuss the rationale for this, and suggest ways to cultivate a personal practice in chapter 3.

Mindfulness-Based Stress Reduction

The mindfulness-based stress reduction program (MBSR) was developed by Jon Kabat-Zinn at the University of Massachusetts Medical Center to help patients manage stress-related disorders and chronic pain conditions. In the past thirty years, more than eighteen thousand people have completed the eight-week MBSR program at the University's Center for Mindfulness. Tens of thousands more have completed one of hundreds of MBSR programs that are available around the world. Kabat-Zinn has written several books describing MBSR (J. Kabat-Zinn, 1990, 1994, 2005).

MBSR teaches thirty or more patient-participants in a structured group format with one instructor. Each weekly class lasts two and one-half hours. One additional daylong class allows for more intensive practice. Many centers offer regular daylong "booster" classes, open to all MBSR graduates. Instructor training programs are available for those interested in teaching MBSR.

If you do not already have an established mindfulness practice, we strongly encourage you to begin by participating in an MBSR course. MBSR teaches participants to practice bringing awareness to ordinary everyday experiences and provides guided instruction in various meditation practices, including mindfulness of the breath, mindfulness of the body (body scan), and mindfulness of movement (simple yoga postures). Guided inquiries follow each practice—bringing attention to the thoughts, feelings, and body sensations that influence our experiences. Participation in an MBSR course demands a significant personal commitment. The program includes forty-five minutes of daily home practice, six days each week. For some, finding the time to do this can be a challenge. The struggle to develop a daily discipline is, in itself, a mindful awareness practice and, we believe, one reason that an experiential understanding of mindfulness is essential.

Research has shown that MBSR can enhance stress management skills (Chiesa & Serretti, 2009) and reduce stress for people with serious medical disorders like cancer (Carlson, Ursuliak, Goodey, Angen, & Speca, 2001; Kwekkeboom, 2001; S. L. Shapiro, Bootzin, Figueredo, Lopez, & Schwartz, 2003) and HIV (Creswell, Myers, Cole, & Irwin, 2009; Sibinga et al., 2008), as well as general hospital and pain patients (J. Kabat-Zinn, Lipworth, & Burney, 1985), and patients with anxiety disorders and panic (J. Kabat-Zinn et al., 1992; Miller, Fletcher, & J. Kabat-Zinn, 1995). MBSR is also effective for individuals in high-stress situations, such as K–12 teachers (Anderson, Levinson, Barker, & Kiewra, 1999), medical students (S. L. Shapiro, Schwartz, & Bonner, 1998), prison inmates (Bowen et al., 2006; Samuelson et al., 2007), and inner-city residents (Roth & Robbins, 2004). Although MBSR was not originally intended to be a psychiatric intervention, today, it is widely used in the treatment of a range of psychiatric disorders.

Mindfulness-Based Cognitive Therapy

Major depression is a recurrent disorder. For patients with more than two previous episodes, relapse rates are over 80 percent (Teasdale, et al., 2000). Zindel Segal, Mark Williams, and John Teasdale (2002) sought a non-pharmacological intervention to remediate this high rate of relapse. Working closely with Jon Kabat-Zinn, they integrated aspects of cognitive therapy for depression into an MBSR model. Like MBSR, MBCT is conducted in groups with eight weekly two-and-a-half-hour sessions followed by daily home practices. Since MBCT is customized for clinical populations, the groups are smaller—generally no more than twelve participants with one therapist. Some therapists now incorporate an all-day session into MBCT.

MBCT teaches individuals who are in remission from a major depressive episode to become more aware of and cultivate a different relationship to thoughts, feelings, and body sensations. Mindful awareness helps to manage inevitable low moods by decentering from the negative cognitions before they spiral into a full-blown episode of depression. As with MBSR, ordinary daily experiences provide multiple opportunities to stay present with difficult thoughts and emotions. MBCT includes some techniques and worksheets adapted from cognitive therapy intended to help patients recognize mood-related thoughts, better understand the relationships between thoughts and moods, and learn to choose a skillful response to whatever thoughts, emotions, or situations may arise. At present, many therapists conducting MBCT are also trained cognitive therapists. Unlike cognitive therapy, however, MBCT does not attempt to restructure maladaptive cognitions.

A number of clinical trials have shown that MBCT can significantly reduce relapse rates for patients who have a history of three or more episodes of major depression (Crane et al., 2008; Eisendrath, et al., 2008; Kenny & Williams, 2007; Kingston, Dooley, Bates, Lawlor, & Malone, 2007; Kuyken et al., 2008; Ma & Teasdale, 2004; Ree & Craigie, 2007; Teasdale et al., 2000; Williams, Duggan, Crane, & Fennell, 2006; Williams, Teasdale, Segal, & Soulsby, 2000). MBCT has been shown to offer protection against depressive relapse on par with pharmacotherapy (Segal et al., 2010). Research has also been conducted using MBCT to treat patients with binge-eating disorder (Baer, Fischer, & Huss, 2005), generalized anxiety disorder (Evans et al., 2008), treatment-resistant depression (Eisendrath et al., 2008), anxiety (Finucane & Mercer, 2006), bipolar disorder (Williams et al., 2008), anxiety and insomnia (Yook et al., 2008), and primary insomnia (Heidenreich, Tuin, Pflug, Michal, & Michalak, 2006). Studies are underway to evaluate the effectiveness of a mindfulness-based relapse prevention program for alcohol and substance use disorders (Witkiewitz, Marlatt, & Walker, 2005). Developed more recently than MBSR, MBCT has fewer resources available for therapist training, but training opportunities are expanding.

Mindfulness-Based Cognitive Therapy for Children

Mindfulness-based cognitive therapy for children was adapted directly from MBSR and MBCT. Although the specific interventions used with children are different, the underlying theory, aims, and approaches are consistent with those programs. In chapter 4, we will describe the specific adaptations we made in order to work with children in this model and why those changes were necessary.

Mindfulness-based cognitive therapy for children (MBCT-C) is based on the premise that thoughts and emotions are not facts. A child first learns to observe and identify thoughts and emotions, then explores how the thoughts and emotions are related to her experiences. We aim to enhance the child's ability to construct a dot-picture that is more accurate to reality. Distortions in the dot-picture are likely to escalate anxiety. Engagement in mindfulness practices may interrupt habituated reactions, increase the opportunities to respond with greater awareness, and foster appropriate choices about how to respond (or not respond) to events. Enhanced awareness can strengthen the child's capacity to tolerate difficult thoughts, accept strong emotions, and manage more skillfully the situation at hand.

Before we discuss the aims of MBCT-C and how to work in this model of therapy, it's important that we take a closer look at childhood anxiety. This will be the focus of the next chapter.

CHAPTER 2

Understanding the Problem of Anxiety

Anxiety Got the Best of Me

Anxiety got the best of me
And made short work of my dreams
And stole my treasure
Taking this moment and whisking it away

Denis Kucharski (2008)

Throughout our lives, large and small stressors are inevitable, inescapable, and, for some, chronic. Worry, stress, anxiety, and perhaps even fear or terror are encountered in daily life. Children may feel pressured to excel in academics or competitive sports. They may live in poverty or crime-infested neighborhoods. Across psychological models of anxiety, such stressors contribute to the development and maintenance of anxiety spectrum disorders (see, for example, Kessler & Greenberg, 2002; Spielberger & Sarason, 1978; Watson, Mineka, Clark, & Starcevic, 1999). Children may feel vague, generalized apprehensions; develop specific worries and anxieties; experience stress-related physical symptoms; or engage in behavioral acting out. An anxiety disorder is more likely if a parent also has an anxiety disorder (Merikangas & Low, 2005). Estimated rates of heritability across the spectrum of anxiety disorders are 30 to 40 percent (Hettema, Neale, & Kendler, 2001). Genetics and the individual's temperament, family environment, and personal experiences become interacting contributors to anxiety. Feeling helpless to manage stressors is likely to exacerbate a child's anxieties even more. As mental health professionals, we can't change the genetic risk factors or (usually) change the child's family or environment. Mindfulness-based interventions offer an alternative approach that may help the child cultivate an intrinsic resiliency to stress. Enhanced self-awareness can lead to greater capacity and effectiveness in navigating difficult situations and circumstances.

ANXIETY IS GOOD?

Anxiety prepares us to meet the ordinary and extraordinary challenges encountered in day-to-day life. A well-documented finding is that moderate amounts of anxiety enhance physical and cognitive performance (Broadbent, 1971). Athletes "psych" themselves up before an important sports competition. Students study harder before exams. With too little anxiety, they are not motivated to perform their best. Anxiety also provides a built-in warning system that alerts us to dangers and potential threats.

The physiology of anxiety is particularly relevant when working with children. For many children, the somatic components of anxiety are more prominent than the cognitive or affective symptoms. Let's explore the physiology of anxiety and how it functions to protect us.

THE PHYSIOLOGY OF ANXIETY: TOO MUCH OF A GOOD THING

Human beings are hardwired to feel anxiety. Anxiety allowed our caveman ancestors to survive long enough to reproduce—when a bear showed up, only the anxious cavemen ran fast enough, fought hard enough, or hid quickly enough to survive. Anxiety helps to protect ourselves or our loved ones from danger. We have all heard tales of superhuman feats done under life-threatening circumstances. Anxiety is a good thing—except when we have too much of it.

The "fight-or-flight response," first described by Walter Cannon (1929), evolved as a system to ensure our safety and survival. It primes our bodies to mobilize, handle a perceived threat, and then return to baseline. The sympathetic nervous system (SNS) is central in activating this acute stress response, and the hypothalamic-pituitary-adrenal axis (HPA) is a primary component of this response system. When danger is anticipated, the brain sends warning messages to the hypothalamus, starting a sequence of events that releases adrenaline and norepinephrine from the adrenal gland. Adrenaline and norepinephrine make the heart pump faster, the lungs breathe faster, the muscles tense, the digestive system shut down, the body sweat and produce heat, and the attention concentrate on the potential threat. The entire HPA activation sequence is quick—happening within one second. Extreme HPA activation can trigger panic attacks. Chronic muscular tension, hypervigilance, and strong feelings of apprehension are common in children experiencing somewhat less acute or generalized anxiety.

Researchers now prefer the term "allostasis" to describe the stress reaction (McEwen, 2002). Allostasis refers to the body's ability to adapt to changes or stressors, whether life threatening or not. In today's modern world we rarely meet a bear face-to-face. We frequently find ourselves in less life-threatening situations that can trigger the stress reaction. We may work under stressful conditions, care for an ailing family member, or be in other circumstances where neither fight nor flight is viable. As a result, our systems become overtaxed, causing wear and tear on our bodies, and setting up conditions for physical illness. Bruce McEwen (2002) described this stressed-out state as "allostatic load." Here, anticipation can play an important role because of the strong connection between perception and physiology. In the absence of a real threat, simply imagining oneself in a threatening situation can precipitate the stress reaction. Our minds, as powerful as they are, can overburden our allostatic systems to the point of exhaustion and illness.

When working in a model of mindful awareness, it is important to notice the attention bias that often occurs with an acute stress reaction. Attention can be focused on a perceived threat to such a degree that other, equally relevant information in the environment is misinterpreted or missed altogether. When a child experiences distressing physical symptoms, such as panic attacks, some psychoeducation is appropriate. However, as a mindfulness-based therapist, you do not intend to change the child's experience. Instead, you help him to remain present and aware of the entire experience as best he can, redirect his attention from the perceived threat, and refocus instead on the experiences of the present moment. For example, asking the child to describe discrete body sensations may help maintain a present-focused awareness. Mindful awareness is a practice of attending to discrete body sensations from moment to moment, and even the strong physiological responses of a panic attack provide opportunities to cultivate mindful attention.

BIOPSYCHOSOCIAL MODEL OF ANXIETY

Anxiety is a basic universal emotion that we all experience at different times and to differing degrees. Anxiety serves a number of adaptive purposes. For example, anxiety facilitates our ability to plan for the future. Anxiety can signal impending threat or danger, and alert us to take action to avoid or cope with that potential danger. Moreover, philosophers have suggested that existential anxiety is universal and that facing this deep-seated spiritual angst enhances self-actualization (Kierkegaard, 1844/1944).

Biological Contributions to Anxiety

About 20 percent of children seem to be born with a temperamental bias that predisposes them to be overly reactive and avoidant of unfamiliar events and people (Kagan & Snidman, 1999). Traumatic experiences in early life may establish a disposition toward physiological reactivity throughout life (Quirin, Pruessner, & Kuhl, 2008). Children with genetic or biological factors that put them at risk to develop anxiety disorders show increased startle reflexes, autonomic reactivity, and stress reactivity (Kagan & Snidman, 1999; Merikangas, Avenevoli, Dierker, & Grillon, 1999). These factors may help explain the generally early onset and chronic course of anxiety disorders in many children.

Cognitive Contributions to Anxiety

An acute stress response requires that two events occur together. The first event is that a serious threat or danger occurs or seems imminent. The mere anticipation of a stressful event is often sufficient to activate allostatic processes. The second event is that the individual believes he has inadequate skills or resources to manage the perceived danger (Lazarus & Folkman, 1984). Attentional biases, inaccurate beliefs, and distorted cognitions are instrumental in initiating, maintaining, or escalating an acute stress response (Eldar, Ricon, & Bar-Haim, 2008; Hunt, Keogh, & French, 2007; Kallen, Ferdinand, & Tulen, 2007).

Traditional Buddhist texts suggest that with our thoughts, we create the world (Bhikkhu Bodhi, 1993). Anxious thoughts create anxious worlds. The following example illustrates how thoughts may influence the perceived level of threat and the perceived ability to cope with that threat.

⚘ Katie and Sam Standing on a Board

Two children are standing on three-foot-high boards ready to dive into a swimming pool below. The first child is an experienced diver. Katie has done this many times and is confident that she has the skills to execute a graceful dive. She feels some sympathetic nervous system response—perhaps a heightened awareness of her body and how it's positioned on the board. She feels energized in a way that has an alert, pleasant, anticipatory quality to it. While Katie waits, her mind may be visualizing the practiced movements of her dive, now just moments away. As she begins to move, her thoughts, emotions, and body awareness are in the present moment. Her thoughts are concentrated on the physical experience. Katie maintains a present-focused attention that excludes awareness of the spectators or the memory of a fight she had with a friend yesterday. She takes her last step, bounces, and executes a lovely dive. Feeling pleased with herself, Katie swims to the side of the pool.

Sam swims well but has never been on a diving board. Standing on the board, he is very nervous. His mind conjures up images of all the ways he might fail: he could trip and fall, land on his back, make a belly flop, or do something else painful or embarrassing. Sam's thoughts are anxiously focused on the future—the moment of the failed dive, the pain in his back, the embarrassment. His thoughts alone have created these imaginary catastrophes. There is little actual danger or even potential danger present. Diving off that board is similar to the dives he has done many times from the edge of the pool. Some part of him knows these things. Nevertheless, Sam's anxious thoughts and vivid imagination precipitate an acute stress response. He feels short of breath, light-headed, and dizzy. He feels his heart pounding, and he becomes nauseated. Embarrassed and ashamed, Sam refuses to dive off the board and runs back down the ladder.

Katie and Sam had completely different emotional experiences, yet the environmental circumstances were nearly identical. Katie had a few more skills to draw upon and greater confidence in her own ability. Sam had perfectly adequate skills, but his thoughts created a series of imaginary disasters that bore little resemblance to reality.

A traditional cognitive therapist would intervene by working toward changing Sam's thoughts—perhaps by examining his automatic thoughts and attributions, or by identifying distortions in his thinking. In contrast, a mindfulness-based therapist would help Sam refocus his attention to the actual experiences of the moment. Sam might bring mindful attention to his thoughts, feelings, and body sensations without trying to change them in any way. Instead of attending to the negative self-judgments and fantasized disasters, Sam could attend to each element of the experience. From that practice, Sam might discover that his thoughts were just thoughts and not accurate reflections of reality. By attending to each moment, Sam might gain a stable foundation from which to appraise the situation, ascertain the skills necessary to manage it, evaluate his own skill level, and perhaps make a different choice. Even with no intention to change thoughts or behaviors, the behavioral outcome may well have been quite different.

Psychosocial Contributions to Anxiety

Parenting style appears to account for very little of the variance in childhood anxiety, although some theoretical models have focused on the role of parenting in modeling anxiety-related behaviors (McLeod, Wood, & Weisz, 2007). The incidence of anxiety has increased dramatically in recent decades and the most likely explanation appears to be related to changes in our sociocultural environment. Jean Twenge (2000) found that the incidence of childhood anxiety was strongly correlated with social indices, such as rates of unemployment, divorce, and crime. She suggested that decreases in social connectedness and increases in environmental dangers may be responsible for the rise in anxiety over the past few decades, and concluded that childhood anxiety strongly reflects what is happening in the culture as a whole. She cautioned that, until children feel both safe and connected to others, anxiety in our culture will likely remain high.

CHILDHOOD ANXIETY

Childhood is characterized by developmental changes and transitional periods. Different thoughts, emotions, motivations, and behaviors are age appropriate at different developmental stages. For example, we do not usually consider occasional aggressive behavior in a toddler to be problematic. This child does not yet have sufficient cognitive development to see another person's perspective or to make cause-and-effect attributions (for example, hitting causes pain to another person). As he matures, however, the normal egocentrism of the toddler would become increasingly problematic.

Throughout childhood, but particularly when developing abstract reasoning abilities, a child's perceptions and cognitive appraisals of potential dangers will change. Fears that are appropriate at one age may be indications of psychopathology at a different age or in a different context. For example, we observe a child of five attending his first day of kindergarten. When his mother leaves the school, the child becomes extremely distressed, cries, and displays intense anxiety. This behavior alone would not generally be evidence of psychopathology or future emotional problems. The same behavior exhibited by a ten-year-old boy would likely provoke greater concern about a possible anxiety disorder.

The cultural and social context, and familial expectations, may also be considered. To offer an extreme example, a well-cared-for adolescent from a financially stable, middle-class family living in a comfortable suburban home who chronically steals food from the local market might be diagnosed as having a conduct or impulse control disorder. The same stealing behavior, however, might be perceived differently when done by an adolescent living in an impoverished, third-world country who is taking food to feed his family.

Another factor is the transitory nature of many childhood anxieties. Children of all ages can express transient fears or anxieties. Many well-adjusted children demonstrate unusual or idiosyncratic behaviors for a few days or a few weeks with no obvious rationale or purpose. In other cases, a sudden change in behavior may be precipitated by an acute environmental stressor or herald the onset of more serious affective or behavioral problems. This is why diagnostic criteria for children and adolescents often include caveats that the behavior must last for at least six months or be inconsistent with the child's developmental level. Our challenge as therapists is to recognize when the anxiety, or anxiety-related behavior, occurs more frequently, is more severe, or is longer lasting than the fluctuations seen in the normal course of development.

A BRIEF REVIEW OF ANXIETY DISORDERS

In this section, we review anxiety spectrum diagnoses and how anxiety in children manifests cognitively, affectively, physiologically, and behaviorally. We discuss ways in which mindfulness-based interventions may enhance a child's self-awareness and capacity to navigate the challenges of everyday life.

Panic Disorder

Cognitive theories have emphasized the role of cognitive distortions in the development and maintenance of panic disorder (PD). Increased awareness of and misinterpretations of physical sensations are considered to be key precipitants of panic attacks (Clark & Beck, 1990). Panic attacks represent a clear example of an acute stress reaction that is triggered or exacerbated by cognitive interpretations. During a panic attack, attention is strongly focused on the perceived threat, often excluding awareness of other important and more relevant information in the environment.

During a panic attack, attention is tightly focused on body sensations such as heart palpitations, nausea, trembling, and shortness of breath. When these sensations are misinterpreted, the result is typically cognitive catastrophizing (or thinking the worst), which further escalates the anxiety. Although there is clear evidence that panic attacks occur in adolescents (Ollendick & Pincus, 2008), for many years there was some controversy about whether children were capable of experiencing the cognitive catastrophizing that is characteristic of adult PD. Peter Muris and his colleagues (2007) investigated children's cognitive interpretations of anxiety-related physical symptoms and to what extent those interpretations were influenced by the child's level of cognitive development. It seems that beginning around the age of seven, children are increasingly able to link physical symptoms to anxiety. Muris and colleagues also found that the tendency to infer danger on the basis of physical symptoms was already prominent in children as young as four years old. The ability to apply emotional reasoning in making cognitive interpretations develops very early in childhood (for example, *I feel anxious, therefore something bad must be about to happen*).

Although the mean age of onset in PD is twenty-four (Kessler et al., 2005), elementary-school-aged children can and do experience panic attacks (Doerfler, Connor, Volungis, & Toscano, 2007). Up to 90 percent of children and adolescents with PD also have another anxiety or mood disorder (Birmaher & Ollendick, 2004).

Although we do not try to change the child's experience, bringing mindful attention to the body sensations experienced during a panic attack may help moderate those symptoms in two ways. First, attention is a limited resource. When a child is mindfully attending to body sensations, he cannot also attend to the catastrophic cognitions. Second, close attention to body sensations allows the child to accurately interpret those symptoms as acute stress and not a serious physical problem. Although they may be experienced as real, rarely has a child's heart palpitations ever led to going "crazy" or dying.

One challenge for the therapist may be to avoid making causal inferences between the cultivation of mindful awareness and the reduction of panic attacks. A related challenge for the child who experiences panic attacks is to cultivate mindful responses when anxiety symptoms are absent. A panic attack begins with an intense autonomic nervous system response and escalates rapidly. Through the continued practice of mindful awareness, the child may learn to replace the conditioned catastrophic response with a conditioned mindful response—while the physiological storm is raging. Developing this degree of awareness requires many hours of practice, which is initially learned in a relatively calm emotional space. Attempting to learn mindfulness practices during a panic attack could be compared to attempting to learn how to swim in the midst of a hurricane.

Agoraphobia

Similar to the escalation of panic attacks, catastrophic cognitions play a significant role in the maintenance of agoraphobic avoidance. The "what if-ing" and catastrophic thinking characteristic of agoraphobic avoidance act to restrict the child's behaviors. Noting what is actually present in the environment may reduce avoidant behaviors by promoting overall psychological resiliency—mindful awareness being essentially an "exposure to life." Arising from clear awareness of experiences, the child may develop a different relationship to the catastrophic thoughts, which offers greater freedom to choose his own behaviors.

Obsessive-Compulsive Disorder

Obsessive-compulsive disorder (OCD) can make life very stressful for children. The first symptoms of OCD often begin during childhood or adolescence, but the median age of onset is about nineteen years old. Obsessions and compulsions are often time consuming, resulting in fewer opportunities for the child to develop social skills. OCD behaviors may also appear odd to others, so children with OCD may be vulnerable to teasing or victimization by their peers.

Mindfulness-based approaches may be a useful tool in the treatment of OCD. At least part of the time, obsessive thoughts are likely to be dissonant with the child's self-identity (that is, ego dystonic). John Teasdale (1999) made an interesting distinction between metacognitive knowledge and metacognitive insight. He suggested that the former is the experience of knowing that thoughts are not necessarily accurate, while the latter is the experiencing of thoughts as events in the field of awareness. Children with ego dystonic obsessions may already have metacognitive knowledge—thoughts are seen as independent of the child's self-identity. The intrusive quality of obsessive ruminations may make it easier for the child to develop the metacognitive insight—thoughts experienced as being "just" thoughts. The presence of harsh self-judgments may prompt you to help the child focus mindful awareness and attention on experiencing them as being "just" judgments.

Post-Traumatic Stress Disorder

Post-traumatic stress disorder (PTSD) can develop at any age, including childhood, but research shows that the median age of onset is twenty-three years (Kessler, Sonnega, Bromet, & Hughes, 1995). Common behaviors in children who have experienced a traumatic stressor include regressive behaviors, crying, temper tantrums, somatic symptoms, separation anxieties, and school refusal. Emotional reactions often include depression, withdrawal, fear, or anger (Vogel & Vernberg, 1993).

Mindful awareness may enhance resiliency by strengthening the ability to maintain a calm, relaxed perspective in challenging situations. Trauma-focused cognitive behavioral therapy (TF-CBT) incorporates mindfulness of the breath and body to help children navigate the physiological arousal that often results from trauma (Cohen, Mannarino, & Deblinger, 2006). Mindfulness practices may also enhance the child's ability to recognize maladaptive cognitions as they arise in the moment. To practice mindful attention is to practice seeing clearly what is present. Some symptoms of PTSD are past focused—that is, the child's attention is focused on the past traumatic event itself. Other symptoms are future focused. For example, anticipatory anxiety and behavioral avoidance of places or people associated with the trauma may develop. In MBCT-C, we teach the child to cultivate present-moment awareness by refocusing his attention onto the present and away from past or future events.

Generalized Anxiety Disorder

Generalized anxiety disorder (GAD) may develop at any time, though the median age of onset is in the early twenties. Similar to adults with GAD, children with GAD worry excessively about a multitude of everyday activities. The generalized worries are perceived as being appropriate and reasonable for the circumstances (that is, ego syntonic), which can make GAD difficult to treat.

Children tend to somaticize anxiety and frequently report stomach pains, nausea, headaches, and sleep or appetite disturbances (Muris et al., 2007). Peter Muris and colleagues reported that by age four, children are able to interpret physical symptoms as signs of anxiety, which increases with cognitive development. Childhood worries can be disorganized, distorted, or based on catastrophic "what if" reasoning: *What if a spider comes into my room…and what if it gets into my bed and bites me…and what if it happens to be a poisonous spider…and what if I get sick and have to go to the hospital in an ambulance…and what if I miss so much school that I have to repeat my classes…,* ad infinitum.

Several researchers are evaluating mindfulness-based therapies for the treatment of GAD with adults, and early results look promising (Evans et al., 2008; Orsillo, Roemer, & Barlow, 2003; Roemer, Salters-Pedneault, & Orsillo, 2006; Wells, 2002). Several characteristics of GAD may be responsive to a mindfulness intervention, for example, by strengthening tolerance for ambiguity and by increasing awareness of everyday experiences (Evans et al., 2008).

Social Anxiety Disorder

Children with social phobia or social anxiety disorder (SAD) fear being judged and evaluated by others. SAD generally begins in late childhood or early adolescence and increases with age (Chavira & Stein, 2005). Older children often are increasingly self-conscious in the context of developmental and environmental transitions, such as reaching puberty, dating, attending new schools, and sensing increased peer pressures. Genetic factors can contribute to the development of social anxiety. Behavioral inhibition (BI), a temperamental trait with a strong genetic basis, is the tendency to react negatively to new people, situations, or things (Kagan & Snidman, 1999). Behaviorally inhibited children are fearful, shy, withdrawn, or irritable when in a new situation or with new people. In one important study, 61 percent of the children who were identified as behaviorally inhibited at age two had developed SAD by age thirteen (Schwartz, Snidman, & Kagan, 1999). Children and adolescents with SAD frequently show impairments in their family lives and social relationships; they have poorer social skills, less social support, and impaired academic performance (Khalid-Khan, Santibañez, McMicken, & Rynn, 2007).

Mindfulness approaches may be beneficial for children who have SAD for several reasons. First, bringing awareness to the sensations may help moderate the physiological symptoms of social anxiety, such as blushing, sweating, and trembling. A child may be able to approach anxiety-provoking social situations with greater awareness (Miller et al., 1995). Second, the self-focused attention seen in those with SAD tends to increase anxiety (Woody, Chambless, & Glass, 1997). Mindfulness training may help a child shift his attention from this self-focus to an external focus (Rapee & Sanderson, 1998). Third, a high frequency of self-critical thoughts can impair performance in social situations. Mindfulness training may reduce the negative self-judgments that fuel anxiety as the child learns to decenter from self-critical thoughts.

Specific Phobias

Some fears are normal and common in children of all ages. However, phobias may produce intense, long-lasting anxiety and significantly disturb a child's daily routine. The feared object does not need to be present to trigger distress. Even very young children can have thoughts that produce anticipatory anxiety (for example, *What if there is a dog at my friend's house?*). Avoidance is the most common behavioral response, but a child may also experience situation-specific panic attacks, cry, have a temper tantrum, freeze, or cling to an adult for comfort or safety. Specific phobias usually begin in early childhood, although the nature of the feared object or situation tends to change over time. Infants and very young children often experience fears of strangers, falling, and loud noises. Fears of the dark, small animals, and imaginary creatures generally begin a few years later.

O. Hobart Mowrer's two-stage model (1960) suggests that avoidant behaviors reinforce many anxiety problems. Exposure with response prevention (ERP) is a "probably efficacious" treatment for a variety of anxiety disorders, including specific phobias (Silverman, Pina, & Viswesvaran, 2008). Mindfulness practices may be thought of as a type of intrapsychic exposure with response prevention. The child's practice of mindful attention is to stay present with whatever thoughts, feelings, and body sensations arise in his experience. In shifting from judging and resisting to simply noting experiences, the child may habituate to the presence of the feared object or experience.

Mindfully observing the feared thoughts may also increase the child's capacity to recognize cognitive distortions or exaggerations. Walking into a darkened room, two children step on a soft, long cylinder. One child reactively interprets the object as a snake and runs screaming from the room. The mindful child breathes and stays present long enough to recognize the object as a harmless piece of rope. Staying present, without judging, may make the difference between a reactive or avoidant behavior and an appropriately responsive mindful behavior.

Separation Anxiety Disorder

At least one in twenty-five children experiences separation anxiety disorder (SA), and for about one-third of these children, the anxieties will persist into adulthood (Shear, Jin, Ruscio, Walters, & Kessler, 2006). For about 80 percent of those children, onset is before age twelve. SA represents a major risk factor for other childhood mental health disorders (Lewinsohn, Holm-Denoma, Small, Seeley, & Joiner, 2008). Children with SA have a high risk of developing panic disorder, agoraphobia, specific phobias, generalized anxiety disorder, obsessive-compulsive disorder, and bipolar disorder (Brückl et al., 2006).

During MBCT-C, a child is taught to observe and describe anxious thoughts, feelings, and physical reactions that arise in response to anxiety-provoking separations. Observing thoughts includes noting those that are present focused and descriptive, and those that are future focused and judgmental. As with all the practices, cultivating a present-focused awareness is intended to enhance the child's ability to see experiences clearly and allow him opportunities to make appropriate choices.

School Refusal

Although school refusal is not a diagnosable disorder, it occurs frequently enough to warrant a few comments. Nearly 28 percent of American children refuse to attend school at some point during their education (Kearney & Albano, 2000). Fears related to school achievement or pleasing teachers and parents sometimes become so pervasive that academic performance is impaired, which then creates a vicious cycle of self-fulfilling prophesies and escalating anxieties. Separation from a caregiver, academic or athletic failures, and test anxieties are common in children who refuse to attend school. As a child approaches adolescence, his problems may be exacerbated by fears of physical injury in sports or anxieties about interpersonal skills and social performance (Marks & Gelder, 1966; Sheehan, Sheehan, & Minichiello, 1981). As with other anxiety-related problems, mindful awareness of thoughts, feelings, and body sensations may provide a stable emotional foundation from which the child can choose more adaptive coping behaviors.

Observations

When a child is brought in for therapy, it is all too easy to focus on deficits or problems and fail to recognize the child's strengths. We conceptualize mindfulness as a strength-based approach to therapy and focus on cultivating existing strengths within the child. MBCT-C does not explicitly teach coping skills. MBCT-C invites children to tap into their own inner resources to actively engage in caring for themselves.

We have learned that children seem to have a truly remarkable ability to adapt to changing demands in their lives. We respect and honor this natural ability and we express that respect in our interactions with them. Mindful awareness simply provides a stable foundation so that the child can stay present long enough to see clearly, learn to call upon the natural resiliencies that already reside within him, and then make conscious choices that may be more appropriate to the situation or event. Over time, the child gradually experiences greater self-empowerment. His self-esteem and self-efficacy may be enhanced. With the practice of mindfulness comes the discovery of freedom—freedom to choose his own behaviors without being helplessly tossed around in a turbulent storm of constantly changing emotions.

In the next chapter, we will further explore mindfulness as a different way of being in the world. The aims and goals of mindfulness-based interventions are unlike most other therapies and may require you to adopt a new perspective on therapy in general.

CHAPTER 3

Different Paradigms and Different Goals

So Just Be

Your hopes and desires,
Your expectations
Bring tension and stress.
There is no peace.

You look for happiness
With old thinking
So it cannot arrive.

You want one thing,
And the world
Gives you something else.

Your present moment wonders
Are taken away.
So just be
With your out breath.

William Menza (2007)

The aim of mindfulness-based cognitive therapy for children is to reduce anxiety and suffering by enhancing awareness. With awareness, we discover more opportunities to choose how to respond to the events in our lives rather than be pushed and pulled by thoughts and emotions. We practice bringing attention to the actual experience. When we stop paying attention to the experience itself and instead start thinking about it, our attention can become captured by the thoughts themselves. A moment of mindfulness arises when we realize that the thoughts carried us away. Then we return attention to the present moment—over and over and over again. Thus we accept ownership of our own lives.

HAPPINESS IS...

Our ultimate goal is to help children realize their potential to be happy, fulfilled human beings. Most philosophers and psychologists agree that the desire for happiness is a universal human impulse. Aristotle suggested, "Happiness is the meaning and the purpose of life, the whole aim and end of human existence." In his seminal treatise on religion, William James (1902) declared, "How to gain, how to keep, how to recover happiness is in fact for most men at all times the secret motive of all they do, and of all they are willing to endure" (p. 77). Yet, happiness remains one of the most elusive of all concepts to define. Jean-Jacques Rousseau (1782/1979) offered one definition that seems to capture the spirit of what we aim to teach, writing that happiness is "… a state where the soul can…establish itself and concentrate its entire being…with no need to remember the past or reach into the future…where the present runs on indefinitely…the simple feeling of existence…" (pp. 88–89).

Most of us probably agree that happiness is something essentially subjective, perhaps some quality of mind or affective state characterized by absolute well-being. Beyond that, thousands of years of debate have produced no consensus on what happiness is or how to achieve it. However, we can all agree that life is not always comfortable, idyllic, or satisfactory. We all get sick. We all will die. We all have feelings of anxiety, sadness, anger, or frustration. In fact, it may sometimes feel as if our lives—as well as the lives of our families, friends, and clients—are filled with more unhappiness than happiness. This also applies to children.

Adult clients come to us saying, essentially, "I am unhappy, can you help me?" Sigmund Freud (1895) felt that our maximum therapeutic effectiveness would be achieved "if we succeed in transforming our [client's] neurotic misery into common unhappiness" (p. 305). But we've just said that the ultimate purpose of MBCT-C is to increase children's sense of happiness. Freud's second piece of advice might be more in harmony with a mindfulness-based approach: "With a mental life that has been restored to health, [your client] will be better armed against that unhappiness (p. 305)."

Living in the Nowscape

We believe that the essential nature of happiness can best be realized by empowering children to see more clearly the moment-by-moment events of their lives. We do this by helping them cultivate a practice of observing and experiencing fully in the present moment. The past is unchangeable, and the future is unknowable. The present is all we have. Jon Kabat-Zinn (2005) wrote, "Everything that unfolds, unfolds now, and so might be said to unfold in the nowscape" (p. 237). The nowscape is this present moment and all that's in it. For each child, as for each of us, the nowscape is a unique and ever-changing environment.

Body sensations and movements are somatic and kinesthetic phenomena that exist only in the nowscape. Each touch, taste, smell, sight, and sound is experienced only in the nowscape. Our identity and conscious sense of self exist only in the nowscape, as does that sense of personal continuity described by William James (1890) as the "stream of consciousness." The nowscape also encompasses every action or behavior, every situation, every event, and all of our interactions with others. The nowscape is actually a remarkably busy place—filled with vibrancy and many wonders. Everything that happens, happens in the nowscape.

Living in the Past

Some children struggle to avoid living in the nowscape. They may try escaping to the past by living in their heads, ruminating over past events, replaying conversations, reliving behaviors done or not done, or reanalyzing choices made or not made: *I should have said this instead of...* or *Why did I do that? It was so stupid...* Reflecting on the past in order to learn from experience is a normal and healthy part of development and psychological growth. Those reflections are an integral part of the nowscape.

For some children, however, efforts to remake the past go beyond reflective contemplation and become unhappy struggles to escape the present. This sort of rumination tends to be dysphoric; characterized by an internalized focus on personal problems; and accompanied by pessimism, self-criticism, and self-blame. It erodes the child's optimism, self-confidence, and perceived ability to cope with circumstances (Nolen-Hoeksema, 1998). More often than not, dysphoric rumination is also unproductive and unrewarding. It does not solve whatever problems precipitated the worries, and it likely impairs the child's ability to find effective solutions. In adults, Lyubomirsky, Tucker, Caldwell, and Berg (1999) found a direct relationship between negatively biased content of ruminative thoughts and decreased willingness to solve one's problems.

Childhood is a time of intense learning where some developmental tasks must be mastered before others can even be attempted. The child who tries to avoid the nowscape by engaging in chronic rumination may have more difficulty mastering the developmental tasks that are essential to the child's functioning and happiness. Since all efforts to change the past necessarily fail, a child who engages in this sort of rumination may become pessimistic, harshly judgmental, and self-critical. This sort of chronic negative self-talk is a strong component of childhood anxiety and depression (Ronan & Kendall, 1997).

Living in the Future

The future is unknown. For very good reasons, humans have evolved to fear the unknown. Throughout history, those who more quickly anticipated or identified threats were better prepared to escape the danger when it appeared. Consequently everyone alive today is descended from those who were very good at anticipating threats. In chapter 2, we discussed how anxiety might arise when this useful survival characteristic is overused.

Anxious children spend a substantial amount of time worrying, often trying to anticipate possible future threats. Anticipatory anxiety can serve to avoid the nowscape because anxious attention is biased attention. A more realistic evaluation may be missed because the relevant cues exist only in the present moment. Future-oriented worries and fears often increase anxiety and perpetuate unsuccessful attempts to change or control the present. Living in the future appears to undermine the child's confidence in herself or in her ability to effectively cope with the now. "What if-ing" and catastrophizing are common: *What if I fail the math exam…?* or *What if my mom gets into a car accident…?* Similar to dysphoric, past-oriented thinking, anticipatory rumination is unproductive. Chronic hypervigilance is physically exhausting—much energy is invested with little or no beneficial outcome.

Children with anxiety will typically experience some combination of debilitating anxious, worried, or fearful thoughts; demoralizing negative self-talk; and both anxious and depressive affect. We all spend part of our lives lost in thought and not living in the present moment. The anxious child's efforts to escape the present may become pervasive, chronic, distressing, and functionally impairing. Mindfulness-based therapy may reduce distress by cultivating greater awareness of the present.

LETTING GO OF—GOALS?

The paradox inherent in any "acceptance" model of psychotherapy is the core assumption that all things in life are acknowledged exactly as they are. As we use it here, acceptance does not imply emotional resignation or behavioral passivity, but may be better construed as an attitude of nonresistance to experience—a nonjudgmental recognition of experiences just as they are. Mindfulness is seeing clearly and acknowledging what is in the present moment, just as it is. In contrast, a goal is directed toward a purpose in the future. We strive to achieve something in the future, so a goal by definition cannot be present in this moment. This rationale suggests that MBCT-C can have no goals. So it doesn't—and yet it does. We practice mindful awareness by accepting the present moment and by letting go—moment by moment—of everything that arises in the nowscape. We can only be fully present in the next moment by letting go of this one. Letting go. Being present. That's all. We already possess everything we actually need, and there is nothing more to attain. Ironically it seems that the harder we struggle to achieve the "goals" of mindfulness, the less likely we are to attain them.

Deikman (1996) suggested that practicing mindfulness enhances the ability to respond appropriately to the ordinary, everyday experiences of life. Mindful awareness is the practice of looking closely at the multitude of events that arise in the nowscape. Looking closely simply helps us see clearly what is happening—right here, right now. In this moment, we can then say, "Okay, now what do I do?" The moment now contains a "choice point." We'll discuss the importance of choice points later in this chapter, but for now, understand that *choice points* represent those moments in which mindful choices can be made. Mindfulness involves opening up to and accepting our lives as they are, which includes accepting our choice points and the choices we eventually make. Ultimately this is the aim of MBCT-C.

GOALS FOR THE THERAPIST

For you as the therapist, having an intellectual understanding of concepts associated with mindfulness is a necessary beginning. Understanding the objectives and goals are essential too. With most therapies, knowledge about that particular therapy is acquired by attending classes or workshops, reading books, or engaging in discussions with more experienced therapists. This, however, is not how we learn to teach mindful awareness. The teaching of mindfulness practices begins with somewhat different assumptions than other therapy models. These core assumptions may well challenge us to make significant changes in our own lives.

Letting Go of Wanting Change

Letting go of the need for change is a fundamental difference between mindfulness-based approaches and other therapies. Cognitive therapists are trained with the aim of helping the client change in some way. As cognitive therapists, we teach cognitive restructuring. We teach social skills to change behaviors. We explore schemas to change their influence on the child's emotions. Most of us became therapists so that we might help children make positive changes in their lives. Most individuals begin therapy with the hope and expectation that positive change will occur.

Unlike most other therapies, however, MBCT-C is not about making changes. One of the greatest challenges for us as therapists teaching mindful awareness practices is letting go of our innate or professionally trained desire to effect changes in our clients. Despite our best efforts, this deeply ingrained expectation for change is likely to subtly influence our descriptions, actions, and verbal exchanges with the children we serve. Mindful awareness cultivates an acceptance of what is, without wishing for change. Yet acceptance is not static. What "is" changes constantly, and indeed, change is possible only within the present moment. Staying present with what "is" then becomes an active and dynamic process of learning and growth—mindfulness embraces change because actions and choices occur in the present moment.

Embodying Mindfulness

MBCT-C differs from many other therapies in its expectation that what you teach is an integral part of your own personal life. Like many others who have adopted a mindfulness-based approach, we believe that for MBCT-C to be an effective intervention, you must first establish your own practice and then teach mindfulness through your own embodiment of mindfulness. We also believe that your understanding will emerge mainly from many hours of your own experiences practicing mindful awareness. In order to teach mindfulness, you must practice mindfulness in your own life.

You may have read every book there is about playing a violin. You might be the world's most knowledgeable scholar of violin music. With all that knowledge, however, if you want to play a violin, you must actually pick one up and practice playing it. You will not "get it" by reading or thinking about it. Like playing the violin, the only way you will understand mindfulness is to invest many hours of personal, experiential practice.

Mindful awareness is learned by practicing being aware. This type of practice is not done in preparation for anything else. If we take care of this moment, the next moment will be different. In this way, "practicing" mindfulness is never a rehearsal. Practice simply means returning awareness to this moment—moment by moment.

Practice, Practice, Practice

We believe that if we as therapists do not embody mindfulness in our teachings, the effectiveness of this treatment will be limited. When Zindel Segal, Mark Williams, and John Teasdale began developing MBCT (Segal et al., 2002), only one of them had any personal experience with meditative practices. Although they sought guidance from Jon Kabat-Zinn and staff at the Center for Mindfulness, they were unsure about the advice. They later revisited this issue and then offered an unambiguous recommendation:

> Our own conclusion after seeing for ourselves the difference between using MBCT with and without personal experience of using mindfulness practice is that it is unwise to embark on teaching this material until instructors have extensive experience with its personal use. We therefore recommend that, as a minimum, prospective

instructors have gained experience of using mindfulness in their own daily lives before they embark on teaching it to clients. (p. 84)

For some excellent therapists, the time commitment needed to develop a personal practice may make mindfulness-based therapies difficult to access. Should you conduct therapy in this model without making that commitment to a personal practice, you may find MBCT-C to be a relatively ineffective treatment.

We do not prescribe the model, mode, duration, or frequency of personal practice necessary. An eight-week MBSR course can provide an excellent beginning, and advanced MBSR teacher-training courses are available. MBCT therapist training workshops and courses are offered throughout the United States and Canada. The MBCT workshops offered generally assume that participants have some experience with both cognitive therapy and some form of mindfulness practice. These workshops focus more on learning the MBCT intervention model and somewhat less on the development of your own practice. Appendix A lists some resources that may be helpful as you cultivate your daily practice.

GOALS FOR THE CHILD

The goals of MBCT-C are not necessarily presented or explained to the children. They are demonstrated when the therapist embodies mindfulness. Mindfulness arises from within. The most significant therapeutic improvements emerge from your own embodiment of mindfulness. This flows from experiential understanding gained from your own personal practice.

Acceptance vs. Change

MBCT-C represents neither a traditional didactic teaching model nor a traditional psychotherapy change model. It differs from traditional cognitive therapy in that there is no emphasis on restructuring thoughts or modifying beliefs. Unlike behavior therapies, there is no attempt to teach specific behavioral skills or promote behavioral changes.

MBCT-C is an acceptance-based approach. Acceptance, as we use it, does not mean a dull passivity toward one's life. Marsha Linehan (1993) developed another mindfulness-informed intervention, dialectical behavior therapy (DBT), in which clients seek unconditional self-acceptance *while* making changes in their lives. Our young MBCT-C client learns to accept herself and her life just as it is—and, at the same time, work toward cultivating mindfulness that may catalyze growth, insight, and balance.

Understanding Obstacles

Psychological influences will almost always pull our attention away from practicing mindfulness. During one thorny year in my own meditation practice (RJS), I sat, day after day, watching my mind invent literally hundreds of different reasons to stop meditating and go do something else, right now. Anything else. Even cleaning the cat box seemed more important than sitting on a cushion watching my breath. I also watched another part of my mind judge myself harshly for not being disciplined enough to "control" my own thoughts. Then I watched a third part of my mind criticize me for judging myself so harshly and with so little self-compassion. Why would my own mind work so hard to sabotage my mindfulness practice? It is helpful to have clear reasons to maintain a daily meditation practice in order to understand and work through these sorts of obstacles.

In a short essay titled "Why I Sit," Paul Fleishman (2005) explored the personal influences that led him to develop and maintain a daily meditation practice. He suggested that there is something inherent in our psychic makeup that seems to shy away from giving sustained attention to the events that make up our lives:

> Most of our lives are spent in externally oriented functions that distract from self-observation. This relentless, obsessive drive persists independently of survival needs such as food and warmth, and even of pleasure. Second for second, we couple ourselves to sights, tastes, words, motions, or electronic stimuli, until we fall dead. It is striking how many ordinary activities, from smoking a pipe to watching sunsets, veer towards, but ultimately avoid, sustained attention to the reality of our own life. (pp. 21–22)

Having an intellectual understanding of this resistance might lead to insights about the self and the world. It is more important simply to recognize that the obstacle exists. A clear personal understanding of what motivates the practice of mindfulness can help both children and adults find the commitment and discipline to sustain a consistent practice.

The group process of exploring obstacles that may interfere with daily practice provides opportunities for the children to offer compassionate support to one another. The acts of giving and receiving strengthen group cohesiveness, which is essential in creating the safe environment necessary for the cultivation of mindfulness. Further benefits can arise for the anxious child who suffers from poor self-esteem or lacks self-confidence. For example, having an opportunity to help another child can be an empowering experience.

Discovering Personal Motivations

Developing a sustained mindfulness practice is a discipline that requires clarity about why we do these practices. The personal motivations for children to practice mindfulness may be different from those discovered by adults. We suspect that it may be even more important for children to explore their reasons to practice because, unlike adults, children generally do not seek this or any other type of therapy on their own initiative.

A key aspiration of MBCT-C is to help each child discover personally meaningful reasons to do this practice. The first two sessions include opportunities for the children to explore this question for themselves. Through interactive discussions, the children help each other define and clarify their motivations for committing to practice mindful awareness. As you express a mindful, supportive, and accepting attitude, you will facilitate this process of discovery.

Children tend to express motivations that are relatively concrete and usually related to some specific difficulty experienced in their lives. For many children, navigating social anxieties and other common fears can be a helpful introduction to the benefits of the program. Children who struggle with test anxiety may discover that mindful breathing before an exam can be calming and focusing. Children who find it difficult to manage anger may realize that acting out the emotion is not helpful to them or to those around them. As their understandings grow, they come to realize more subtle ways in which mindful attention may be helpful.

Other children may have a harder time getting clear about ways in which mindfulness practices might be personally meaningful. For example, a child who participated in the MBCT-C program suffered the recent death of his mother and was having difficulty functioning at home and in school. Steven cried frequently, was distant and inattentive, and couldn't talk about his grief or accept comfort from his family or friends. His grief seemed wordless and overwhelming. When Steven's intense sadness emerged unchecked during a session, the intensity of the experience was acknowledged, respected, and mindfully explored—by the other children. Until he experienced how that compassionate exploration could help ease his grief, Steven was unable to conceive how mindfulness might be applied in his own life. By becoming more mindful of their anxiety or anger or sadness, children can see more clearly what contributes to strong emotional fluctuations. They may learn ways to make friends with their own emotions without feeling overwhelmed.

You may find it challenging to discuss potential benefits of mindfulness practices with children. It may be difficult to avoid the use of terms associated with forced affective or behavioral changes, such as "regulation," "self-control," or "self-management." Remember that mindfulness is the practice of attending to thoughts, feelings, and sensations without trying to change them—while recognizing that change nevertheless occurs.

Mindfulness of Thoughts, Feelings, and Body Sensations

Intrapsychic events are central to all our experiences. Paying mindful attention to thoughts, feelings, and body sensations (particularly sensations of breathing) facilitates staying present long enough to see clearly what is happening in the moment. Mindfulness practices help our clients clearly observe their own thoughts, emotional states, and physiological sensations. The difficulty arises because we are so easily captured by our thoughts and emotions. How many times each day do you become "lost in thought" and temporarily oblivious to your surroundings? Have you ever needed to ask a friend to repeat something he or she just said because your "thoughts were elsewhere"? Where do our minds go during those moments of being "absent-minded?" Where are we when our "thoughts are elsewhere"?

Sometimes we function as if we are on "automatic pilot." In some situations, this can be useful. It probably isn't necessary, or even desirable, to give your full attention to the contraction of your right brachioradialis muscle when raising your arm to engage the turn signal of your car while driving. Letting your muscles function on automatic pilot allows you to pay more attention to the road conditions, which decreases the likelihood of having an accident. But much more of our daily functioning happens on automatic pilot than we might ever imagine.

Thoughts, feelings, and body sensations easily capture our attention, so we may not see as clearly as we could. Giving disproportionate attention to these experiences, we may give less attention to how we are interacting with people or perceiving the situation at hand. How clearly do we see when we are so angry that we are "seeing red"? Have you ever been "deadened" by grief? Or "blinded" by love? The fact that phrases like this are so common in our language reflects one way that we avoid experiencing anticipated unpleasantness in the nowscape. Emotional states—whether pleasant or unpleasant, strong or mild—color our perceptions and interpretations of events. Being more aware of emotions—as emotions—lets us see the moment-dot picture more clearly, which results in more opportunities to make skillful choices.

Traditional cognitive therapies frequently teach children to identify body sensations as a means of providing clues about their affective state. This can be particularly effective for the child who experiences her anxieties primarily as somatic symptoms. Body sensations occur only in the present moment, so focusing attention on the body is a practice of mindfully observing what is in this moment. Both the MBSR and MBCT programs use techniques that involve increasing awareness of the body, for example, the body scan and basic yoga postures.

In MBCT-C, an abbreviated body scan (see J. Kabat-Zinn, 1990) promotes awareness of body sensations. Observing and noting body sensations can help ground a child's thoughts and emotions in the present moment. Children become more aware of their thoughts, feelings, and body sensations as separate, interrelated phenomena. They work to understand better how those thoughts, feelings, and body sensations interact to influence their perceptions of day-to-day experiences. This theme is consistently reinforced throughout the course of the program. There are no times, places, or circumstances in which mindfulness cannot be practiced. Ordinary everyday experiences provide all the material necessary with which to practice. As Jon Kabat-Zinn observed, "The little things? The little moments? They aren't little."

Judging Is Not Noting

Many of us have strong tendencies to judge ourselves, judge others, and judge the world around us. We make hundreds or even thousands of judgments every day and are mostly unaware of them. We like pancakes. We don't like gaining weight. We like a friend. We don't like his shirt. We like our cars. We don't like paying for car repairs. Like. Don't like. Like. Don't like. Daniel J. Siegel (2007), who has explored some neural correlates of mindfulness, commented on both the pervasiveness of judging and the extreme difficulty of disengaging from the judging mind. Once again, we suggest simply accepting—that we seem to be extremely judgmental beings.

"ME? I'M NOT JUDGMENTAL!"

Each time you look at a piece of your life and wish it were otherwise, you are being judgmental. We tend to do this so chronically and so habitually that we are like fish swimming in oceans of judgments, oblivious to the judgments that surround us. What might happen if we could stop being quite so judgmental? Siegel (2007) writes:

> Without judgments, what are we? If we "just" are curious, open, accepting, and even loving, where has our identity gone? These may sound like curious questions, but it seems that top-down influences like judgments, memories, emotional reactivity, and identity do not so readily loosen their grip on our minds. What are we without them? (p. 151)

Siegel suggested that one benefit of suspending judgments is the possibility that life will become more "rewarding, engaging, exciting, flexible, and psychologically healthy" (p. 151). Suspending the process of judging can allow different experiences to arise...without our having to do anything at all.

A key insight of MBCT-C is to help a child be more mindful of her automatic pilot habit of immediately judging her experiences. MBCT-C seeks to strengthen her ability to see clearly by noting the details that create her nowscape. The practice of noting, instead of judging, is applied to intrapsychic events (for example, thoughts, feelings, and body sensations) and other events (for example, interactions with other people, objects, events, or situations) "in the moment." Remember that at any given time, we have a limited amount of attention. The model of mindfulness that we promote is awareness based, not thought based. We can increase awareness of our judging without needing to do anything about it at all. Increasing awareness in the nowscape, however, seems to leave fewer attentional resources available for judging.

THREE TYPES OF REACTIONS

We react to events in our lives. Our choices are limited to three possible reactions, which can be described as moving toward, moving away, or being unmoved. Every reaction begins with first experiencing an event and then appraising it (judging it). The appraisal is a cognitive elaboration that triggers one of the three reactions. We move toward an experience that we define as pleasant or are attracted to, move away from an experience we define as unpleasant or are averse to, and are unmoved by an experience to which we have no particular attraction or aversion. These attitudinal reactions arise in response to the appraisal of the event (the judgment), not the event itself. The appraisal is an intermediate process that is often automatic, preconscious, and pre-emotional. Appraisals are subjective, frequently biased by past experiences, and not necessarily accurate to the realities of this situation at this moment.

In MBCT-C, we invite children to see clearly that each moment includes an affect or feeling tone (*vedana*), which may be pleasant, unpleasant, or neutral. Noting emotions cultivates a simple, nonjudgmental awareness of this feeling tone. Emotions become accompanied by awareness. With increasing awareness, emotions become familiar (albeit varied) experiences. Despite their great variety, emotions are all the same in one respect: they are in ever-changing flow—coming and going without leaving traces. By observing this repeatedly, emotions can begin to arise without precipitating a cascade of cognitive elaborations. Moderating the escalation of cognitive elaborations allows the child to know herself better and may reduce the power of emotions to influence perceptions and behaviors. Let's take a closer look at each of these affective reactions.

Moving toward. This reaction is an affective movement toward an event, idea, feeling, object, or person we judge positively. To say that someone is judgmental is commonly considered a pejorative, and typically equated with being identified as a negative or overly critical person. But just as frequently, judgments can be positive or praiseworthy. Believing that a red rose is beautiful is as much a judgment as thinking that your friend's shirt is ugly. We feel attracted to the rose, want it to last longer, or want to have more roses. Ice cream tastes good. We want more ice cream. We like you. We want to be your friend and spend more time with you. We want to be happy. Therefore, we move closer to whatever we think might increase happiness. Yes, this may temporarily allow us to feel happy—until that transient external source of happiness changes, disappears, or we decide that something else will make us even happier. Positive judging does not appear to increase happiness.

Moving away. When an emotion or idea emerges that we define in a negative way, we typically react with a wish that it go away as quickly as possible. Anxiety, sadness, anger, guilt, and shame feel "bad" and must be suppressed or pushed away. Some adults are so uncomfortable with their "negative" emotions that they self-medicate with alcohol or drugs. When we can't avoid unpleasantness altogether, we tend to choose the least unpleasant option. Physically and emotionally, we move away from objects, events, and people we judge to be unpleasant, bad, or uncomfortable. Sometimes this can be useful—touching a hot stove hurts, so we pull away quickly. Pulling away from something that induces pain is sometimes the wisest thing to do. But what of the multitude of things that do not create physical pain or things that may involve necessary pain (for example, going to the dentist)? Judgments affect behaviors. If a child decides that visiting the dentist is an uncomfortable experience, she will seek ways to avoid going. Judgments are not only subjective but also they are variable. When the child gets a toothache, a dentist visit may be judged more favorably if it can provide relief from the pain.

Being unmoved. Indifference is the reaction to an event that is perceived as neutral. We are unmoved and therefore untouched by the experience. We have no particular attraction or aversion to the person or object or event. When we write, "The ink on this page is black," you are unlikely to feel any particular like or dislike for either the statement or the fact of the black ink. This event is affectively neutral. It is neither good nor bad. In daily life, neutrality may be the most common of our reactions.

"OKAY, SO WHAT IF I AM JUDGMENTAL?"

One problem with judging is that, when something is not completely pleasant, then by definition something about it is not pleasant. Few things are ever completely pleasant. So our emotions are pushed and pulled by a multitude of constantly changing judgments. We love our dog—until she chews our favorite shoes. Chocolate cake is wonderful—until we get a stomachache. Even with the most pleasurable of events, there is usually something that can be judged as aversive, even if only slightly so. If nothing else, the most idyllic moment imaginable must always come to an end. The most wonderful of relationships carries the seeds of great unhappiness, for nothing is ever permanent. The first noble truth of Buddhism suggests that, "Birth is suffering; decay is suffering; illness is suffering; death is suffering. Presence of objects we hate is suffering; separation from objects we love is suffering; not to obtain what we desire is suffering."

Judgments are simply subjective, evaluative statements about events. If that were all they were, they would cause few problems. Problems arise because judgments are capricious and constantly changing. Judgments distort perceptions and interpretations of events, interfere with seeing clearly what is happening in the present moment, easily escalate emotions, restrict the child's ability to see her choice points, and often precipitate unwise behavioral choices.

Child: I don't like [judgment] that TV show. I want to change the channel.

Friend: No. I want to watch this.

Child: That's not fair [judgment]. We always watch what you want. I don't ever get to watch what I want.

Friend: That's not true. We watched your favorite movie the last time you were here.

Child: (*whining a little*) But the ball game is much more exciting [judgment], and we're missing it right now.

Friend: (*getting irritated*) Look, this is my house, so if you want to watch something else, why don't you just go to your own house?

Child: (*becoming angry*) You're a jerk [judgment]. If you were really my friend, you'd do what I want to do [judgment].

Friend: (*sad and hurt*) That wasn't a nice thing to say. I thought we were friends. Please go home now.

Child: (*standing up, crying, and slamming the door on the way out*) I will. You're a terrible friend [judgment]. It's all your fault [judgment] that I'm so upset now.

This vignette illustrates how the act of judging obscures and distorts reality. The judgments made are characteristic of the observer, not of the object or event being judged. The map is not the territory. Evaluations of experiences are not the same as the experience itself. Describing a giraffe as being beautiful or ugly interferes with seeing the creature as it is, because it adds an additional layer of affective response that does not belong to the giraffe. When children judge some event as being "good" or "bad," they are likely to be less open to and less present with the experience.

A child generally doesn't have words adequate to describe the richness of her nowscape. Sometimes children find it hard to understand why a word is a judgment and not a descriptor. For example, the statement "John is tall" is a judgmental statement. Tall by whose standards? Relative to what? Alternatively, the statement "John is six feet tall" is descriptive. Six feet in height is an objective characteristic descriptive of John, not a characteristic associated with the observer. John will continue to be six feet tall no matter who is looking at him. The English language is filled with words that are descriptive and words that are evaluative, and by helping children navigate this challenge, you can help them learn to describe without judging.

We can choose to judge experiences or we can choose to observe experiences. When we note our nowscape, we are simultaneously less likely to be judging it. Practice in first observing (awareness) and then noting (labeling) can be one way to interrupt this endless stream of judgments. Many of the sensory exercises used in the MBCT-C program are followed by discussions in which the children practice describing their experiences. Therapists invite children to practice distinguishing words that describe from words that judge. Children begin to develop a language that observes, without judging, their internal states—seeing clearly their thoughts, feelings, and body sensations.

Judgments are such conditioned habits that it is sometimes difficult even to be aware of their presence. We train awareness in two steps. First, children practice identifying judgments as they are being made, moment by moment. With continued observation, it becomes clear that judgments are subjective, habitual, learned from previous experiences, and often applied indiscriminately in inappropriate situations. Second, children learn to note mindfully the nowscape rather than to judge it, then observe the ways in which noting may transform the quality of the experience.

Decentering

Decentering may be described as experiencing one's own thoughts as "just" thoughts, feelings as "just" feelings, and body sensations as "just" body sensations. Thoughts, feelings, and body sensations are presented as phenomena to observe rather than to judge (including observing the experience of being judgmental) and as events to be noted rather than changed. Thoughts, feelings, and body sensations may be seen as transient and continually shifting internal events rather than evidence of an objective truth. Decentering occurs when thoughts, feelings, and body sensations are experienced simply as components of one's ever-changing nowscape.

Mindfulness practice can be viewed as a type of exposure with response prevention, a commonly used technique in the treatment of anxiety disorders (Foa & Kozak, 1986). Prolonged mindful exposure to intrapsychic events is practiced over and over—without numbing the senses or pushing away from the event, no matter how unpleasant. Many repetitions of this cycle shift the mental representations that shape an individual's relationship to her own anxious thoughts, feelings, and body sensations (Teasdale, 1999; Teasdale, Segal, & Williams, 1995).

Decentering allows for greater clarity in seeing the moment as it is. Children perceive their thoughts as passing events in the mind. Simply to accept thoughts as "just thoughts" means that thoughts are no longer defined as reality. Decentering involves greater acceptance of, and a nonavoidant relationship to, thoughts, feelings, and body sensations.

Decentering should not be confused with dissociation. Decentering involves conscious awareness. Dissociation is a disruption of conscious awareness. Decentering is looking directly at a thought and seeing it as a thought. Dissociation is a state of avoiding being present with an experience. Decentering connects us to our experiences. Dissociation severs the connection to an individual's thoughts, feelings, and body sensations. Decentering is empowering. Dissociation distances the mind from experiences that are appraised as being too difficult to face.

Discovering Choice Points

Choice points, as we mentioned earlier, are all those moments in which mindful choices can be made. In everyday life, choice points occur hundreds of times each day. Previously unknown, unseen choice points also may be discovered by learning to see more clearly. Recognizing the existence of a choice point increases the ability to respond to events with mindful awareness. When feelings of anxiety, fear, anger, or sadness arise, the aim is to observe and note the entire experience.

❧ Rick and His Choice Points

Rick is a twelve-year-old boy who is very bright, has several close friends, and has no significant academic problems. He has struggled for months to manage his anger. He often feels irritated by others' actions and has a low tolerance for frustration. Rick fights with his classmates and argues with his teachers. He has had multiple school suspensions and been labeled a troublemaker by his parents and teachers. This bothers him because he always feels that his actions are justified by the circumstances in which he finds himself.

He is walking across the school playground when two girls sitting on a bench begin teasing him. In the past, he would have snapped back with a scathing remark, escalating the situation further. Today he is practicing mindful breathing [choice point], so he just notes the irritability begin to grow without saying anything [choice point]. His face feels hot, his jaw tightens, and his fingers begin to clench. He knows that if he gets in another fight this semester, he will again be suspended from school. He chooses to keep walking [choice point] without saying anything to the girls [choice point]. Keeping his breathing clearly in his awareness [choice point], he shifts his attention to his thoughts [choice point]. In less than three paces, he notes four different judging statements. He keeps walking [choice point] as he focuses on observing sensations in his body [choice point]. The girls make another comment. He now observes that he feels no desire to react [choice point]. He reaches the far side of the playground without being captured by his thoughts or emotions. He walks inside, feeling pleased at having discovered so many choice points.

Choice points epitomize the different paradigm and un-goal-like "goals" of MBCT-C. In a sense, clarity to see choice points becomes the "fruit" of this practice and inspires constructive changes. We emphasize freedom to choose one's own choice points throughout the program.

Choice points only occur in the present moment. In order to make choices, Rick first must observe that choices are available. Rick can choose how to respond by being mindful of the moment. His behaviors may become less influenced by reactive judgments, emerging instead from conscious awareness and acceptance of the full experience. Awareness then enables the potential and freedom to change.

SUMMING UP

As you work toward cultivating mindful awareness for yourself and with your clients, it may be helpful to remember these important points:

- What may be most important initially is to allow each child to discover personally meaningful motivations to practice mindful awareness. Oftentimes, learning that mindful awareness can influence experiences becomes the intrinsic motivation.

- Without experiential understanding, the child may be less likely to practice or embrace any potential benefits from the program.

- Thoughts, feelings, and body sensations are separate (but related) intrapsychic events constantly flowing in and out of the nowscape.

- There are many other events in the nowscape as well.

- Judging is not the same as noting.

- Thoughts are "just" thoughts.

- We have choices and the freedom to choose how to respond to events in our lives.

Remember that it is not hard to be mindful, but it is hard to remember to be mindful. With that knowledge, practice mindful compassion for yourself and others while remembering to cultivate your own practice.

In the next chapter, we describe how we adapted the adult MBCT program so that it is developmentally appropriate for children. This will conclude our discussion of the theory, rationale, and development of MBCT-C. In part 2, we will offer details and specifics of conducting the program.

CHAPTER 4

Adapting Mindfulness-Based Cognitive Therapy for Children

There are only two lasting bequests we can give our children.
One is roots, and the other is wings.

Hodding Carter

Unlike children, adults don't often have spontaneous wrestling matches or a game of tug-of-war over a box of crayons. Adults generally don't protest too loudly when they are asked to take turns ringing the meditation bells. Adults typically don't construct a fort out of yoga mats or see how long they can balance a zafu (meditation cushion) on top of their heads. At least, not when other adults are watching.

Anyone who has the privilege of working with children knows that effective child therapy generally requires a flexible and creative approach, a healthy dose of patience, and a robust sense of humor. In this chapter, we'll discuss how mindfulness-based cognitive therapy for adults (MBCT) was adapted to meet the needs of children. We will describe the rationale for the changes we made and offer suggestions to consider when implementing your own program. (Please note: All handouts and signs mentioned in this chapter can be found in appendix C as well as on the accompanying CD-ROM.)

DEVELOPMENTAL CONSIDERATIONS: THREE PRIMARY DIFFERENCES

In creating a child-friendly adaptation of the successful MBCT adult program (Segal, Williams, & Teasdale, 2002), we considered how children differ from adults in their cognitive, affective, and physical development. The simple act of sitting on a cushion and watching the breath may be interesting, engaging, and personally meaningful to an adult who willingly chooses to do so. Most children, however, do not enter therapy voluntarily and may begin with little interest or understanding of mindful awareness.

We wished to find creative ways to make MBCT-C fun to children and help them discover personally meaningful reasons to engage in the practices. We wanted to adhere closely to the theoretical model described in chapter 3, while retaining the playfulness and compassionate spirit of MBSR and the therapeutic aims of MBCT. Keeping all this in mind, three fundamental developmental differences from adults informed our adaptations. First, children are at earlier levels of affective and cognitive development. Second, children have less capacity for sustained attention. Third, children are more dependent on family support and relationships. Let's take a closer look at each of these domains and explore the changes we made to address these differences.

Affective and Cognitive Development

Most adult therapies depend on the client's ability to identify and verbalize thoughts and feelings. Children have relatively undeveloped metacognitive awareness (that is, awareness of one's own cognitive processes), and so they tend to be less adept at describing their intrapsychic experiences or labeling their feelings (Bailey, 2001). If you ask an adult how she is feeling, she may reflect a moment and respond, "I'm feeling frustrated" or "very anxious." A child may be less able to describe his internal states with words. Instead, he may cry when he feels sad or scared. He may throw down his toys when he feels angry or frustrated. While young children often wear their hearts on their sleeves, translating their thoughts and emotions into words is sometimes a challenge.

Adult mindfulness programs, such as MBSR and MBCT, help the client learn to identify thoughts and feelings by cultivating awareness of the breath, body sensations, and other sensory experiences. These core practices are retained in MBCT-C. Like adults in MBSR and MBCT programs, the children in MBCT-C learn the practice of mindful awareness through experiential and interactive practices that engage all of the senses.

In addition, we developed short activities intended to help the child cultivate mindful awareness within specific sensory modes (that is, sight, sound, touch, smell, taste, and kinesthetics). These practices are presented in simple, age-appropriate language. They are accompanied by visually appealing materials to engage the child's attention and interest.

Attentional Capacity

Unlike the average adult, most children find it difficult to stay engaged with a single activity for an extended period without getting restless or bored. In developing MBCT-C, we made four structural changes to MBCT in order to address children's attentional differences.

First, we expanded the program to twelve weeks and shortened each session to ninety minutes. MBCT consists of sessions of two to two-and-a-half hours, conducted over eight weeks. Shorter sessions and longer program duration accommodated children's attentional differences within a similar programmatic structure.

Second, long sittings were replaced with shorter, more frequent practices. MBCT for adults traditionally incorporates breath meditations and body scan practices lasting up to forty-five minutes. Most children would find it difficult to sit quietly for this long without feeling the urge to giggle, move, or nudge the person next to him. In MBCT-C, sitting meditations are initially practiced in three-minute blocks, a few times within each session. We found that nearly all children can sit quietly, bringing awareness to the breath, for three minutes. Over several weeks, breath meditations increase to ten minutes. Later we'll describe the Three-Minute Breathing Space, a breathing practice borrowed directly from MBCT.

Third, a lower child-to-therapist ratio was implemented because children can require greater individual attention than adults. MBCT groups for adults typically have up to twelve participants with one therapist. MBCT-C was planned for groups of six to eight children, facilitated by one or two therapists.

Fourth, the program activities were enlivened and diversified in order to engage the child's attention and provide frequent opportunities for the child to stretch and move around. MBCT-C practices are more varied than MBCT practices. MBCT-C session activities alternate between focused sensory practices, short breath meditations, mindful movement, mindfulness of the body practices, visualization, drawing or writing exercises, and interactive discussions.

Family Interrelatedness

MBCT-C was designed so that parents are an integral part of the program. Children are dependent on their parents or guardians in ways that most adults are not. They rely on adults for all their basic survival and security needs—physically, emotionally, socially, and spiritually. When parents are engaged in the child's treatment and support the child's mindfulness practice outside therapy, benefits are likely enhanced. MBCT-C is structured to engage parents throughout the program.

Parents begin by attending a two-hour group orientation session shortly before the program begins, called Introduction to Mindfulness. Parents have an opportunity to meet one another and ask questions of the therapists in a relaxed group setting. During the orientation, the therapist provides a brief overview of the program and discusses some potential benefits of mindfulness meditation. Next, parents are guided through several of the experiential practices that the children will be learning in upcoming weeks. In the therapist-guided interactive group discussion that follows, parents are invited to discover the benefits of cultivating mindful awareness along with their children. They are encouraged to actively support the child's practice and to model mindful speech and behavior at home.

After this initial orientation to MBCT-C, some parents may wish to start their own meditation practice. We provide an information sheet (handout A) that describes the program, and its purpose and benefits, and also includes a few reading suggestions and additional resources. In the programs we conducted, we presented each parent with a complimentary copy of the book *Everyday Blessings: The Inner Work of Mindful Parenting* (M. Kabat-Zinn & J. Kabat-Zinn, 1998). This small gift, graciously accepted by the parents, became a tangible expression of our shared commitment to the children and to the practice of cultivating mindful awareness. In chapter 5, we describe the parent orientation session in more detail and provide practical strategies to incorporate MBCT-C into your clinical practice.

Parents and therapists are typically in regular contact throughout the twelve-week program. Therapists may telephone parents to discuss a specific clinical issue involving their child, inquire about a missed session, or make program announcements. We encourage you to invite parents to call you throughout the program to ask questions or offer feedback.

Each child receives written materials to take home in "travel folders" that they carry to and from the sessions. Children are encouraged to share these written materials with their parents. The handouts include poems and stories, a summary of each session, home practice instructions, and daily recording sheets. With the handouts, parents develop a systematic understanding of the aims of each session and the ways in which we practice mindful awareness in everyday life. The materials give parents the opportunity to participate in the home-based practices with their child.

At the end of the program, a parent review session is held. Parents are invited to share their experiences of the MBCT-C program and discuss ways to cultivate and support their child's continued practice. The review session is less structured than the orientation session. Parents have used this time to discuss their experiences with the program, speak about changes they may have seen in their child's emotional state or behaviors, and help us to understand how the program might be improved. In most child treatments, therapists naturally forge a bond with the parents of child clients, so the review session also provides therapists and parents the opportunity to say farewell. The parent review session will be described more in chapter 13.

STRUCTURAL CONSIDERATIONS: ESTABLISHING THE FOUNDATION

The adaptations above address the developmental differences between adults and children in cognition, attention, and family involvement. Here we discuss key considerations in structuring and establishing the foundations of the MBCT-C program.

While group therapy is a preferred modality for MBCT-C, we offer a number of suggestions for modifications necessary to adapt each session for individual therapy. In practice, forming a therapy group may involve logistical challenges that make it impractical or unfeasible for many clinicians.

Group Therapy

Similar to MBSR and MBCT, group dialogues are integral to MBCT-C. The children learn practices of mindful awareness from each other by sharing their unique perspectives in a group setting. In early sessions, group dialogues focus on identifying the barriers or obstacles to completing the home practices. Children are invited to share their personal stories of integrating mindful awareness into their daily routines. One child, for example, may suggest posting the home practice record on his refrigerator door as a reminder to practice every day. Others may share personally relevant ways they discovered to enhance mindful awareness in their lives. Rather than telling the children what to do, we encourage you to offer your clients ample opportunities to share their insights and suggestions for the benefit of the entire group. Through shared dialogues, the group dynamic evolves, establishing the group as a safe and secure environment.

GROUP SIZE

MBCT-C groups consist of six to eight children, facilitated by one or two therapists to provide each child with greater individualized attention. If necessary, groups of up to twelve participants with two therapists are feasible. If only one therapist is available to lead the group, an upper limit of eight children is recommended. Beyond that, you may not be able to provide each child with sufficient individual attention.

GROUP COMPOSITION

This program is specifically developed for children nine to twelve years of age. Children at opposite ends of this age range, however, can be worlds apart in their development because of the tremendous strides in physical, cognitive, social, and emotional development that typically occur during this period. If feasible, you may want to consider conducting separate groups for younger children (aged nine and ten) and older children (aged eleven and twelve) so that you can tailor your interventions more appropriately. A twelve-year-old may be familiar with the word "anxiety," while a nine-year-old may be more responsive to the words "fear" and "worry." A twelve-year-old may be preoccupied with peer problems at school, while the nine-year-old may be more concerned with staying out of trouble at home. Younger children may require more structure or guidance than older children. You may find that working with different age groups shifts your perspective, creating subtle changes in how you speak or interact with the children.

Even among twelve-year-olds, significant differences can be found. One example is the onset of puberty. In our research program, we worked with several twelve- and thirteen-year-olds in the throes of obvious physical changes, towering over their peers and exhibiting secondary sexual characteristics that made them easily mistakable for older adolescents. These physically more mature clients were less engaged with the group process. The differences in physical maturity compared to their peers may have contributed to their early termination from the program. For this reason, we recommend selecting children at similar stages of cognitive, emotional, and physical development in composing your groups. We offer further suggestions on identifying appropriate clients in chapter 5.

Individual Therapy

In individual therapy, a child will not have the opportunity to learn from his peers as he does in a group setting. The dyad between the therapist and client, however, can be considered a group in its own right, albeit a very small group. The most significant change when modifying MBCT-C from group to individual therapy is that a greater degree of active participation on the therapist's part will be necessary. Nearly all activities will take less time with one child than with a group, so for the most part, reducing the ninety-minute group format to a sixty-minute individual format will still allow sufficient time to complete the activities described in each group session. Suggestions for adapting specific group activities, alternative activities for a few practices that can't be readily adapted, and example practice inquiries for individual therapy are provided at the end of each session description.

ENVIRONMENTAL CONSIDERATIONS: DEFINING THE SPACE

Children spend many hours in school, and most know what is expected of them: sit in their assigned seats, face the front of the classroom, listen to the teacher at the blackboard, and follow her instructions. They also know what they are not supposed to do: roam the halls without a pass, eat in class, or play video games. Children are expected to follow rules that are outlined by teachers and school administrators. Most, of course, are necessary for the school to function properly and to ensure the safety of the children.

A special kind of environment differentiates MBCT-C from a classroom setting, yet MBCT-C retains sufficient structure to foster a secure therapeutic environment. This delicate balance between the need for structure and the need for playful exploration is renegotiated continuously between the children and the mindful therapist.

Cultivating a Different Space

In traditional therapies, hierarchical power differences exist between the therapist and the client, generally with the therapist having a higher level of authority. We encourage you instead to be an integrated participant, one who participates in, as well as supports, the children's process of self-discovery. You may encourage the children to remove their shoes and sit on floor cushions while doing so yourself. You may sit with the children, so that you are all together in an inward facing circle. You may include your name on the attendance board alongside the children's names. You may actively participate in all program activities, complete the home practices, and, as appropriate, share relevant personal experiences with the group. With two therapists (possibly alternating roles), one therapist is available to guide a practice activity while the other serves as a "supportive participant," practicing with the children and available to a child in need of individual attention.

This different kind of space is further cultivated by interacting less formally with the children than do most teachers. In MBCT-C, we prefer to invite children to call us by our first names, further differentiating this program from a school environment. This informality subtly emphasizes an experiential approach to learning rather than a didactic method of teaching, and establishes you as active participant rather than instructor. In some settings (for example, universities, hospitals, or community agencies), it may not be customary for children to address adults by their given names. In this event, please invite the children to address you in whatever way is comfortable for you.

The Quiet Space

A central tenet of MBCT-C emphasizes freedom of choice. We all have the freedom to respond to situations with greater awareness. Creating a special space for a child who does not want to participate in a given activity supports this concept. A designated chair is placed in one corner of the room, identified with a sign that reads "Quiet Space". If a child does not want to participate in an activity for any reason, he may sit quietly in this space until he wishes to rejoin the group. The space is regarded as a safe retreat. It is not intended to be used for "time-outs" or be monitored by the therapist. The children are not instructed to go to the space; rather, it is offered as a place where they can choose to rest or be alone as needed. Some kids spontaneously spend a few minutes there and then seamlessly rejoin the group when they are ready. A child is not expected to explain why he needs a few minutes to be alone. The group members are encouraged to understand that using the Quiet Space is a personal choice and that a decision to do so requires no explanation.

Guidelines for Mindful Behavior

When a group of children gets ready to play a game together, the first thing they do is make sure everyone is clear about the rules. Children generally feel more comfortable when they understand the rules of the game, the procedures involved, and the behaviors that are expected of them. This is especially true when they are thrown into a novel situation. When working with children in groups, it is usually necessary to offer more explicit guidelines than when working with adults. For example, most adults comply with the social convention not to interrupt while another person is speaking. Children, however, may need occasional reminders.

Cultivating compassion and mutual respect begins with the first session, when you will discuss and agree upon the group's guidelines. Our suggested Guidelines for Mindful Behavior (handout D) can be distributed to each child:

Guidelines for Mindful Behavior

1. We choose to act and speak to other people with care and kindness.

2. We can remember not to talk when another person is talking.

3. We can remember to raise a hand to share our ideas with the group.

4. We agree not to talk during mindful awareness practices so as not to disturb others.

5. We agree that if anyone does not wish to take part in an activity, one person at a time may sit in the Quiet Space.

There likely will be times when children momentarily fail to remember the guidelines. You may choose to ring the meditation bells, or ask a child to ring the bells, thereby inviting the group to return to the present moment. The bells offer a gentle but compelling reminder to return awareness to experiences in the here-and-now. With several groups, we've seen dynamic social norms quickly emerge in which mindful behaviors from one child elicit mindful behaviors in the others. This *esprit de corps* likely arises from freely offered cooperation, where "behavioral management" of the group is taken care of by the children themselves.

We have experienced momentary lapses of the guidelines ourselves, for example, by inadvertently addressing the children in an authoritarian manner. When the children were becoming a bit rambunctious or restless, our tone of voice may have conveyed our fears that we were losing control of the group. In retrospect, our asking a child (as we suggest you not do), "Are you being mindful right now?" was a question that arose more from our own insecurities and fears than from our genuine interest in the children's well-being. We had not yet learned to trust the process. Therapists learning this approach may also become more aware of their own insecurities. The mindful therapist learns to trust the wisdom gained from her personal practice to support and guide the group. Knowing that she, too, will have occasional lapses, she can still form intentions to embody mindful behaviors, and speak to others with care and kindness.

Worry Warts Wastebasket

The presence of the Worry Warts Wastebasket sends a message that all experiences, positive, negative, or neutral, are welcome in the therapeutic setting. The Worry Warts Wastebasket is a small container supplied with pencils and paper. It is placed just inside the door of the therapy room. At the beginning of each session, you may invite each child to write down his current worry on a piece of paper and then put it in the wastebasket for the duration of the session. The inclusion of this child-friendly activity serves several purposes. First, it helps the child identify and articulate his anxieties. Second, it informs the child that he can bring his worries with him to the session, and emphasizes that he has a choice in deciding what to do with them. He can, for example, choose to leave them in the wastebasket or retrieve them later. He can choose not to discuss them, or he may decide to share them with the group. Third, it supports the notion that the child can decenter from the worries and that it is possible simply to let them go. Finally, a small catharsis is often achieved by the action itself. Many children delight in crumpling up their worries and getting rid of them (at least temporarily) by "scoring a basket."

Bells of Mindfulness

In MBCT-C, as in adult MBSR and MBCT programs, we use meditation bells to signal the beginning and end of each mindfulness practice. Bells, small cymbals, or bowls that produce a clear, long-lasting tone may be used. Using the bells of mindfulness helps cultivate an awareness of the transition into each mindful awareness activity. Children have a natural curiosity and often develop an affinity for the bells and what the bells represent. As the therapist, you will demonstrate how the bells are to be handled—not as toys, but with respect. Ringing the bells signals a clear intention to practice being present.

PROCEDURAL CONSIDERATIONS: ADOPTING A PLAYFUL, BALANCED APPROACH

The MBCT-C practices are presented in a child friendly way. We offer a balanced approach that provides structure and guidance while cultivating playful procedures and practices.

Being Present (Attendance Record)

Attendance is recorded each week on the Being Present Board, a board that lists names and session dates. Instead of having the therapist "take attendance," the group practices "being present" each week. At the start of each session, each child places a colored sticker next to his name for that particular session. This activity can be a small ceremony to mark the beginning of each session. Some children may express satisfaction at the number of sessions they have attended. Some compete in a friendly way with each other for the most sessions attended. The Being Present Board allows children to chart their progress through the twelve-session program. The visual reminder of the Being Present Board may also increase treatment compliance.

Feely Faces Scale

As mentioned earlier, children may not have the cognitive and verbal capacity to express how they feel. A feelings scale is typically used in various forms of child therapy as a way to help the child identify how he's feeling by using pictures. In MBCT-C, the Feely Faces Scale (handout E) displays seven different flower faces ranging from "very relaxed" to "very worried." The child places a colored sticker in the box that corresponds to the appropriate face on the scale. Using two Feely Faces scales (pre and post) encourages the child to pause for a moment, observe, and note his feelings at the beginning and end of each session. It helps him focus attention on his present experiences and learn that emotional states change over time.

Transforming Home "Work" into Home "Practice"

Home practice assignments are an integral component of MBCT-C. "Homework" is a word that few children like to hear, so it is simply referred to as "home practice" in MBCT-C. The home practices for each week are short exercises that require about fifteen minutes each day, six days each week. The activities, first introduced and practiced in session, are intended to be fun and relaxing. They provide clear guidance to help the child integrate mindful awareness practices into activities of daily living. You may choose to underscore the importance of "everyday" practice that creates continuity between sessions.

For the home practice, encourage the children to identify a quiet space at home if possible and set aside a consistent time for their practice. Obstacles inevitably arise: the presence of an exuberant sibling, lack of privacy, a noisy household, or an overly full schedule. During the home practice review at the beginning of each session, children have opportunities to share their personal experiences and challenges. To guide this discussion, it can be helpful for the children to record their daily practices on the worksheets provided (reproducible record forms are provided in appendix C and on the CD-ROM).

Obstacles are an integral part of practicing mindful awareness. All experiences are considered "grist for the mill." Interruptions can be defined simply as more events to be aware of, rather than as distractions to the practice of mindful awareness. When the group members share challenging experiences, children learn from their peers, discover new ways to carve out the necessary time and space, and transform challenges into more opportunities to practice mindful awareness.

Practicing mindful awareness, children learn that changes may not be immediately noticeable. The development of mindfulness is often compared to cultivating a garden. A seed does not bloom into a flower overnight. First, the ground must be prepared and tilled. Then the seeds must be planted. With the proper amounts of water, food, and sunlight, sprouts will gradually appear. Through forming the intentions, cultivating patience, and practicing mindful attention, eventually the sprouts grow and flowers bloom. In the same way, the therapist can invite the children to approach their practice with curiosity and patience, knowing that the fruits of their efforts may not be immediately apparent, but may grow over time.

Growth of the Therapist

As we developed and began conducting MBCT-C, we became aware of certain decisions we made that may have inadvertently undermined some of the messages we intended to convey. Here, we offer some lessons we learned along our own journey, with the hope that, in similar circumstances, you may learn from our mistakes.

We initially provided smiley face stickers for the children to record their attendance. The use of smiley faces may have conveyed a subtle message that positive emotions were valued more than other emotions. We also offered cartoon stickers for the completion of home practices. Although we never actually withheld a sticker from any child, the use of stickers as "rewards" may have expressed a message of striving for external goals rather than conveying an unconditional acceptance of what is present.

Upon reflection, we believe that these choices emerged from our own uncertainties. We did not yet trust ourselves or the process. We did not know if we could adequately engage the children or trust them to complete the home practices on their own. We believed (and still do) that the children would benefit more by completing the home practices than not. We recognized the need to help each child find personally meaningful reasons to engage with these practices; however, a part of us didn't really believe that they would. Much of our own work during this time involved letting go of our expectations and allowing the children the freedom to choose their own paths. We discovered that children, if given the choice, often choose wisely. The true "reward" for the child is in discovering for himself personally meaningful reasons to practice mindful awareness. No amount of smiley faces or cartoon stickers will help him arrive at this realization. Although the stickers may have encouraged the children to practice long enough to find their own meaning, we learned that the therapist's own personal preparation and ongoing practice is the most important ground from which the child's own discoveries grow. In conclusion, we encourage you to practice, trust yourself, trust the process, and believe that children are capable of making wise choices.

SUMMING UP

In its final form, MBCT-C has retained the theoretical underpinnings of MBSR and MBCT. It adapted many of their central practices to be more accessible to a young child. The adaptations we made are based on differences in affective and cognitive development, capacity for attention, and family dependence. We gave careful consideration to the therapeutic environment and the creation of a safe space.

In working with children in either group or individual therapy, balance is maintained when we provide nominal structure while allowing plenty of room for playful discovery. This balance is fluid, ever changing, and in constant negotiation. Children are diverse in their needs and personalities. Every group member, including yourself, will offer unique contributions to the overall identity of the group—whether a large group of eight or ten members, or a small group of one child and one therapist. The process will never be the same from week to week or from group to group. Implementing greater or lesser structure depends on many factors. Most therapists are already adept at listening carefully to the specific needs of each client and adapting her interventions as the therapeutic relationship evolves. Cultivating your own mindful awareness is the practice of seeing clearly and trusting your own wisdom—moment by moment.

In part 2, we explain how to conduct MBCT-C. For each of the twelve sessions, we include a session overview, an outline, and identified treatment goals. Descriptions of each mindfulness practice with sample dialogues, along with a list of the handouts and materials needed, are provided. We also offer suggestions for adapting the group practices for individual therapy. Before we go into session-by-session details, however, let's explore some of the practical issues associated with implementing the program and gain a more thorough understanding of the overall approach and intentions of MBCT-C.

PART 2

Mindfulness-Based Cognitive Therapy for Children

CHAPTER 5

Overview of the Twelve-Session Program

The faculty of voluntarily bringing back a wandering attention, over and over again, is the very root of judgment, character, and will... But it is easier to define this ideal than to give practical directions for bringing it about.

William James (1890)

In this chapter, we provide an overview of the program and offer practical guidelines to work with children in group or individual therapy. The program begins with an orientation to mindfulness, shifts to cultivating mindful awareness across the senses, and ends with an integration of the lessons. Each session is supplemented with handouts, including session summaries, home practice worksheets, and poems or stories. Table 2 shows a summary of the twelve sessions and lists follow-up materials to be sent to participants three months after the final session. The written materials and handouts are included in appendix C and on the CD-ROM packaged with this book.

The aims of the initial phase (sessions 1 to 3) are to provide an orientation to mindfulness, establish program expectations, review parameters for the program, and address barriers to maintaining the home practice. These sessions also focus on cultivating mindfulness of the breath and body.

The middle phase (sessions 4 to 10) deepens mindful awareness with sensory-based practices. Children learn that their own thoughts, feelings, and body sensations can contribute to increasing or decreasing anxiety. They may learn to differentiate judging from noting, and to see more clearly what response choices are available to them. These core themes are repeated across a variety of sensory modes and activities.

The termination phase (sessions 11 to 12) addresses the integration of mindful awareness across the senses and maintenance of mindfulness practices in daily life. In any therapeutic work, whether in group or individual therapy, we need to address termination issues. You may wish to help children prepare for this parting by taking the time to celebrate the shared journey. We also recognize that remembering to practice mindful awareness can be more difficult than actually being present and aware. To encourage the maintenance of daily practice, we suggest sending a letter to each child three months after the program ends. Intended as a friendly reminder to practice mindful awareness, each letter will have been written by the child to herself.

As we guide children through each session, we can sometimes become so engaged in an activity that we momentarily lose sight of its purpose. It is one thing to listen to a song or eat a raisin with mindful awareness. Helping to transform these experiences into something applicable to the child's everyday life is the task of the mindful therapist. How might a mindful listening activity help a child feel less anxious when taking an exam? How can practicing mindfulness of the body help her feel less nervous and more competent when interacting in social situations? Mindfulness practices are inherently relaxing. Relaxation, however, is a secondary benefit. The primary aim is to support the child in developing a different relationship to her thoughts and feelings, and to help her adopt a new way of being in the world.

Table 2. Overview of the Twelve Sessions and Follow-Up

Session and Theme	Key Points	In-Session Practices	Poems, Stories, and Other Handouts	Home Practices
1 Being on Automatic Pilot	• We live much of our lives on automatic pilot. • Mindfulness exists, and it is a different, more helpful way of being in the world.	• Getting to Know You • Discovering Awareness in a Cup • What Mindfulness Means to Me • Taking Three Mindful Breaths	• Mindful Breathing Is the Best Practice • Mindfulness Is Cultivating Attention	• Mindful Breathing Lying Down • Mindful Breathing Sitting Up • Living with Awareness
2 Being Mindful Is Simple, but It Is Not Easy!	• Living with awareness isn't easy, so why are we doing this anyway? • We give attention to the barriers to practice. • Understanding the importance of practice. • Bringing awareness to the breath and body.	• Taking Three Mindful Breaths • Raisin Mindfulness • Mindfully Moooving Slooowly • Taking Three Mindful Breaths	• Flight from the Shadow • Practicing Mindful Awareness • Instructions for Mindful Breathing	• Living with Awareness • Mindful Breathing • Mindful Eating
3 Who Am I?	• Thoughts arise in the present, but are often about the past or future. • Thoughts may not be accurate to the present reality. • Thoughts are not facts.	• Taking Three Mindful Breaths • Mindfulness of the Body • Hey, I Have Thoughts, Feelings, and Body Sensations! • Listening to the Sounds of Silence • Taking Three Mindful Breaths	• Have You Ever Gotten a Thought? • Breathing • Who Am I?	• Mindful Breathing • Mindfulness of the Body • Pleasant Events

Session and Theme	Key Points	In-Session Practices	Poems, Stories, and Other Handouts	Home Practices
4 A Taste of Mindfulness	• We have thoughts, feelings, and body sensations, but these are not who we are. • Thoughts, feelings, and body sensations are not exactly the same as the events they describe.	• Introduction to Three-Minute Breathing Space • Opening to One Orange • Mindful Yoga Movements • Three-Minute Breathing Space	• Ode to a Grape • Three-Minute Breathing Space	• Three-Minute Breathing Space • Mindful Yoga Movements • Tasting Fruits
5 Music to Our Ears	• Thoughts, feelings, and body sensations often color how we experience the world. • With our thoughts, we create individual and unique relationships and experiences. Awareness holds it all.	• Three-Minute Breathing Space • Do You Hear What I Hear? • Mindfulness of the Body • Three-Minute Breathing Space	• The Door	• Three-Minute Breathing Space • Mindfulness of the Body • Mindful Listening
6 Sound Expressions	• Practicing mindful awareness helps us recognize that thoughts, feelings, and body sensations influence how we express ourselves. • We can choose to express ourselves with mindful awareness.	• Three-Minute Breathing Space • Sounding Out Emotions—Mindfully • Mindful Yoga Movements • Three-Minute Breathing Space	• Hearing	• Three-Minute Breathing Space • Mindful Yoga Movements • Unpleasant Sounds

Session and Theme	Key Points	In-Session Practices	Poems, Stories, and Other Handouts	Home Practices
7 Practice Looking	• Judging is not the same as noting. • If we simply observe experiences rather than judge them, the experience may change. • We can choose to observe or note our experiences instead of judge them.	• Three-Minute Breathing Space • Visualizing with Clarity • Mindful Yoga Movements • Seeing What Is in the Mind's Eye • Three-Minute Breathing Space	• Looking	• Three-Minute Breathing Space • Seeing the Little Details • Stressful Events
8 Strengthening the Muscle of Attention	• Judging often changes how we experience the world. • Becoming more aware of judgments may change how we relate to thoughts and feelings. • Discovering "choice points."	• Three-Minute Breathing Space • Seeing Through Illusions • Moving Mindfully • Seeing What Is Not There • Three-Minute Breathing Space	• Choices	• Three-Minute Breathing Space • Choosing to Be Aware • Seeing Five New Things
9 Touching the World with Mindfulness	• We have little control over most events that occur. • We do have choices in how we respond to events. • Choice points exist only in the present moment. • Bringing greater awareness to this moment, we may see more choice points.	• Three-Minute Breathing Space • Being in Touch • Mindfulness of the Body • Three-Minute Breathing Space	• Touch	• Three-Minute Breathing Space • Mindfulness of the Body • Mindful Touching

Session and Theme	Key Points	In-Session Practices	Poems, Stories, and Other Handouts	Home Practices
10 What the Nose Knows	• We often react to events by moving toward things we like or judge as "good" and moving away from things we don't like or judge as "bad." • Judging an experience may interfere with seeing clearly what is present in each moment. • We have choices in how we respond to events.	• Three-Minute Breathing Space • Judging Stinks! • Mindful Yoga Movements • Three-Minute Breathing Space	• To Be or Not to Be. • Things We Can Learn from a Dog	• Three-Minute Breathing Space • Mindful Yoga Movements • Mindful Smelling
11 Life Is Not a Rehearsal	• Mindfulness is available in everyday life. • We can practice mindful awareness using all our senses.	• Three-Minute Breathing Space • Thoughts Are Not Facts • Feelings Are Not Facts Either • Raisin Mindfulness • Mindfulness Is… • Three-Minute Breathing Space	• Slow Dance • Letter to My Self	• Three-Minute Breathing Space • Letter to My Self

Session and Theme	Key Points	In-Session Practices	Poems, Stories, and Other Handouts	Home Practices
12 Living with Presence, Compassion, and Awareness	• Mindful awareness can be helpful in our daily lives. • Bringing greater awareness to our lives is a personal choice. • Living with awareness requires commitment, compassion, and continued daily practice.	• Three-Minute Breathing Space • Exploring Everyday Mindfulness • Program Evaluation (optional) • Three-Minute Breathing Space • Graduation Ceremony • Graduation Party! • Three-Minute Breathing Space	• Little Gidding • Living with Presence, Compassion, and Awareness • Letter from Therapist to Child • Daily Practice Calendar • Program Evaluation Questionnaire (optional)	
Three-Month Follow-Up	• Support for maintaining a daily practice of mindful awareness.	• No session • Therapist mails Letter to My Self and Daily Practice Calendar to each child	• Letter to My Self (written by the child after session 11) • Three-Month Follow-Up Letter from Therapist to Child • Daily Practice Calendar	

GETTING STARTED

Before you begin, we would like to offer our thoughts about a few key issues. These include identifying children who are appropriate for group or individual therapy, gathering the necessary materials, structuring the sessions, cultivating a mindful space, and working with parents.

Identifying Appropriate Children: The Initial Interview

When identifying children to be included in a group, we recommend that an initial interview be held with each prospective child and her parents. The main purpose of the meeting is to evaluate whether or not the child is likely to find MBCT-C meaningful and worthwhile at this time.

GROUP THERAPY

The decision to enroll a child in group treatment depends on several factors. During the initial interview, you will identify the child's strengths, as well as symptoms and problem areas, and then explore the suitability of the program for this child at this particular time. (We'll look at specific questions to consider below.) This initial discussion also provides you with an opportunity to explain MBCT-C to the parents and discuss how mindfulness can allow the child to stay present with anxious thoughts and feelings, and then respond more effectively to stressful situations. If it appears that the child could benefit from MBCT-C, inform the parents about Introduction to Mindfulness (the parent orientation session) and the child's session schedule.

As you explore with the parents whether their child might benefit more from group or individual therapy, the consideration of certain issues may be useful. Some questions to consider during the initial interview include these:

- Is the child experiencing a significant level of distress?

- What is the level of commitment of the parents?

- What is the level of motivation of the parents and the child?

- Does the child have attention deficit/hyperactivity disorder (ADHD)?

- Does the child have any food allergies?

Let's take a closer look at some issues raised by each of these questions.

Is the child experiencing a significant level of distress? Part of your assessment is a consideration of whether the child might be better served in group or individual therapy. Are her symptoms interfering with activities of daily living? For example, if significant distress related to her anxiety makes it difficult for her to attend school, individual therapy may better support a problem-focused intervention. Some MBSR and MBCT instructors will not admit individuals into the program if they are actively suicidal and have no other form of counseling support (Segal et al., 2002). We take a similar stance with children who are actively suicidal or experiencing psychotic symptoms. Children or adolescents who are using alcohol or drugs will be better served by therapies aimed at treating these specific behaviors.

What is the level of commitment of the parents? Parents are responsible for providing transportation for their child to attend therapy sessions. Will they bring their child to group therapy every week or make alternative transportation arrangements? Irvin D. Yalom (2005) notes that consistent attendance is important for a cohesive group and recommends excluding those who may not be able to attend regularly. Parents are also expected to attend the Introduction to Mindfulness (orientation) session before the program begins, and a parent review session after the program ends. Are they committed to attending these sessions? These expectations need to be clearly explained during the initial interview.

What is the level of motivation of the parents and the child? Although motivation is considered the most important inclusion criteria for adult psychotherapy (Yalom, 2005), this is not necessarily the case with children. Some children may not fully understand therapy—what it is, how it might be useful, or why they need to go. We cannot rely solely on the child's initial motivation to determine her suitability for group therapy. Instead, we engage the parents and establish our expectations for their involvement. Are they motivated and willing to be actively involved in the child's weekly home-based practices? Explain to the parents that participation in MBCT-C encourages shared home practice time for all twelve weeks of the program.

Parents are expected to review the home practice assignments with their child every week and participate in the experiential activities. If they are not prepared to be involved and engaged, it may be best for them to defer beginning the program until they feel ready for this level of commitment.

Does the child have attention deficit/hyperactivity disorder (ADHD)? Although preliminary research supports the feasibility of group mindfulness meditation for adolescents with ADHD (Zylowska et al., 2008), it is unknown whether those results generalize to younger children or to diagnostically mixed groups. Evaluate each child on a case-by-case basis, assess symptom severity, and consider how the child might fit in with group members whose primary problem is anxiety. The child may be better served in individual therapy with its greater degree of personalized attention.

Does the child have any food allergies? It is wise to ask the parents about any food allergies their child might have, either in the initial interview or during the Introduction to Mindfulness session. MBCT-C includes several mindful eating exercises using oranges, raisins, and other dried fruits. If a child is allergic to any of the foods you plan to use, you might ask the parents to provide substitute food items. Similarly, some children may experience allergic responses to certain scents. Assorted scents are used in the mindful smelling activities. You may ask the parents if the child has had adverse reactions to any smells. Some scents like ammonia may be best avoided altogether. Less important for the purpose of these exercises is the child's preference for specific foods or scents. Mindful eating and smelling practices offer opportunities for the child to observe her likes and dislikes, while learning to see them as simply judgments about experiences.

OTHER SUGGESTIONS FOR CONSTRUCTING THERAPY GROUPS WITH CHILDREN

An in-depth discussion of the art and science of constructing therapy groups is beyond the scope of this chapter. Yalom's (2005) seminal book on group psychotherapy offers a comprehensive discussion of this issue. Suggestions we have found most useful in our clinical work with children include these:

- When possible, create groups that include similar numbers of girls and boys.

- When possible, restrict the age range within a group. For example, create one group with nine- and ten-year-olds and a separate group of eleven- and twelve-year-olds.

- When a child acts much older or younger than her chronological age, determine the best fit on an individual basis. An eight-year-old who cognitively and behaviorally acts more like an eleven-year-old might fare better with a slightly older age group.

INDIVIDUAL THERAPY

In individual therapy, you do not need to consider the fit with other group members or how individual dynamics affect the therapeutic process (Yalom, 2005). The central question is whether the child is likely to benefit from a mindfulness-based therapy. You should assess the potential to establish a working alliance with the child and her parents, and determine their level of motivation. An essential question is this: are the parents willing to participate in their child's home-based mindful awareness practices and activities? Children often benefit more when the parents actively engage in daily practice. After conducting the initial interview with parents and child to assess the child's appropriateness for this therapy, schedule a separate session with parents for the Introduction to Mindfulness (orientation) session.

Gathering Needed Materials

Here we describe general materials needed for all sessions. Additional materials specific to each session will be listed with that session.

- *Mats:* Exercise or yoga mats are used for activities done on the floor, for example, mindfulness of the body and mindful movement activities.

- *Cushions:* Use small, firm pillows or meditation cushions designed specifically for children. Choosing cushions that are all alike reduces the likelihood that a child might feel possessive about a specific cushion. In group therapy, cushions are organized in a circle in the center of the room. In individual therapy, two cushions can be arranged to face each other. Appendix A provides information about purchasing children's meditation supplies.

- *Meditation bells:* Each session begins and ends with a brief sitting meditation. A meditation bell or gong is used to signal the beginning and end of the mindfulness practices.

- *Being Present Board for attendance:* An attendance board can be made of heavy poster paper or foam board. First names (of children and therapist) run down the left side, and session numbers run across the top. In a group setting, the Being Present Board can be placed in the center of the circle, and at the beginning of each session, each child chooses a colored sticker to place next to her name. In individual therapy, you may create a smaller version of the Being Present Board or choose to dispense with it altogether. Individual therapy allows greater flexibility, and a child can complete each session at her own pace. It can still be useful to recognize this child's "being present" each week to help remind her of her progress through the program.

- *Three-ring binders or notebooks:* Each child receives a book, *Mindfulness in Everyday Life*, to hold the session materials. Binders with transparent front and back cover pockets (view binders) are recommended. The child completes a drawing activity in session 1: "what mindfulness means to me" for the front cover. In session 11, the same exercise is repeated to create the back cover (front and back cover templates for these are included with the handouts in appendix C).

- *Binder dividers:* The notebook is separated into five sections by dividers:

  1. *How I Feel:* This section includes the Feely Faces scales described later.

  2. *Session Summaries:* We suggest preparing this section in advance for all the notebooks so that the session summaries are organized in sequence.

  3. *Home Practices:* Home practice information and practice records for each session are in this section. We suggest preparing this section in advance as well.

4. *Mindfulness Poems, Stories, and Other Materials*: For each session, a poem or short story supports the main theme and therapy goals. The poems are distributed and read aloud by group members at the end of each session, and then added to this section. Some sessions have additional handouts, usually informational, that can be included in this section.

5. *My Experiences of Mindfulness*: This section includes a few sheets of lined paper for the written activities that are completed in-session.

• *Home practice record form for parents (handout B)*: The use of practice records for parents is optional. They may be used to record home practice compliance for research purposes or for parents to track their own personal practice.

• *Travel folders*: Some therapists may wish to review the child's notebook materials between sessions. Researchers who are evaluating the MBCT-C protocol may prefer that the notebook information be accessible as well. If the notebooks are left with you between sessions, travel folders allow the child to transport session summaries and home practice assignments to and from each session. Pocket folders can be labeled with each child's name. You can invite the child to remove the materials for each particular session and place them in her travel folder. Materials are returned to the notebook the following week.

• *Colored paper for session handouts*: Using one color for each session is an easy way to organize materials. For example, use blue paper for session 1 handouts, yellow for session 2, and so on. This also gives both you and the children an easy reference point. You may describe handouts from a previous session as the "green handouts."

• *Art supplies*: You will need an assortment of art supplies for the in-session drawing activities. These may include crayons, colored markers, colored pencils, lead pencils, pens, construction paper, scissors, tape, and a three-hole punch.

• *Stickers*: You will need colored dot stickers for the child to record her attendance on the Being Present Board and her present emotional state on the Feely Faces scales.

- *Whiteboard, chalkboard, or easel:* A whiteboard, chalkboard, or easel with poster paper will be useful during a number of the discussions that follow the activities.

- *Worry Warts Wastebasket:* Place a small container, along with pencils and notepaper, just inside the door of the therapy room. You may introduce the Worry Warts Wastebasket in session 1. In subsequent sessions, as the children arrive, they are invited to write down their worries on paper and put them in the wastebasket. This symbolic decentering from anxious thoughts may help a young child comprehend that the worried thoughts are "not me" and that she has choices in how to relate to the worries. The child is invited to deposit her worries in the wastebasket for the duration of the session and pick them up before she leaves, or she may choose to leave them behind.

- *Feely Faces Scale:* This scale allows the child to identify her subjective level of well-being at the beginning and end of each session. Seven different emotional expressions, from "very relaxed" to "very worried," are arranged vertically to correspond to a seven-point Likert-type scale. The child is asked to rate her overall mood and record this by placing a sticker in the appropriate box. One scale is used to record the presession mood state and a second to assess postsession mood state (see handout E).

Therapy work with children generally requires additional materials or resources. You will need to prepare some supplies for most sessions, but there are ways to manage costs. Children can be asked to bring their own mats and cushions. See what supplies you already have at home. Rummage through your attic or stop by a local yard sale. Commercial meditation supplies are not required. You can substitute less costly materials to stay within a budget.

Structuring Group Sessions

Each ninety-minute group session follows the same general procedure:

1. Complete the initial Feely Faces Scale.

2. Take attendance with the Being Present Board.

3. Guide the first brief sitting meditation.

4. Briefly review the previous session.

5. Introduce the agenda for the current session.

6. Review home practices from the previous week.

7. Conduct experiential mindful awareness practices and activities.

8. Guide the second brief sitting meditation.

9. Read the poem or story as a group.

10. Complete the second Feely Faces Scale.

11. Distribute and read session handouts.

12. Review home practices for the upcoming week.

Steps 1 through 6 take about fifteen to twenty minutes. The experiential activities in step 7 take about forty-five to fifty-five minutes. The closing steps 8 through 12 generally take about fifteen minutes.

Structuring Individual Sessions

For individual therapy, we recommend sixty-minute sessions when possible. This gives you time to review the child's home practices from the preceding week, conduct the experiential activities, and discuss the home practices for the following week. We will suggest procedures to omit if there is insufficient time and describe specific modifications required for individual therapy.

CULTIVATING A MINDFUL SPACE

Planning and preparing to conduct MBCT-C sessions require a substantial commitment of time and energy. Besides the logistical aspects above, some mental planning and preparation is necessary. You need a clear understanding of the program as a whole and a clear road map for each session. This means conveying unambiguous messages from one session to the next, maintaining continuity across sessions, reviewing the goals of previous sessions, and consistently reviewing home practice assignments. Planning involves adopting a mindful approach to teaching styles and intervention techniques. In the sections that follow, we offer suggestions for cultivating a mindful space.

Crossing the Threshold

When a child crosses the threshold into the therapy room, she encounters a new environment. Here she will make discoveries, learn mindful awareness practices, and experiment with a new way of being in the world. Before the first session, you may greet the child, escort her to the therapy room, and stop at the threshold to bring her attention to a sign on the group room door: "Slow, Mindfulness in Progress." Crossing the threshold, the child enters the room with mindful awareness. She stops by the Worry Warts Wastebasket, writes her worries on a piece of paper, and puts the paper in the wastebasket. She quietly takes off her shoes, gets her notebook (*Mindfulness in Everyday Life*), and takes her seat on a cushion. During the first few minutes, she sits quietly, checks her current mood state, and records it on the Feely Faces Scale. This may sound complicated, but the child quickly learns to follow the rhythms of this mindful sanctuary.

Fostering a Safe Environment

We often talk about therapy as being a "safe place," but exactly what does this mean? First, therapy is safe when it is confidential. As with other group treatments, MBCT-C emphasizes a safe, respectful, and confidential environment. The rules of confidentiality are explained to both parents and children during the consent and assent process. Group members are reminded periodically of the need to respect each other's confidentiality outside the therapy room. Second, therapy is safe when it gives children choices. Earlier we introduced the Quiet Space, a designated chair placed in one corner of the room that a child occupies if she needs a moment alone. This safe retreat offers the child freedom to choose whether to participate in the activities.

Intellectual Understanding Is Not Experiential Knowing

MBCT-C encourages children to develop and practice mindfulness skills in an experiential way by participating in guided activities and practicing mindful behaviors. In the beginning, the therapists briefly introduce the concept of mindfulness and offer opportunities for the child to express her (intellectual) understandings of the program. Cultivating this awareness begins during the first session with several brief activities intended to expand the child's (experiential) understanding of mindfulness.

The style of the therapist can be described as nonjudgmental interest in the shared process of discovery. Explanations and instructions provided by therapists are minimized. The experiences themselves speak to what is deepest and best within each child. It seems more helpful to say too little than to say too much. Instead, the child is encouraged to explore and learn from her own present-moment experiences. The therapist's role is to elicit descriptions of the experiences from the child rather than to offer explanations, analyses, or intellectualized interpretations about the experiences. If the child should begin to interpret or analyze her own experiences, she can be gently guided back to describing the experience itself.

This emphasis on experiential learning is aimed at empowering the child. Learning based on experience becomes imbued with personal meaning. The child learns that she can relate to her thoughts and feelings in a different way and that she can respond to stressful events with mindful awareness. We are respectful of the child's process and assume that every child already has the necessary internal resources to cope with the many vicissitudes of life. As therapists, we simply guide the child to discover this resilience and awareness within herself.

Opportunities to Practice Mindfulness

We can choose to be present at any moment of any day. We can choose to be mindful when we're brushing our teeth, putting on clothes, taking out garbage, or washing dishes. Throughout the program, cultivating mindfulness is incorporated into every activity, mundane though it might initially seem. The child takes off her shoes, walks into the room, and sits down on a cushion—with mindful awareness of each action. At the end of each session, she mindfully puts away the meditation cushions, yoga mats, and art supplies. She is encouraged to be present and aware of whatever she is doing in each moment.

Bells of mindfulness are rung at the beginning and end of each activity, and at other irregular intervals, as a reminder to be present in the moment. When noticing that the noise level and distracted energy in the room has increased, a child may spontaneously choose to ring the meditation bells. The soft chimes gently "re-mind" us to return the mind's attention to the present moment. The bells soon acquire special meaning for the children. Children usually show consideration for the other children by taking turns ringing the bells.

Being Mindful of What Is Present

Segal, Williams, and Teasdale (2002) acknowledge that the therapist's ongoing mindfulness practice allows flexibility in teaching styles. Therapists may choose to respond to the most salient aspect of the child's experience, even by temporarily setting aside the session agenda. It is important not to let the curriculum undermine your emphasis on freedom of choice. When therapists are attuned to the present and flexibly adapt to the needs of the group, children see how mindfulness can be applied to events in everyday life.

☆ Emily's Return to the Present

Emily arrived at one session in a visible state of distress. She shared with the group how she was unable to sleep the previous night after viewing a disturbing horror movie. She could not separate the fictional account of the film from the reality that she was safe, right here, right now. There was power in how the group responded. The other children chose to spend part of the session offering compassionate support to help bring Emily's attention back to the present moment. Her peers suggested that she focus on her breath, watch and note her thoughts, and practice noticing how her emotions were being expressed in her body. Emily's distress dissipated as the realization arose that the movie was only a movie and that she was safe in this very moment.

Spontaneous experiences can illustrate the practice of mindfulness in the midst of stressful events. Teaching opportunities that arise in the nowscape (in the moment) often have a lasting impact on the group. The children get to see firsthand how these skills are applied in daily life.

Embodying Mindfulness

To teach mindful awareness is to embody mindful awareness. If you approach children with a "do as you're told, not as I do" attitude, you will likely face resistance in the therapy room. You must be a full-fledged participant in the program, learning and sharing along with the children. Your guidance of the children is grounded in your own present-moment experience.

Therapists exemplify mindfulness through their general approach, attitude, actions, behaviors, language, and attentiveness to the child's experience:

- Foster acceptance by refraining from criticism, judgments, or judgmental language.

- Adopt and convey an attitude of curiosity and openness. Segal, Williams, and Teasdale (2002) aptly note, "The instructor's curiosity about participants' experience can invite participants themselves to become curious about their own experience" (p. 90).

- Invite participation rather than call on children to respond. Open each dialogue with an invitation (for example, "I invite you to share your experiences...") to emphasize freedom of choice. Children learn that they can choose what to share, or choose not to share at all. If there are no volunteers, you may choose to start the dialogue by sharing your own experiences.

- Whenever possible, use the present participle when describing actions you would like the children to take, for example, "... as you practice bringing your attention back..." rather than the command form "Bring your attention back..." (Segal et al., 2002).

- Offer encouragement and acceptance with the phrase "as best as you can." Many children with anxiety are habitually self-critical.

Our best is all that any of us has to offer. Recognizing this can sometimes help the child to moderate unrealistic or unhelpful self-expectations.

• Gently guide the mindfulness practices and activities without reading the instructions verbatim. Transcripts presented are only general guidelines. You will find your own voice and cultivate your unique ways of embodying mindful awareness.

Children can be sensitive to the emotions of the adults around them— more than we might imagine. Anxious children in particular are likely to detect an adult's stress or anxiety and respond to it by becoming increasingly anxious themselves. Children are likely to sense when you rush into a session feeling hurried and harried. Allowing time and space to attend to your own meditation practice before each group session will enhance your presence and ability to teach mindful awareness to the children.

Conducting Practice Inquiries

Segal, Williams, and Teasdale (2002) found that the optimal time for reflection on session exercises is immediately after the experience. MBCT-C stays with an activity until the child has had opportunities to reflect on her experiences. The inquiry, modeled after both MBSR and MBCT, follows three specific lines of questioning (Z. Segal, personal communication, August 17, 2009). First, ask about the experience itself (for example, "What was the experience like?" "What did you observe?"). Second, inquire how the experience was different from our usual way of being (for example, "How is mindfully eating a raisin different from how you usually eat?"). Third, explore how the experience can be applied in everyday life (for example, "What does mindfully eating a raisin have to do with helping deal with worries?"). As a mindful therapist you will inquire with respectful attention, compassion, and nonjudgmental interest. We offer a few more suggestions:

• Foster dialogue by asking open-ended questions to help the child reflect on experiences.

• Encourage the child to describe her actual experiences rather than talk *about* her experiences.

- Help the child differentiate thoughts, feelings, and body sensations, and then inquire, "Does bringing greater awareness to thoughts, feelings, and body sensations change how you experience the activity?"

- Highlight distinctions between observing or noting an actual experience versus judging, evaluating, analyzing, or comparing it to other experiences.

- Help the child look for other available choice points.

Allowing adequate time at the end of each exercise for the practice inquiry is important for several reasons. First, describing the experience clarifies and reinforces the child's understanding. Second, the children learn from each other. Hearing others describe experiences rather than judge them supports learning a new, less judgmental vocabulary. Finally, as a child observes that other children's thoughts and feelings make their experiences unique, so she may learn that her own thoughts and feelings create her unique experiences. While it's often easy to see how other people create their own suffering, it's sometimes harder to see how we create our own.

PARENTS' INTRODUCTION TO MINDFULNESS

We invite parents to attend a ninety-minute Introduction to Mindfulness session a week or two before the program begins. This orientation session allows the parents to meet in an informal group setting with the therapist. We prefer to arrange chairs in a circle to facilitate interactive discussion and convey a spirit of collaboration among therapists and parents.

Outline of Parents' Orientation Session: Introduction to Mindfulness

1. Self-introductions (15 minutes)

2. Brief introduction to MBCT-C with time for questions (20 minutes)

3. Experiential mindfulness practice: Three-Minute Breathing Space (10 minutes including the practice inquiry)

4. Experiential mindfulness practice: Raisin Mindfulness (15 minutes including the practice inquiry)

5. Group dialogue to discuss experiential mindfulness practices and to understand how mindfulness can help all of us (children, parents, and therapist) respond more effectively to anxiety and strong emotions (20 minutes)

6. Discussion about expectations for parental involvement (10 minutes)

Therapists who intend to conduct individual therapy may follow a similar format. If you are working with the parents of just one child, you may wish to shorten this session to forty-five minutes.

Coming Together

Parents have vastly different reasons for seeking a mindfulness-based treatment for their child. They may have relatively little knowledge of mindfulness, or they may arrive with a wealth of personal meditation experience. The program may have been recommended by a friend, or they may have sought out the program knowing exactly how it could benefit their child. It's helpful to gain an understanding of each parent's experience of mindfulness and any expectations they might have of the program. After parents have a chance to settle into the room, open the dialogue by introducing yourself and explaining the purposes of this session. Invite the parents to introduce themselves, and share any personal experiences with mindfulness and any expectations they may have.

What Is Mindfulness-Based Cognitive Therapy for Children?

It can be useful to begin simply with Jon Kabat-Zinn's (1994) definition of mindfulness: mindfulness means "paying attention in a particular way; on purpose, in the present moment, and nonjudgmentally" (p. 4). You may choose to introduce MBCT-C as an approach that is based on MBSR, a program designed to help clients cope more effectively with physical and psychological stress; and MBCT, a therapy originally created for adults who experience recurrent episodes of depression. You can explain that MBCT-C is an adaptation of the adult program, which focuses on helping the anxious child establish a different relationship to her thoughts and feelings. We encourage the child to expand her ability to respond with awareness rather than automatically react to stressful situations. Invite parents to ask questions and share their thoughts or reactions with the group.

Experiential Practices and Group Discussions

We would like parents to experience some of the practices their child will be learning. Start by introducing the Three-Minute Breathing Space as a basic breathing practice that is done regularly throughout the program. Guide them through the Three-Minute Breathing Space (described in chapter 8, session 4).

The next practice is Raisin Mindfulness (described in chapter 7, session 2). Eating is an ordinary activity that illustrates how we often function on automatic pilot. Bringing mindful attention to the present, we may notice that the quality of the experience changes. Present-moment awareness helps us engage more fully with the experience. Distribute a few raisins to each parent and invite them to assume a mindful posture. Verbally guide them through the experience of eating a single raisin mindfully. We don't label the raisin as a raisin; instead, we refer to it as "the object." This supports decentering from thoughts about the object.

The practice inquiry begins with your invitation to share their observations and experiences. Invite parents to describe how this experience was different from the way they usually eat. Most people can relate to mindless eating. We often multitask while we eat—talking, reading, watching TV— with little awareness of the food or the act of eating itself. Bringing mindful awareness to the present, we become reacquainted with the experience of eating. The Raisin Mindfulness activity may offer parents some experiential understanding of the profound transformations that can be brought about through mindful awareness.

How Can Mindfulness Help Your Child?

Therapists need to make clear connections between practicing mindful awareness and responding more effectively to worries, anxieties, and daily stressors. Invite the group to reflect on the question, "How can mindfully eating a raisin help us in our daily lives?"

Just as we practice being present with the experience of eating a raisin, we practice bringing our thoughts into the nowscape. Falling into past-oriented thinking, we ruminate about events that have already happened. When thinking about past events, we can relive the experience. Thoughts, feelings, and body sensations can emerge as if the event were happening in this moment. We vividly remember the time when a flight delay left us sitting in an airport for twelve hours. We feel the anger and frustration all over again. The body tenses as we think about how the delay wreaked havoc on the rest of our week. We relive the grievance and upset of what can't be changed. The event isn't real; it exists only in the mind. We are not sitting at an airport waiting for a flight. We are right here, right now—living in the nowscape. With future-oriented thinking, we occupy the mind with speculations about events that have not yet happened and may never happen. Creating a multitude of "what if" scenarios, anxious thoughts may turn into an endless ticker tape in the mind: What if I can't sleep tonight? If I don't, then I'll be terrible in the job interview tomorrow. What if I blow it? What if the interviewer doesn't like me? If I don't get this job, my life is ruined. How could we not feel overwhelming anxiety? Muscles tense. The heart beats faster. We begin to sweat or feel nauseated. Eventually we return to the present and find ourselves lying comfortably in our own bed. We were nearly overwhelmed by an event that hasn't happened. Yet, in the mind, it feels so real.

A child's concerns are different but no less distressing. She is upset when she thinks about the fight she had with her best friend last week. She gets butterflies in her stomach worrying about the report she must present in class tomorrow. When she refocuses attention on the present moment, she can learn to observe thoughts and feelings without identifying with them. She gradually learns that she does not need to suffer by replaying a past that is unchangeable or anticipating a future that is unknowable. Repeating a variety of activities done with mindful awareness, a child cultivates mindfulness. Being in the moment, she may *discover that she has choices. She doesn't need to react thoughtlessly to stressful events. She may learn that she is capable of holding the thoughts and emotions in awareness, then choosing to respond with mindfulness.*

Parents Are Your Cotherapists

Parents have already made a commitment to their child's mindfulness practice during the initial interview. During the orientation session, remind and encourage parents to participate actively and support their child's home practices. Ask them to review the session summaries. Invite them to participate in the home practice activities along with their child. You wish to convey a clear message that they are integral to the program.

Ending the Session

Distribute handout A, which briefly describes the program and lists a few books and other resources. You may wish to add local resources, classes, or workshops. Appendix A lists some national resources relevant to the therapist, which may also be of interest to some parents.

THERAPIST'S PERSONAL PREPARATION

Through our hectic days, our minds saturated with an endless list of things to do, we sometimes forget to reserve space to care for ourselves. If you've ever had a clinical emergency with one client arise just when you were about to go into session with another, you understand the challenges of staying focused in the moment. The person begins to speak, but we're not listening. We're preoccupied with thoughts about the other incident. Thoughts can fill the mind, leaving us few resources to attend to the present. The mind is everywhere except where it needs to be—with the person who is sitting in the room. Simply by creating the space for our own daily practice, we may discover that we can help our clients as well as ourselves.

Segal, Williams, and Teasdale (2002) discussed how each MBCT session needs a significant amount of preparation—the therapists' personal preparation. Reviewing videotapes, they could easily identify the sessions when they rushed in from a previous meeting, compared to the sessions in which they took time to prepare themselves. Preparation includes practical arrangements that facilitate a smoothly run session. It also includes the therapist's preparing to "embody the balance of openness and 'groundedness' that participants are invited to experience for themselves" (p. 84).

You will need ample time to set up the room, review the session materials, and prepare yourself through your personal practice. Two therapists coleading groups may choose to "check in" with each other and practice together. Children sometimes become aware that therapists have a practice time before the session. Occasionally one may arrive early and join the pre-session meditation. Children see that the therapists have the same personal commitment that they ask of the child. For the therapist working in individual therapy, this commitment is equally important. Even a few minutes of sitting before a session helps create a grounded space in the room.

Allowing postsession time for cotherapists to debrief is also important. This discussion is essential to a good cotherapy relationship (Yalom, 2005). With cotherapists, the possibility of splitting exists where children may align with one therapist more than the other. Some children quickly learn which therapist will allow them more latitude. A brief postsession discussion allows cotherapists to discuss group dynamics, bring awareness to interpersonal processes unfolding in the session, identify specific clinical concerns, and modify their approach as necessary.

REFLECTIONS ON CHILDREN AS OUR TEACHERS

On this shared journey of working with children, they will teach us many lessons. They will invent new yoga postures. They will discover that a raisin makes "a neat little clicking sound" when rolled between two fingers, and so may teach us how to listen to our own raisin with a different kind of awareness. They will see things we don't and bring new perspectives to our view of the world. They will challenge us and sometimes push our limits. They will teach us patience. Most of all, they will inspire us to explore mindfulness—playfully and creatively—as we practice seeing the world through the eyes of a child.

On the shared path that is therapy, we inevitably encounter peaks and valleys. There are obstacles to navigate and triumphs to celebrate. We expect to find fascinating new avenues to explore and distant places where novel ideas lie waiting to be discovered. We become mindful therapists as we accept all this as being the process of therapy. Guide one another and allow the journey to unfold as it will.

READY TO BEGIN

The next eight chapters describe how to conduct MBCT-C. For each of the twelve sessions, we offer an overview, therapy goals, essential questions, and key points. Each chapter includes a session outline, materials needed, and a list of handouts. All of the handouts used (shown in appendix C) are provided in reproducible form on the CD-ROM included with this book. You will also find detailed descriptions of each mindful awareness activity, sample dialogues, and suggestions for adapting MBCT-C for individual therapy. MBCT-C involves a great deal of repetition of a few simple lessons. We wrote each session as if we were speaking directly to the child, so necessarily, there is repetition in the writing across sessions. We use different words to convey similar messages. We hope that these different ways of communicating the same message helps you find your voice as a mindful therapist.

CHAPTER 6

Introducing a New Way of Being in the World

No-Man's Land

Paradox
Ambiguity
Uncertainty
Helplessness
Impermanent change
Emptiness
No-man's land,
No control
Even of my thoughts,
This is how it is,
This is the Way,
So be kind to yourself
And others.

William Menza
(2002)

A child in an MBCT-C group may develop greater awareness of his own identity, develop more adaptive social-emotional skills, increase his awareness of other's needs, and practice communications skills. As the child improves his ability to tolerate distressing or uncomfortable thoughts and feelings—learning to accept them as they are—he may be less inclined to react thoughtlessly to emotional triggers. The child who is friends with his thoughts and feelings may experience greater happiness and self-confidence than the child struggling to escape those thoughts and feelings. Emotional resiliency supports the cultivation of mindfulness, and mindfulness may cultivate emotional resiliency. The emotionally competent child is less likely to experience clinical anxiety.

SESSION 1 OVERVIEW: BEING ON AUTOMATIC PILOT

Mindful awareness is the practice of living in the present moment, which lets us experience our lives with clarity, compassion, and acceptance. *Automatic pilot* is speaking or acting with little awareness of the internal experiences of thoughts, feelings, and body sensations. As we bring greater awareness to these internal experiences, we discover how often we live on automatic pilot. We begin to see more clearly what's really happening in this moment. We can then choose how we want to respond. We cultivate awareness by awakening to the present moment, moment...by moment...by moment. In this session and the next ones, we will explore how practicing mindful awareness might be helpful to each of us.

Our intention is the foundation upon which we cultivate mindfulness. As we learn to turn off automatic pilot, we experience our lives in different ways. We each have compelling, personal reasons to practice mindfulness. We may discover that liking or disliking our experiences rarely solves problems. We may discover that we are more comfortable in our lives when we stop judging experiences. This is what it means to cultivate mindfulness. The goal of this session is to discover that we can increase mindful awareness simply by forming the intention to do so.

Therapy Goals and Essential Questions

- Foster a secure, cohesive group environment devoted to the cultivation of mindfulness.

- Elicit the child's understanding of mindfulness and how mindful attention differs from ordinary attention. Raise awareness of how frequently we function on automatic pilot.

  - What is mindfulness?

  - How is practicing mindful awareness different from what we do every day?

- Explore ways that mindfulness might be helpful in daily life. Motivate home practice by appealing to playfulness, curiosity, and the delights of exploring this new way of being in the world.

  - How is mindfulness cultivated by observing what is happening in the present moment?

  - Can practicing mindful awareness help us become happier with ourselves and others?

Key Points

- The aim of MBCT-C is to cultivate mindful awareness. We do this simply by bringing our awareness to the present moment.

- As we purposely attend to the body and the breath, we learn how simple and how challenging this practice can be.

- In cultivating mindful awareness, a fundamental change can occur in how we relate to thoughts, feelings, and body sensations. Practicing mindful awareness may bring about new, sometimes radically changed perspectives and can transform how we interact with the world.

Session 1 Outline

Preparation

- Use your personal mindfulness practice to prepare for the session.
- Welcome each child by name. Take attendance with the Being Present Board. Allow each child to select and place a sticker by his own name.
- Introduce the Feely Faces Scale (checking in and being present with emotions). Ascertain that every child understands how to use the scale as a measure of current emotions, particularly anxiety.

List of Mindfulness Practices

- Getting to Know You
- Discovering Awareness in a Cup
- What Mindfulness Means to Me
- Taking Three Mindful Breaths

Concluding the Session

- Read the poem: Mindful Breathing Is the Best Practice.
- Ask children to complete the Feely Faces Scale.
- Review session 1 summary and the handout Mindfulness Is Cultivating Attention.
- Review the home practices.

Materials Needed for Every Session

- Being Present (attendance) Board
- Stickers for attendance board and Feely Faces Scale
- Bells of mindfulness

- One firm cushion or pillow for each child and therapist

- One yoga or gym mat for each child and therapist

- Worry Warts Wastebasket, paper, and pencils

- One notebook (three-ring binder) for each child and therapist

- Session handouts

Materials Needed for This Session

- Preprinted template for the front cover of *Mindfulness in Everyday Life* (see CD-ROM). Copying the template onto sixty-seven-pound cover-stock paper in light colors works well. One for each child and each therapist to personalize.

- Pencils, crayons, colored pencils, or felt-tip pens.

- One small, nonbreakable cup (for example, five-ounce plastic cup) and water.

List of Handouts

1.1 Poem: Mindful Breathing Is the Best Practice

1.2 Session 1 Summary: Being on Automatic Pilot

1.3 Home Practices

1.4 Breathing Practice Record

1.5 Handout: Mindfulness Is Cultivating Attention

Introduction to Mindfulness-Based Cognitive Therapy for Children

Begin the session with the Getting to Know You activity. While introducing and defining mindfulness, bear in mind that the practice of mindfulness is best understood experientially. Less time spent offering explanations and instructions allows more time for experiential practice. We offer sample explanations and dialogues (shown in italics) along with descriptions of each activity. We do not intend for the provided scripts to be memorized or read verbatim. Your unique verbal and behavioral expressions of mindfulness will emerge naturally from your own experiences.

We all have some moments that we like and some moments that we don't like. Some moments are fun or exciting, while others feel scary, sad, or boring. We each live with all kinds of different moments. Practicing mindful awareness can make it easier to accept all of our moments, not just some of them. Being mindful of our moments, we learn to see more clearly and can choose how to respond.

This mindfulness program for children offers practice in actively attending to the moments of our lives. Over the next twelve weeks, we will practice becoming more aware of what goes on inside us. Moment by moment, we will learn to be more aware of thoughts, feelings, and body sensations. We will explore being more observant of things in our daily lives, and do many fun and interesting activities. We will explore how our moments might feel very different when we choose to bring greater awareness to them.

Some moments may not feel very exciting. Others may feel so uncomfortable that we want to get away from them. In those situations, we may sometimes go for hours without being very aware of what we are doing. Our thoughts can be miles away without our even knowing it. Have you ever daydreamed in class and then realized that you missed hearing what your teacher just said?

You may wish to elicit personal experiences of being on automatic pilot.

- "I ate breakfast while watching TV, and when I finished, I realized that I didn't even know what kind of cereal I had eaten."

- "I went to school yesterday so upset with my little brother that I walked right past my classroom without knowing it."

Sometimes we don't pay attention to what we're doing, feeling, or thinking. We'll call that being on "automatic pilot." When we're on automatic pilot, we aren't paying attention to our lives. We can sometimes be like robots that aren't aware of what they do. When we're on automatic pilot, we sometimes act in ways that leave us feeling worried, angry, or sad. Without even knowing it, we might act in ways that make other people feel sad or mad. By becoming more aware of our own thoughts, feelings, and body sensations, we see that we don't have to do the same old things that made us feel sad, scared, or angry in the past. With mindful awareness, we learn that our behaviors are sometimes pushed and pulled by thoughts and feelings in ways that may not be helpful to our families, our friends, or ourselves. Sometimes the thoughts and feelings even get in the way of our doing things we really want to do. Practicing mindful awareness may allow us to see more possibilities, giving us the freedom to make appropriate choices and choose actions that might be helpful to ourselves and those around us.

Developing mindful awareness also helps us become more aware of moments that may otherwise slip right by unnoticed. Allowing pleasant moments to pass by unnoticed may mean that our lives aren't as rich as they might be. As we practice new mindfulness skills, we will learn to make friends with all the thoughts, feelings, and body sensations that are part of all our experiences. We practice mindful awareness to learn that paying attention in a particular way (that is, intentionally, in the present moment, and without judgment) can change the nature of our experiences.

WHAT IS MINDFULNESS?

The way that we use the word "mindful" or "mindfulness" in this program may be a little different from how some of you may have used it before. Being mindful means being aware. Mindful awareness practices are simply practices in becoming more aware. Mindful awareness is a special type of awareness that is focused on what's happening in the present moment, right here, right now—without judging or rejecting it. One teacher defined mindfulness as "paying attention in a particular way: on purpose, in the present moment, and nonjudgmentally" (J. Kabat-Zinn, 1994). Mindfulness means accepting all our moments—without judging them or trying to push them away—accepting that it's okay to be right where we are. It's the only place we can be—here in the present moment.

Mindfully exploring our present moments can be exciting and fun. We may learn new and interesting things about ourselves and our world. We are explorers—making marvelous new discoveries right here in our present moments. This is how we cultivate mindfulness—one moment at a time.

WHY ARE WE IN THIS GROUP?

This explanation will be specific to the children in your own group. We don't assume that parents have explained to their children why they are in therapy. We grant every child respect by clearly discussing the reasons they're in the group. Here are some common reasons for referral:

- Learning to better manage specific worries about school, reading, exams, or other academic events

- Learning to respond more effectively to generalized anxiety, worries, or fears

- Learning to cope more effectively with challenging or stressful situations

- Learning ways of interacting socially with other children and adults with less anxiety and more skillfulness and compassion

- Enhancing the ability to tolerate and accept intense emotions

- Learning to respond to thoughts and feelings that may motivate inappropriate behaviors

- Cultivating mindful acceptance to increase happiness, fulfillment, and general contentment with themselves and their lives

DEFINING THE STRUCTURE AND GUIDELINES FOR THE GROUP

We learn and practice mindful awareness in a comfortable, safe, and confidential environment. Each child needs to feel free to discuss his thoughts and feelings without fear of ridicule or rejection. Most anxious children are more at ease when they understand the structure and what is expected of them. After the introductions, you may review the general organization and structure of the group, and its guidelines for mindful behavior. We usually mention that every child is free to choose his own behaviors as long as those behaviors do not interfere with another child's participation. It can be helpful to emphasize that mindfulness begins when each child enters the room and that mindful behaviors include mindful speech.

Guidelines for Mindful Behavior. Responding to children who expressed a desire for clarity, we developed five guidelines for mindful behavior (see chapter 4 and handout D). During session 1, the guidelines are reviewed and discussed. We cultivate a compassionate environment, expressing respect for others by speaking with kindness and care. We encourage children to refrain from judging, criticizing, invalidating, insulting, or rejecting themselves or another child.

The Quiet Space. The Quiet Space is simply a comfortable chair placed in one corner of the room (facing partly away from the group, not directly into the corner). The space is defined by a sign on the chair. At any time, a child may choose not to participate in a group activity and instead sit quietly in the Quiet Space.

Bells of Mindfulness. We begin and end every session and every mindfulness practice by ringing a meditation bell. The act creates a clear boundary around these moments and expresses, "I intend to bring greater awareness to my experiences right now." The sound becomes a call that awakens an intention to be mindful. We teach children that the sound of the bells can be a reminder to take three mindful breaths and return awareness to the moment. The bells of mindfulness may be rung by any child at any time and when he himself wishes to return awareness to the moment. Should the noise or activity in the room increase to where it becomes difficult to remain present, any child (or therapist) may choose to ring the bell. Children are also invited to take turns ringing the bells of mindfulness to signal the beginning and ending of each activity. Appendix A lists some places to purchase meditation bells.

Worry Warts Wastebasket. The Worry Warts Wastebasket can be placed (with paper and pencils) just inside the group room door. As each child enters the room, he is invited to write down his current worries, fold or crumple the paper, and throw the worries in the basket. Consequently he doesn't need to worry about them during the session. At the end of the session, he may choose to pick his worries out of the basket and take them with him. In our experience, very few children choose to do so.

Other Issues for Discussion. Some groups may have specific issues that are relevant only to that group. For example, if sessions are conducted during school hours, then children might need to obtain a signed permission slip from the therapist each week before returning to class. There are several issues, however, that should be discussed during the first session with every group.

- Confidentiality and privacy within the group.

- General information about the program: duration and frequency of sessions, outline of the session structure, use of the handouts and *Mindfulness in Everyday Life* book, and the importance of home practice.

- Attendance: being present, arriving on time for sessions.

- Respect for the group process: entering the therapy room mindfully, removing shoes at the door, speaking in quiet voices, moving quietly, and not disrupting the group activities by words or actions.

Mindfulness Practices

Practice: Getting to Know You

A new setting with unfamiliar people can be quite anxiety provoking for many children, especially those with separation or social anxieties. Knowing something about each child in the group may help lessen the anxiety. Learning something about others can be an important step toward cultivating a supportive environment within the group. You may opt to use name tags for one or two sessions.

Invite the children to pair off and introduce themselves. A child may choose to share his name, age, information about his family, where he goes to school, and other basic demographics. Encourage him to share some personal information if he feels comfortable doing so; for example, what he did during the last school vacation, his favorite things (color, food, book, movie, and so on), or an activity that he enjoys (games, art, music, dance, and so on). Invite him to share one thing that he does well (music, art, sports, and so on). With an odd number of children, one group may consist of three children. Allow about five minutes to exchange information. Each child then introduces his partner to the group, sharing the interesting things that he just discovered about his new friend. It becomes an act of mindfulness to listen respectfully and attentively to another.

Practice: Discovering Awareness in a Cup

This activity follows the orientation discussion. Beginning the program, some children may believe that they are already as mindful as they can possibly be. This introductory practice allows a child to experience shifts in mindful attention as we place increasing demands on his intentions to be present and aware. Children and therapists are seated in a circle, sitting close enough together so that each can comfortably reach the hand of the person on either side. The group members generally sit cross-legged on the floor or on small cushions.

Fill a small cup of water about half full. Explain that this activity is to experience how we practice enhancing mindful attention. The initial challenge is for each child to hand the half-full cup to the next child, passing it all the way around the circle, being careful not to spill any water. At this point, not spilling the water does not demand a great deal of mindful attention.

After the cup has been passed once around the circle, fill it nearly to the brim with water. Then pass the filled cup of water around the circle again. Handing the cup to the next child without spilling now requires a greater degree of mindful attention. To accomplish this task now requires attention to our own movements and awareness of the coordinated movements of those sitting next to us.

Next, pass the full cup of water around the circle for the third time, this time with window shades closed and the lights turned off. In a dim or near-dark room, each child has an opportunity to experience bringing a high degree of mindful attention to a simple activity. If darkening the room is not possible, the child may be invited to close his eyes. Passing a cup of water to another person in this context requires precise attention to one's own body movements and to the coordinated movements between two children. What if some water is spilled? Well, a little water sprinkled with a few giggles never actually hurt anyone.

Practice Inquiry

Invite the children to describe their experiences of this activity. The intent of most practice inquiries is to elicit descriptions of the experience. Should a child begin talking about, judging, or evaluating the experience, you may gently redirect him back to simply deszcribing the thoughts, feelings, and body sensations. With a group of children who are comfortable expressing themselves, the dialogue will mostly be carried out between the children with some guidance from the therapist. During these dialogues, your essential aim should be to support each child in describing his experiences.

If the children seem restless, you may wish to take a few moments before the next exercise to stand up and practice mindful stretching. This can help them remain present during the latter part of the session. Simple stretching movements, done slowly and with awareness of each movement, help cultivate mindfulness of the body.

Practice: What Mindfulness Means to Me

Every session, children receive handouts—poems or stories, session summaries, and home practice assignments. The book, *Mindfulness in Everyday Life*, compiled from the handouts and written assignments, is personalized with the child's own writings and drawings. Handouts may be put into the books before the program begins or handed out at each session. We suggest preparing the books in advance, except for the poems or stories. Passing these out and reading them together near the end of each session is a pleasant and meaningful group activity. Children typically enjoy this experience; however, deciding to participate in the readings is a personal choice, not a requirement. The poems are decorated with unique artwork. Handing them out at each session is meant to enhance the child's appreciation of the wisdom they contain.

During this drawing activity, each child will personalize the front cover of his book with his name plus any images or words that express what mindfulness means to him. Directions for this activity are simple: "Draw whatever mindfulness means to you." Allow ten to fifteen minutes. You may wish to encourage the group to give the same degree of mindful attention to their drawings as they did to the Discovering Awareness in a Cup Practice. The intent of this activity is to offer the child an opportunity to express what mindfulness means to him. The quality of the artwork is irrelevant. Remember to prepare your own cover while encouraging the children's activities. You will be compiling your own book of *Mindfulness in Everyday Life* as you participate in activities and home practices with the children.

Practice Inquiry

During this inquiry, each child may choose to show the group his new cover and describe what mindfulness means to him. You may wish to focus the discussion on descriptions of the covers, the experience of mindful drawing, and what mindfulness means to each child. Some children may denigrate their own drawings or compare them negatively to other children's drawings. At this early stage of the program, the difficulty of avoiding judgments can be normalized—perhaps with the gentle observation that thoughts about the drawing are separate and not the same as the drawing itself. The child's self-criticisms are just more thoughts. The mindful therapist avoids judging the quality of the drawings, including her own, either by praise or criticism. Offering accepting and descriptive adjectives embodies mindful awareness more than expressing personal judgments. This is not to say that encouraging and supportive comments can't or shouldn't be offered. As a general guideline, however, encouraging the child's natural presence and innate capacity for mindfulness is likely to be more helpful than praising the product of his efforts.

We suggest that children be encouraged to volunteer rather than be called upon to speak. On occasion, asking about specific elements in his drawing may help the very shy or reticent child to express himself, but he should not be required to speak if he prefers not to. After a child describes his drawing, you may begin to inquire about thoughts and feelings. Be aware that in this initial session, it may be more difficult for an anxious child to express himself as easily as it may be in later sessions.

Practice: Taking Three Mindful Breaths

Breathing is a particularly valuable practice for developing mindfulness. It is always present, simple to observe, and hardly ever done with awareness. Bringing awareness to the simple act of breathing offers the child practice in relating to an ordinary experience in a different way, and opportunities to contrast that experience with the usual automatic pilot way of doing things. Mindfulness of the breath is one of the foundations of this program.

Our breath is always with us. To observe the breath, we need only form the intention to attend to it. To maintain an ongoing awareness of each breath can be, however, more of a challenge. Taking Three Mindful Breaths helps children understand how interesting and how challenging the practice of mindfulness can be, because our attention is continually distracted by thoughts, feelings, and body sensations. Experientially the child quickly learns how frequently these internal experiences can divert attention from the breath. An important first step in the learning process is recognizing the difficulty (shared by all of us) in holding our attention where we *will* it to be.

Wandering thoughts are inevitable. The moment in which we become aware that the thoughts have again wandered is a moment of awakening. Like training an exuberant puppy, mindful awareness is cultivated with gentle, compassionate, and patient repetition. When we notice the thoughts wandering, gently and kindly, we simply return attention to the breath—over and over again. With each moment of awakening, the child deepens his understanding while learning to navigate obstacles and maintain mindful attention in his life. In session 2, we will work at identifying and approaching those obstacles.

With children who are new to mindfulness practices, we've found it best to keep the introductory practices very short. The initial breathing exercise, called Taking Three Mindful Breaths, is done again at the beginning and end of sessions 2 and 3. Depending on the group's engagement in this activity, you may choose to repeat Taking Three Mindful Breaths two or three times.

> *Being mindful means becoming more aware of what is happening in this moment. It is the opposite of being on automatic pilot. When we're aware, we can respond to each situation with free choices instead of acting like robots. We practice bringing awareness to the present moment—over and over again. One way to practice mindful awareness is by bringing attention to our breath—one breath at a time.*
>
> *Let's begin this practice by intending to be more mindful. We may start by sitting up comfortably and straight. It might help to imagine that your head is like a balloon gently floating up toward the sky. We'll call this "taking a mindful posture." When we do this, we tell ourselves that we intend to practice being mindful. If you wish, you may close your eyes.*

You may want to add that closing eyes is optional, because some children may feel uncomfortable doing so. An alternative is to ask them to have a "soft gaze" (unfocused eyes) and look at a spot on the floor about three feet in front of them.

> *We practice bringing attention to one full breath. While you breathe in, you may choose to say to yourself,* I know that I am breathing in. *While you breathe out, say to yourself,* I know that I am breathing out. *When you pause between your breaths, say*

to yourself, I know that I am pausing between my breaths. *If your attention wanders, that's okay—just note that it wandered, and then come back to your breath. Rest for a moment, then practice being mindfully aware of one more full breath. Rest again. Then take one more in-breath—pause—and out-breath, bringing your full awareness to the experience of breathing.*

Practice Inquiry

It is essential to conduct practice inquiries with genuine interest and uncritical acceptance of the child's experiences. Convey an attitude of open and enthusiastic exploration of experiences as best you can. Facilitate this attitude by asking open-ended questions and inviting participation. We suggest that you avoid calling on a specific child to respond. Here are some sample questions:

- Would anyone like to describe what you experienced during this exercise?

- What about this experience was different from the way you usually breathe?

- The breath arises in the body. Can you describe some of the body sensations you might have noticed while watching the breath?

- Awareness allows us to see that the mind keeps wandering off thinking about other things. Did anyone experience this?

Concluding the Session

As we've discussed, participating in the group poetry reading is strictly up to the individual child. No stigma or disapproval should ever be directed at a child who chooses not to participate in this or any other activity. This can be an opportunity for the therapist to demonstrate acceptance. The invitation to read may be extended to the group as a whole without calling on any individual.

For the first few sessions, you may wish to remind the children to complete the second Feely Faces Scale. This is another opportunity to cultivate mindful awareness—a moment to look inward and ask, *How am I feeling right now?*

Session summaries and home practices are reviewed at the end of every session. Although the home practices are described in the handouts, every week the therapist needs to review the activities. Invite each child to ask questions until he clearly understands them. The home practices are related to what was practiced during the session. If time permits, you may also read the supplementary information handouts provided for sessions 1 to 4. A child is encouraged to practice bringing greater awareness to thoughts, feelings, and body sensations for a few minutes every day. Just as in cognitive therapy, written assignments can facilitate remembering to practice each day, but may sometimes feel like school homework to a child. Adopting the attitude that home practice is fun and interesting tends to facilitate the practice. This is why it's important for you to complete each week's practices, just as the children do.

MINDFULNESS IN EVERYDAY LIFE

- Mindful Breathing Lying Down
- Mindful Breathing Sitting Up
- Living with Awareness

ADAPTING SESSION 1 FOR INDIVIDUAL THERAPY

In a sixty-minute session with one child, the natural flow of each activity will move more quickly than when working with a group of six to eight children for ninety minutes. Some exercises will need to be shortened. Others require adaptations, which we will suggest as we go along. Getting to Know You becomes simply a mutual introduction between you and the child, which reduces the time by ten to fifteen minutes. Discovering Awareness in a Cup is practiced between the child and you. The cup can be passed three or four times at each step rather than just once.

Without having the feedback from other children, you may need to be more interactive with the child. During these interactions, be attentive to finding an appropriate balance between offering too much direction and allowing the child to flounder without a real grasp of the intended practice or application. The child's learning needs to be experiential, not intellectual. When you believe that the child has gained this kind of understanding, transition to the next part of the session. One benefit of individual therapy is the opportunity to stay with each activity for as long as necessary.

Few nine- to twelve-year-old children can sit comfortably for sixty minutes without needing to engage in mindful movement practices. Since mindfulness of the body is a core practice, we suggest that you shorten the duration rather than skip it altogether. If time is an issue, the session summaries do not need to be read aloud—instead, invite the child to read them at home.

It is important that the child clearly understand the home practice activities; therefore, they should be reviewed before concluding every session. If you have any concerns about a child's understanding of the exercises, it may be helpful to invite the parents into session to review the summary and home practice assignment together.

CHAPTER 7

Who Am I and Why Am I Doing This?

Magic Show

My I, me, mine fade away,
As I watch the magic show
Of sensations, feelings, thoughts,
Concepts, consciousness,
While resting in my unborn mind.
No more useless thinking, speaking or acting;
So my body and mind are light and free.

William Menza (2005)

MBCT-C engages children in brief experiential activities. Most children are naturally drawn to them because they are fun, interesting, and not hard to do. The anxious child is simply invited to give her attention, as best she can, to whatever activity is presented.

Bringing awareness to the nowscape is not difficult. However, we are accustomed to living on automatic pilot, so practicing mindful awareness initially may feel a bit awkward or strange. When a novel activity is first introduced, a child may respond with fidgeting, giggling, or a rash of questions. This is perfectly natural and understandable. With continued practice, self-consciousness diminishes. During sessions 2 and 3, we explore what it means to live with mindful awareness and discover personal motivations for doing so.

Anyone who has struggled to develop the self-discipline of a daily mindfulness practice knows that it is not easy. The primary aim of session 2 is to explore some barriers to daily practice and discover personal motivations to surmount these barriers. In session 3, a child learns that how she relates to thoughts and feelings might be one obstacle to cultivating awareness. Feelings of anxiety may divert the child's attention toward the perceived threat and, in so doing, interfere with her seeing clearly what is present. Anxious thoughts that are seen as more than "just thoughts" may lead to habitual avoidance or maladaptive behaviors. Part of the problem occurs when the child identifies herself with the thought contents. Believing these internal stories is likely to maintain or exacerbate feelings of anxiety. One solution is to change not the content of the thoughts but, rather, how the child chooses to relate to the thoughts.

SESSION 2 OVERVIEW: BEING MINDFUL IS SIMPLE, BUT IT IS NOT EASY!

Everyone discovers some obstacles to daily home practice. Watching the breath is not difficult. Finding the time and remembering to practice daily can be very difficult. Few of us would continue this if we did not have some compelling personal reason to do so. For a child to engage in mindful practices, she needs to be motivated and have a clear understanding of how practicing mindful awareness may influence her life. Without clear intentions and compelling personal reasons, a child either won't practice at all, or will do so in a perfunctory, "mindless" manner. For this reason, session 2 might be the most important session of the entire program.

In this session, your main goals are to elicit and address present or anticipated obstacles to consistent practice. You will help each child discover personal reasons to choose this way of being in the world. The ongoing practice of mindful awareness may change how she relates to her experiences and allow her to connect more deeply with the nowscape.

Starting with session 2, each session begins with a brief review of the previous session, including the practices introduced in that session. The child has opportunities to explore the meaning of these practices, the obstacles to practice, and the role mindfulness may play in her life. During the home practice reviews, children are invited and empowered to support each other by describing their own obstacles and how they've learned to manage them.

Therapy Goals and Essential Questions

- Living with awareness isn't easy, so why are we doing this anyway?

- Increase awareness of the challenges associated with developing a mindfulness practice and discover reasons to choose this way of being.

  - What makes this practice so challenging?

  - Why is this practice done in everyday life?

- Introduce mindful awareness of the breath, body sensations, and movements. Begin cultivating an experiential understanding that acting with mindful awareness can transform ordinary experiences.

  - What is mindfulness of body sensations?

  - What happens when we try to be mindful of our breath and body sensations?

  - What is mindful eating, and how is it different from what we do every day?

  - How can practicing mindful awareness of body sensations be helpful in our lives?

Key Points

- Mindfulness is a different way of being in the world.

- While mindfulness is easy to practice, it can be difficult to remember to practice.

- Practicing mindful awareness can be helpful in our lives.

- Mindful awareness can be practiced anywhere, at any time. We begin to deepen our awareness by attending to the breath and the body.

Session 2 Outline

Preparation

- Use your personal mindfulness practice to prepare for the session.

- Take attendance with the Being Present Board.

- Have children complete the Feely Faces Scale.

- Give a brief recap of the previous session (introduction to mindfulness).

- Review the agenda for this session.

- Review the home practices from the previous week.

Mindfulness Practices

- Taking Three Mindful Breaths (first practice)

- Raisin Mindfulness

- Mindfully Moooving Slooowly

- Taking Three Mindful Breaths (second practice)

Concluding the Session

- Read the parable: Flight from the Shadow.

- Have children complete the Feely Faces Scale.

- Review session 2 summary.

- Review the handouts: Practicing Mindful Awareness and Instructions for Mindful Breathing.

- Review home practices.

Materials Needed

- A small package of raisins.

- One small bowl and a spoon with which to distribute a few raisins to each child.

- In advance, prepare one baggie for every child and therapist with about a dozen raisins in each. You may choose to use an assortment of Flame (dark) raisins, Sultana (golden) raisins, cranberry raisins (craisins), or dried currants. These raisins will be used in the Mindful Eating activities done at home in the coming week. Distribute the baggies at the end of the session when reviewing the home practices for the coming week.

List of Handouts

2.1 Parable: Flight from the Shadow

2.2 Session 2 Summary: Being Mindful Is Simple, But It Is Not Easy!

2.3 Home Practices

2.4 Mindful Eating Record

2.5 Handout: Practicing Mindful Awareness

2.6 Handout: Instructions for Mindful Breathing

Mindfulness Practices

We cultivate mindful awareness by paying attention to the events around us and bringing awareness to our thoughts, feelings, and body sensations. Practicing mindfulness sometimes isn't easy, but with patience and practice, it can be very helpful in our lives. For example, managing anxiety about taking tests can help us concentrate better— while studying and when taking exams. Staying focused without feeling distracted by anxious thoughts and feelings may make it easier to learn and remember the material.

Introducing the Breath*

Breath is life. We might think of the breath as a thread that connects all the events in our lives from beginning to end. Have you ever noticed how our breath changes with our moods? It can be short and heavy when we're tense or angry, fast and shallow when we're excited, and slow and full when we're happy; and it can almost disappear when we're afraid. The breath can bring stability to the body and mind— when we deliberately choose to become aware of it. With practice, we become more mindful of our breathing. We can use our breath to direct our awareness in different ways than usual. Our breath can help us focus on what needs attention and help us cope with worries and anxiety.

The breath is always here—every moment. We can attend to it whenever we wish. Most of the time, we're not even aware of it—it's just there, forgotten. One of the first things we do when practicing mindfulness is to get back in touch with the breath. We notice how the breath changes with our moods, thoughts, and body movements. We don't need to control it. We just practice watching it and getting to know it—like a new friend. We observe it—with interest—feeling each breath and how it moves in and out of the body.

Mindful breathing takes practice. Bringing awareness to the breath is very simple, but not always easy. The first thing many of us discover is that we have little control over our own thoughts. With the best of intentions, we start to watch the breath. The next thing we know, thoughts have carried us far away. This is natural and just lets us practice bringing mindful awareness back to the breath. Mindfulness can be practiced in other ways as well. We will practice being mindful of body sensations and all the senses as we bring awareness to what we taste, hear, see, touch, and smell each day.

Practice: Taking Three Mindful Breaths
(first practice)

Initially you'll need to provide verbal guidance for each practice, but less as each child develops a natural understanding of it. At the start, you may wish

* Inspired by the work of Karen Ryder, mindfulness instructor.

to limit this practice to the three breaths as described, but Taking Three Mindful Breaths may be repeated two or three times. In·session 4, we will expand Taking Three Mindful Breaths into the Three-Minute Breathing Space.

It can sometimes be easier for a child to focus on her breath at the belly rather than the nostrils—perhaps encouraging her to choose and then stick with one option in any practice. Children may naturally engage in dia-phragmatic ("belly") breathing more frequently than adults. You may invite them to place one hand on the abdomen to help focus attention. You might introduce Taking Three Mindful Breaths like this:

> *I invite you to practice bringing your attention to the breath. We*
> *will start by being mindful of just three breaths. You may choose*
> *to focus on the breath at your nostrils—perhaps noting how the*
> *air feels cool as it comes into your body and slightly warmer as it*
> *leaves. Or you may choose to attend to the breath at your belly—*
> *feeling the belly rise and fall as air enters and leaves your body.*
> *Focusing your attention, as best you can, on the breath. Watching*
> *the air as it comes in and goes out—entering the body and leaving*
> *the body. If your mind begins to wander, that's okay. We simply*
> *practice bringing attention back to each breath—breathing in and*
> *breathing out. Your mind will naturally wander off and get lost in*
> *thoughts. That's just what minds do. When you notice that your*
> *mind has wandered, simply note that this has happened and then*
> *gently bring your attention back to the breath—over and over,*
> *simply noting whenever the mind has wandered, then returning*
> *attention to the breath. You may tell yourself,* Being aware of the
> wandering mind is being mindful, *then return to watching the*
> *breath.*

You may occasionally offer reminders just to note whenever "distrac-tions" occur (as they inevitably do) and then return attention to the breath. Attention that shifts to thoughts, feelings, body sensations, and perceptions (sights, sounds, smells, or tactile sensations) is normal and to be expected. We do not define this as interruptions to the practice of mindfulness. These are just more events about which we practice being aware. For example, children might become distracted by sounds in the room. You may invite the group to mindfully listen to the sounds as "just sounds," rather than ignore them, then return attention to watching the breath. Perhaps a child giggles. Without singling out that child, you might say something like:

Bringing your awareness to the breath, you may also hear sounds in the room. You may simply choose to note, "Here is a sound," then gently bring your attention back to the breath. Sounds will pull us away, thoughts will pull us away, body sensations will pull us away—but what we do is always the same. We simply practice bringing attention back to the breath.

Practice Inquiry

After every practice, each child has opportunities to describe her experiences. Begin by inviting group members to describe the experience of the activity itself: What was it like to watch each breath? What did you observe about the body sensations of breathing? What thoughts and feelings arose? Second, elicit descriptions of how those experiences may be different from ordinary breathing. Third, connect these different experiences to daily events in the child's life.

Note: All the verbal mindfulness instructions are delivered calmly, at a slow, but deliberate pace. Whenever possible, avoid declarative statements in favor of gentler sounding phrases.

Practice: Raisin Mindfulness

Eating is an ordinary daily experience that is often done on automatic pilot or during other activities, such as reading or watching TV. Mindful eating may increase awareness of how often we function on automatic pilot. Raisin Mindfulness explores a different way of relating to everyday experiences. The child may learn that bringing mindful awareness to an activity can change the nature of the experience. Moments experienced in this way can often have a different feel or quality about them. The aim of Raisin Mindfulness is to experience the differences between acting on automatic pilot and acting with mindful awareness. The raisin practice and subsequent inquiry, adapted from one of our earlier articles (Semple &Lee, 2008) and used by permission, is similar to that used in the parent session and in both MBSR and MBCT (see pp. 102–110 in Segal et al., 2002). You may begin by asking the children to assume a mindful posture. Pass out two or three raisins to each child, and invite the group to quietly explore the object while you say something like:

> What is your experience of holding this object in your hand? Looking at it very carefully... as if you are describing it to a Martian who has never seen one before. (pause) As best you can, note the thoughts or images that come up as you look at this object. (pause) Practice noting that they are just thoughts, and then gently return your attention to the object. (pause) Exploring it with your eyes, noting its colors...and any patterns. (pause) Exploring it with your fingers. (pause) Does the object feel dry or moist? Noting if it's bumpy or smooth... soft or hard. Is the texture the same all over the object? How heavy is it? (pause) Exploring the object with your nose and ears...Does this object have any smells? (pause) Does it make any sounds? (pause) With our senses, bringing all of your attention to this object lying in the palm of your hand.
>
> Whenever you're ready, you may place the object in your mouth. I invite you to practice exploring it with your tongue. (pause) Does it taste or feel different in different parts of your mouth when you roll it around? (pause) Is your mouth watering in anticipation of eating the object? What are you tasting before you bite into it? What are you smelling? What are you hearing? Is the texture changing the longer it's in your mouth? (pause) As best you can, keep attending to this object while noting thoughts, feelings, and body sensations. Are the thoughts looking forward to swallowing this object and eating another? Are they attending to all the varied sensations of the one that is in your mouth? Are the thoughts somewhere else altogether?
>
> Bringing your attention back... gently biting the object... tasting its flavors. (pause) Noting if the textures on the inside are different from the outside... bringing awareness to changes in the moistness or flavor. (pause) Slowly chewing the object while noting the sensations. (pause) As you swallow, bringing awareness to the sensations as it slides down your throat. Following the object all the way down to your stomach. (pause) Then, bringing attention back to the sensations in your mouth, noting what's there. Are there different tastes or flavors in your mouth now? Are your thoughts still here with this experience? (pause) Feeling now that your body is exactly one raisin heavier than it was a few minutes ago.

Practice Inquiry

Questions that begin with "what" (for example, "What did you observe as you held the object?") or "how" (for example, "How did your right arm feel when...?") or "where" (for example, "Where in your mouth did you feel that tingling sensation?") are generally more helpful than "why" or "when" questions. "Why" questions can promote intellectualized thinking about the experience and "when" questions sometimes prompt us to reflect on the chronology of the experience, both of which tend to move us away from the moment-by-moment direct experience.

Helping a child to describe thinking as a process may help her cultivate awareness of the experience of thinking. Describing the process of thinking can be facilitated using movement descriptors (for example, thoughts rushing in and out, flowing calmly, marching by), spatial descriptors (for example, thoughts crowded into one corner, spacious, scattered all over the place), auditory descriptors (for example, thoughts shouting, whispering, clamoring), or metaphors (for example, like soap bubbles floating by, like dry leaves falling from a tree, like wild monkeys swinging from vine to vine, like a joyous puppy on a leash, like a stampede of wild horses).

Practice: Mindfully Moooving Slooowly

Children who experience anxiety often find that one thought (for example, *Why can't I keep my attention on my breath?*) is in direct conflict with another (for example, *That was another dumb thought*). When this happens, it can be helpful to bring attention to how all these thoughts affect the body. Increasing awareness of body sensations may help the child decenter from the battle of thoughts. Decentering can moderate the emotional turbulence and allow her to connect more comfortably with the nowscape. Emotions manifest in the body, so noting body sensations may also help a child identify specific emotions. Mindful walking may be especially useful for a child who is physically nervous or agitated. At such times, she may have difficulty settling into the seated breath meditation. Bringing awareness to body movements can allow the child to feel more grounded in the moment and increase awareness of the agitated energy. Overall, movement practices may be more accommodating than a sitting practice when the mind or the body is agitated.

Most of us spend much of our lives "lost in thought." Being in the body instead of the head may offer the child a whole new perspective on her experiences. Simply bringing mindful awareness to body sensations can radically change the experience. For example, tense muscles, shortness of breath, flushed face, or increased heart rate may be misinterpreted as sensations to be anxious about. But body sensations are only felt in the present moment. Noting and identifying the sensations as "just" body sensations may help to de-escalate an imminent anxiety attack or prevent the onset of a panic attack.

Mindfully Moooving Slooowly is done with attention to the plethora of body sensations that accompany each step. Like mindfully eating a single raisin, mindful walking can transform an ordinary, everyday activity into a mindful awareness practice. The room must be large enough for children to walk slowly without bumping into each other. Depending on the size of the room, you may choose to walk in a line around the room or let the children wander more freely. Encouraging the children to lower their eyes and adopt a "soft gaze" (unfocused) may reduce a nervous child's self-consciousness. The aim of this practice is to cultivate moment-by-moment awareness of the body sensations that accompany all our movements.

> We can discover and practice mindful awareness in walking. We can walk to experience walking, just to know that we are walking, not to reach any particular destination. We may use the sensations of walking to anchor ourselves in the present moment. We begin this practice by standing up, slowly and with mindful awareness of the shifting of the body's weight, the movements of the muscles, the feel of the floor underneath our feet. You may choose to stand in place a minute or two before starting to walk.
>
> Feeling grounded in the present. Bringing awareness to the intention to move. Slowly beginning to move. Lifting one foot, slowly, shifting weight, reaching, touching, placing the foot on the ground. Standing still again. Feeling the body at rest and connected with the ground. Practicing noting thoughts that arise about the sensations. Then slowly lifting the other foot, shifting the body weight, reaching, touching, placing that foot on the ground. When you notice that thoughts have wandered, gently bringing your attention back to the sensations in the body.

You will need to guide the mindful walking practice verbally only for the first few minutes, then you may continue for another five to ten minutes in silence. The bells of mindfulness may be sounded to signal the end of the practice as you invite the children to return to their seats.

Practice Inquiry

Initially many children will not have extensive vocabularies with which to describe body sensations. They may use judging words or make comparisons to other experiences rather than describe the actual sensations; for example, "Walking in slow motion felt just like when I was about to jump off a diving board." Offering possible descriptors may help the child expand her vocabulary to describe body sensations.

Child:　　　My right foot fell asleep, so when I first stood up, it felt weird.

Therapist:　　I wonder if a Martian would know what you meant when you say it felt weird. Does that mean that your foot was feeling numb? Or heavy? Or was there a tingling feeling? Was the foot feeling hot or cold? Did you notice if the toes felt any different? Was that feeling the same for each toe?

As a mindful therapist, you are embodying the essence of nonjudgmental awareness through your choice of words. Encouraging feedback can certainly be offered without using evaluative or judgmental phrases. For example, instead of saying, "That was a very good description," you may simply note that the clarity of a description helped you better understand the child's felt experience.

Practice: Taking Three Mindful Breaths (second practice)

Taking Three Mindful Breaths is repeated near the end of the session. This practice and the brief practice inquiry that follows offer a quiet transition into the close of the session. The children end the session seated quietly, relaxed and prepared to share in the poetry reading.

Concluding the Session

Some children will be eager to participate in the poetry reading that ends each session, and some will not. Each child has freedom to choose her own behavior, as is initially discussed in session 1. At the outset of the program, we make known our intention to create an ambience in the room that is different from a typical classroom. This message of freedom of choice may need to be repeated several times in the early sessions.

We invite the children to practice three exercises at home during the next week, two of which are repeated from the previous week. Remember to distribute the prepared baggies of assorted raisins to each child for the Mindful Eating practices. Mindfulness of the breath is central to this program, so we ask the children to practice some variant of mindful breathing at home every week.

MINDFULNESS IN EVERYDAY LIFE

- Living with Awareness
- Mindful Breathing
- Mindful Eating

ADDITIONAL NOTE

After two sessions, if a child still appears to have difficulty engaging in the activities, it may sometimes be helpful to speak privately with her—away from the rest of the group. You and the child can work together to identify what might be interfering with her interest or ability to engage as well as she might wish. Just taking the time to check in with a shy or anxious child may increase her participation. With two therapists, perhaps one can attend to a child who might have special needs while the other attends to the group. Observing other children's engagement and enjoyment may also increase the child's desire to participate. It's not uncommon for children to experience some increased anxiety at the beginning of the program, then become enthusiastic and avid participants.

SESSION 3 OVERVIEW: WHO AM I?

We all have thoughts, feelings, and body sensations. Understanding that these personal experiences are not who we are is called decentering. Decentering is a process of learning to see thoughts as "just thoughts," feelings as "just feelings," and body sensations as "just body sensations." When we see these experiences for what they are, we are less likely to be caught up in them or allow our behaviors to be unduly influenced by them.

Decentering lets us see clearly and, perhaps, discover that we have freedom to choose how we respond.

The mind is always thinking. Much of the time, we think about things that aren't happening right here or right now. Sometimes our thoughts wander around and relive past events. Other times they anticipate something that hasn't yet happened. Frequently they are a million miles away. All these thoughts feel real, even when they don't have much to do with what's really going on. It can sometimes be hard to see that thoughts are "just thoughts."

We all have these things called thoughts, feelings, and body sensations. We also have something we might call "me" that can observe those thoughts, feelings, and body sensations. Thoughts, feelings, and body sensations are not "me"—that is, they are not who we are. Thoughts can seem real. If we believe them, they may affect how we feel and even change our behaviors. Discovering how busy the mind is, we cultivate mindful attention and can see more clearly what's happening in this moment. Thoughts come and go all the time. "Me" is what watches the thoughts coming and going.

Therapy Goals and Essential Questions

- Recognize that thoughts and feelings influence what we experience. With our thoughts, we construct all the unique experiences that make up our lives.

  - Are all those thoughts and feelings really real? Do they accurately reflect reality?

  - In what ways might having thoughts and feelings change how we experience the things that happen in our lives?

- Begin identifying thoughts, feelings, and body sensations for what they are.

  - How are thoughts, feelings, body sensations, and behaviors related to each other?

  - In what ways do thoughts and feelings affect how we live our lives?

  - How might our lives be different if we experienced thoughts as "just thoughts"?

Key Points

- Thoughts are not "me." Thoughts are "just thoughts."

- Thoughts arise in the present, but are often about the past or future.

- Thoughts may not be accurate to the present reality. Thoughts are not facts.

- Thoughts can, however, influence feelings, body sensations, and behaviors.

Session 3 Outline

Preparation

- Use your personal mindfulness practice to prepare for the session.

- Take attendance with the Being Present Board.

- Have children complete the Feely Faces Scale.

- Give brief recap of previous session (dealing with obstacles to practice).

- Review the agenda for this session.

- Review the home practices from previous week.

Mindfulness Practices

- Taking Three Mindful Breaths (first practice)

- Mindfulness of the Body

- Hey, I Have Thoughts, Feelings, and Body Sensations!

- Listening to the Sounds of Silence

- Taking Three Mindful Breaths (second practice)

Concluding the Session

- Read the poem: Have You Ever Gotten a Thought?

- Have children complete the Feely Faces Scale.
- Review the session 3 summary.
- Review the handouts: Breathing and Who Am I?
- Review home practices.

Materials Needed

- None

List of Handouts

3.1 Poem: Have You Ever Gotten a Thought?

3.2 Session 3 Summary: Who Am I?

3.3 Home Practices

3.4 Pleasant Events Record

3.5 Handout poem: Breathing

3.6 Handout: Who Am I?

Mindfulness Practices

Practice: Taking Three Mindful Breaths (first and second practices)

Taking Three Mindful Breaths is done at the beginning and end of the session. You may also choose to repeat it at other times. Each time, the practice can be lengthened by a few breaths, up to two or three minutes. Being attentive to the mood in the room can help you gauge how long to extend this practice. Prolonged for too long, children may become restless, especially in these early sessions, when they're becoming accustomed to these foundational practices. For the remainder of the program, mindfulness of the breath is practiced several times each session. Anyone may request a few moments of mindful breathing by ringing the bells of mindfulness. As we've discussed, mindful breathing provides a foundation upon which to cultivate mindfulness.

Practice: Mindfulness of the Body

Mindfulness is like a spotlight that can shine attention anywhere in the body. A focus on the body can redirect attention to present-moment experiences. In this guided activity, invite the child to observe the sensations inside each part of her body and note how those sensations can change moment by moment. She may wish to observe and note any impulses to move her body and her thoughts about those impulses. She may become aware of judging thoughts about the experience, or thoughts of wanting the experience to be other than it is.

During this practice, the child is instructed simply to pay attention, as best she can, to the sensations in the body. When the mind wanders (as it always does), she may note simply that the mind has wandered and then gently bring her attention back to the body. Mindfulness of the Body begins with the child being invited to lie down on her back with arms and legs comfortably stretched out, palms facing upward. The child should have enough space to comfortably lie down without touching another child. If she wishes to do so, she can gently close her eyes. Beginning with a few moments of mindful breathing increases awareness of the body.

Coming into this moment by becoming aware of the breath.
As you are breathing in, you may tell yourself, "I know that I am breathing in." As you are breathing out, you may tell yourself, "I know that I am breathing out." You may choose to bring your attention to the breath at your belly. If you wish, place your hands on your belly. Feeling the belly rise and fall with each breath. Feeling your hands rise and fall with each breath too. Or you may choose to bring your attention to the breath at the nostrils. Being mindful of the air entering the nostrils, you may notice that it feels cool. What else do you observe? Following the breath as it leaves the nostrils. The air may be a little warmer as it leaves the body. If your mind wanders, that's okay; it's just what the mind does. When you notice this, you are being present and aware. Simply note that the mind has wandered, then gently bring your attention back to your breathing—over and over. We are practicing bringing the mind back whenever it wanders.

Now shifting your awareness to your left foot. Feeling where it touches the floor. Noting all the different sensations where your foot meets the floor. As best you can, being aware of the sensation of air on the foot or the sock against the skin. You are practicing feeling the foot as it rests on the floor. What sensations are inside the foot? Shifting your attention to focus on one toe. Noticing where the toe connects with the foot. Starting with the big toe, bringing mindful attention to the sensations of each toe. Do the different toes experience different sensations? You may choose to be aware of how the sole of the foot feels, or bring your awareness to sensations in the ankle. Are you experiencing feelings of warmth or cold? There might be a sensation of energy flowing through the foot. Are the muscles in the foot relaxed or tensed? When you notice that the mind has wandered, you are being mindful of your thoughts. Just practice noting the thought and then returning awareness to the foot. Noting the top of the foot, the toes, the space between the toes, the sides of the foot, the back of the ankle. Does the ankle feel hot? Or warm? Or cold? Is the foot feeling numb, tired, energetic, or something else? Do you feel blood circulating through the foot? Noting too when thoughts arise that might be commenting on the experience or when the thoughts go wandering off altogether. Then congratulating yourself for noting this and bringing attention back to the foot. The mind drifts away. That's okay—it's just what minds do. Gently bringing your focus back to the sensations in the body.

Gradually guide the shifting of attention to the other foot and then slowly move up the body. Invite the child to shift her attention as you speak. For example, you may say something like this:

As you attend to that part of your body, I invite you to observe all the sensations you experience inside the body and on the body. Maybe you feel sensations of heat or coolness. Or perhaps you might note a sensation of pressure in some part of your calf where it touches the floor. Are you aware of the feel of clothing on your skin or the air where it touches your body?

In only ten or fifteen minutes, we can't attend to the entire body, nor is it necessary to do so. Adults generally practice the body scan for forty-five minutes, but this is typically beyond the capacity of most children. We practice bringing awareness to the small details, so it is perfectly okay if you never move beyond the ankle. The length of this activity is determined by how long the child can remain engaged. Initially this is generally ten to fifteen minutes, increasing gradually. You may wish to close by bringing the child's awareness back to the breath.

Practice Inquiry

Practicing Mindfulness of the Body requires the child to focus her attention inward, so you may allow a few moments for attention to refocus outward again. The child can then choose to share her experiences and engage in the group dialogue. Beginning the practice inquiry, you may wish to invite descriptions of the experiences. Questions that might be relevant include these:

- *What was it like to observe the inside of your body with mindful attention?*

- *How would you describe those sensations?*

- *Were there times when you found yourself thinking about the experience instead of just watching it or simply being with the experience?*

- *Were there times when you became aware that you were thinking about something else altogether? What was that like?*

- *What happens to body sensations when the mind is elsewhere?*

One aim of the inquiry is to help a child identify thoughts, feelings, and body sensations and further develop her vocabulary of descriptive words. Raising her awareness of judging words can begin here.

Child: After a few minutes, my foot felt really bad.

Therapist: Saying it felt "bad" doesn't really help us to understand what you were experiencing. What part of your foot were you attending to?

Child: My toes felt jumpy and twitchy. I wanted to move them.

Therapist: How might you describe what "jumpy" felt like? Was that what you were thinking about or was it an inside-the-body sensation?

Child: It was an inside feeling. A lot of warm energy was moving in my foot. The energy flickered and moved around a little.

Session 3 begins the ongoing practice of clearly differentiating thoughts, feelings, and body sensations. It can be helpful to write in a three-column format (chalkboard, whiteboard, or poster paper on an easel) to identify each one appropriately. Seeing the content divided this way may help a child learn two important lessons: first, that thoughts, feelings, and body sensations are related to each other; second, that these thoughts, feelings, and body sensations are unique to her. Recording descriptions from other children can make it clear that each child experiences the same activity in different ways. The child may learn that these internal events contribute to create unique personal experiences. The focus of the Mindfulness of the Body practice is to increase awareness of body sensations. The next practice focuses on identifying thoughts and feelings as well.

Practice: Hey, I Have Thoughts, Feelings, and Body Sensations!

This is a short activity borrowed from MBCT that is intended to introduce a child to the concept that thoughts, feelings, and body sensations exist, are related to each other, and influence how we experience and respond to the world. Previous practice inquiries likely touched on these ideas; now they are made explicit. You may offer a brief description or definition of thoughts, feelings, and body sensations with an example or two elicited from the previous activity. Each child will be writing in her notebook as part of this practice. She may choose to sit or lie down in a relaxed position. She can be encouraged (but not required) to close her eyes to better visualize the scene. Once the children are comfortably settled, introduce this visualization by saying:

> Begin by relaxing and imagining the following scene as vividly as you can. As best you can, practice seeing the whole thing—all the sights, colors, sounds, and scents. Feeling yourself being in this scene as if you are really there. Experiencing it as if it's happening right now.
>
> Pause for a few breaths, and then describe this scene: You are walking down the street, and on the other side of the street, you see somebody you know. This person is a good friend of yours. You smile and wave. The person just doesn't seem to notice you and walks by.

Encouraging full immersion in the visualization, invite the child to become aware of her thoughts, feelings, and body sensations. Avoid suggesting what those thoughts, feelings, or body sensations might be or should be. After a few minutes, invite each child to open her eyes and record the thoughts, feelings, and body sensations in her notebook. Gently discourage dialogue between children at this time.

Practice Inquiry

The aim of this inquiry is to elicit an understanding that thoughts, feelings, and body sensations contribute to our felt experiences. By inviting one child then another to share her experiences with the group, it typically becomes clear that each child had a different experience. A clearer understanding of this can come from listing the various thoughts, feelings, and body sensations on a blackboard or poster paper during the discussion. The compiled list may resemble table 3 (below). After eliciting descriptions of experiences, you may wish to explore how each child imagined a different encounter, even though everyone in the room heard the same words. During the discussion, you may also inquire how the child might have responded to the event and record their responses in a fourth column. Eliciting and noting different behavioral responses is a simple way to demonstrate how different components of experience are related to one another.

Table 3. Examples of Thoughts, Feelings, Body Sensations, and Behaviors

Thoughts	Feelings	Body Sensations	Behaviors
My friend is mad at me and doesn't want to talk to me.	I felt angry.	My throat felt tight, my fingers curled into fists, and I wanted to cry.	I might start crying.
My friend didn't see me at all.	I felt sad.	My stomach hurt a little, and my body felt heavy all over.	I might go home instead of going to the park with my friends.

Thoughts	Feelings	Body Sensations	Behaviors
My friend doesn't like me anymore.	I felt bad about myself. I felt very anxious.	My heart was beating fast, and my hands were sweaty.	I might not be able to concentrate on my homework.
My friend must have a problem, because she never even looked up.	I felt concerned for her.	I felt warm all over, and my heart felt open toward her.	I might call my friend tonight.

Practice: Listening to the Sounds of Silence

Listening to the Sounds of Silence is a mindful listening practice that can bring greater awareness to a present-focused experience through listening to a specific sound in a different way. This short practice involves ringing the bells of mindfulness one time, then listening with awareness until the sound is no longer heard. Then for a few moments more, continue to listen to the sounds of silence. The instructions are straightforward: "*I invite you to listen with mindful awareness to hear the sounds of silence.*" The children may wish to raise their hands to indicate when the sound of the bells end and the silence begins. This is a simple yet intriguing practice. The intense, concentrated listening in the room is often palpable. You may expect requests for the activity to be repeated. Some children wish to ring the bell themselves. We generally ring the bell (or allow it to be rung) no more than three or four times with at least one to two minutes of silence in between. Practicing mindful awareness doesn't require much sensory stimulation. Ordinary moments provide a multitude of opportunities for mindful awareness. Small moments are all we need.

Practice Inquiry

The inquiry encourages the understanding that there are different ways of being in the world that can lead to different experiences. You may want to discuss how experiencing thoughts as "just thoughts" might affect a child's felt experiences. Remember to ask open-ended questions whenever possible:

- *What was the experience of listening to silence?*

- *What did you note about silence that you might not normally notice?*

- *Did practicing mindful listening change how you might listen to other sounds?*

- *How might this practice help you in other areas of your life?*

Occasionally a child might express that mindful listening is no different from other listening.

Child: I didn't hear anything different from what I hear when I listen normally.

Therapist: Thank you for sharing. The mindful listening practice we just did isn't intended to make us hear anything different. It is just to let us practice being more aware of whatever is happening around us. When we practice mindful listening, we sometimes hear things more clearly—things that we might otherwise miss. This may give us more opportunities and choices about how to respond to events in different ways.

Concluding the Session

We found that the poetry readings quickly became a treasured experience for many children. Reading together can create a sense of warmth and cohesiveness within a group. We selected each session's handout to convey the spirit of each session, but you are welcome to use poems or stories of your own choosing. We don't interpret or explore the meanings of the poems. We offer them to the children simply for their enjoyment. The mindful wisdom contained in the poetry may grow more meaningful over time.

The home practices this week include a Pleasant Events activity. Being mindful of a pleasant event is the practice of bringing awareness to thoughts, feelings, and body sensations. This can help the child understand how our usually unconscious evaluations of an experience wind up defining the quality of the experience. Noting an event usually gives rise to a different state of mind than when judging it. Perhaps because we have a limited attention capacity, as noting increases, the tendency to judge decreases. We hope that the child will eventually come to understand that judgments in both directions—liking and not liking—may result in unhappiness. In session 6, the home practice focuses on bringing mindful attention to an unpleasant event. For now, practicing mindful attention during pleasant events will help engage the child's interest in the activity.

MINDFULNESS IN EVERYDAY LIFE

- Mindful Breathing

- Mindfulness of the Body

- Pleasant Events

ADAPTING SESSIONS 2 AND 3 FOR INDIVIDUAL THERAPY

There are few modifications necessary to fit the described practices for sessions 2 and 3 into a standard sixty-minute session with one child. All of the practices (except Taking Three Mindful Breaths) will take less time to complete with one child than with a group. Stretching and walking activities can be eliminated if necessary, but shortening them is preferable. By practicing a variety of activities, the child learns that she can bring mindful awareness to her experiences in many different ways.

The visualization activity Hey, I Have Thoughts, Feelings, and Body Sensations! needs modifications to convey the message that how we interpret events changes the felt experience of the event. Working with one child, you may begin the activity the same way as with a group. Elicit the child's initial thoughts, feelings, and body sensations experienced in response to the visualization. You may wish to add your own experiences in the three-column format. The next step differs from the group procedure. To create a marked contrast, we recommend selecting an example that is different from the child's experience. For example, if the child felt insulted and responded with anxiety, you might ask:

I wonder what we might feel if we saw that our friend was crying and we had caring and concerned thoughts about him. Let's close our eyes, and imagine that we see our friend again, but now we see that he is crying and we think, My friend looks so sad; I hope nothing is wrong with him.

Help the child explore the thoughts, feelings, and body sensations in the revised scenario. Elicit the child's understanding of how different cognitive interpretations might influence her feelings and behavioral responses. Then repeat this, pairing a different interpretation with another credible emotional response. The practice inquiry can support the child's understanding in two ways: helping the child learn that the quality of an experience changes as the thoughts change; and exploring how this practice of noting thoughts, feelings, and body sensations might be beneficial in everyday life.

CHAPTER 8

Mindfulness to Your Taste

Life consists in what a man is thinking of all day.

> Ralph Waldo Emerson, writer
> and philosopher

On the wooden board outside of the meditation hall in Zen monasteries, there is a four-line inscription. The last line is "Don't waste your life."

> Thich Nhat Hanh, Buddhist teacher

What we taste is affected by our memories and past experiences, just as it is with our other senses. We continually associate emotions with foods. We might wrinkle our noses in disgust upon hearing the word "broccoli" or "liver," or believe that a food described as "nutritious" won't taste good. These emotional relationships evolve and change throughout our lives. What might shift if that dish of broccoli were prepared by a master chef? We rarely reflect on how much thoughts, feelings, and emotional associations influence our daily food choices, or consider whether the foods we eat might affect our moods and emotions.

SESSION 4 OVERVIEW: A TASTE OF MINDFULNESS

We sometimes find ourselves on automatic pilot when eating foods we like. We may sit in front of the TV with a tub of popcorn until the tub is empty—with little recollection of the experience of eating. As noted in session 2, eating is a particularly valuable exercise to illustrate how often we live on automatic pilot. We seldom eat with mindful awareness. Meals today are often eaten on the run or while doing other activities. With no time to simply eat and enjoy the experience, there is less opportunity to practice mindful awareness of eating.

> At school, Mark finds himself in a cafeteria line, waiting to be served. Looking at the selection of foods, he feels frustrated and disappointed. He doesn't see anything he likes. Thoughts run through his mind: *I hate macaroni and cheese. Oh, no, not turkey sandwiches again! Why don't they ever serve us anything good?*

These thoughts put Mark in a negative mood, but he has little awareness that the thoughts affected his mood. The irritable mood precipitates more dissatisfaction. Judging thoughts pile up. At the end of the day, an annoyed Mark leaves school. Judgmental thoughts can easily result in disappointment or negative expectations.

Practicing mindful awareness of the ordinary act of eating can help us understand the transformations that might occur when an everyday act is performed slowly and with intention. We may discover that we have choices in how we experience food. As we reacquaint ourselves with flavors and sensations, eating may feel richer and more satisfying. Over time, we may develop a different relationship to thoughts connected with eating, and realize that thoughts are not the same as the events they describe. Thoughts may become "just thoughts." There can be tremendous freedom in recognizing that our day need not be spoiled by a thought. This insight may be essential to understanding that cultivating mindfulness holds the potential to transform our experiences.

Therapy Goals and Essential Questions

- Enhance awareness that we have thoughts, feelings, and body sensations, but these are not who we are.

  - What does it mean to eat with mindful awareness?

  - How might this be different from what we do every day?

- Understand that thoughts, feelings, and body sensations are not the same as the events they describe.

  - Do thoughts, feelings, memories, expectations, or beliefs influence what we choose to eat or change the experience of eating?

  - How might our everyday experiences change as we become more aware of thoughts, feelings, and body sensations?

Key Points

- We can bring greater awareness to the experience of eating and become more aware of thoughts and feelings associated with the foods we eat. This awareness may change the experience of eating.

- Thoughts and feelings may appear solid, real, and true, but still not accurately describe the events in our lives. We may see events more clearly by increasing our awareness of thoughts, feelings, and body sensations.

- Seeing clearly gives us more freedom to choose how to respond to those events.

Session 4 Outline

Preparation

- Use your personal mindfulness practice to prepare for the session.

- Take attendance with the Being Present Board.

- Have children complete the Feely Faces Scale.
- Present a brief recap of the previous session (identifying thoughts, feelings, and body sensations).
- Review the agenda for this session.
- Review the home practices from the previous week.

Mindfulness Practices

- Three-Minute Breathing Space (introduction and first practice)
- Opening to One Orange
- Mindful Yoga Movements
- Three-Minute Breathing Space (second practice)

Concluding the Session

- Read the poem: Ode to a Grape.
- Have children complete the Feely Faces Scale.
- Review session 4 summary.
- Review handout: Three-Minute Breathing Space.
- Review home practices.

Materials Needed

- Clementine oranges—sometimes called Mandarin, Seville, or Christmas oranges, seedless tangerines, or Cuties—at least one for each child and therapist.
- Paper towels and hand wipes.
- Prepare in advance: Paper or plastic snack bags containing a small handful of dried fruit—one bag for each child and therapist. Small pieces of dried fruits such as apricots, peaches, cranberries, pears, apples, or cherries work well.

List of Handouts

4.1 Poem: Ode to a Grape

4.2 Session 4 Summary: A Taste of Mindfulness

Mindfulness Practices

Practice: Three-Minute Breathing Space

A child is now familiar with the basic breathing practice. He knows how to check in with the breath and focus on the physical sensations of breathing. He has learned to direct attention back to the breath upon becoming aware that the mind has wandered. He may be learning that he can use the breath to reconnect with the present moment when worries or anxiety pulls his attention away.

In session 4 we introduce a longer, multifaceted breathing practice called the Three-Minute Breathing Space. Segal, Williams, and Teasdale (2002) developed it as a "mini meditation" to bring small segments of formal mindfulness practice into daily life. This practice is used to remind us to pause in the midst of a busy day, check in with ourselves, and reconnect with the present. The Three-Minute Breathing Space is practiced regularly throughout the program—in sessions and at home.

The Three-Minute Breathing Space consists of three steps: awareness, gathering, and expanding. Step 1, awareness, begins with an intention to shift from automatic pilot while bringing a greater awareness to thoughts, feelings, and body sensations present in the moment. Begin by inviting the child to adopt a mindful sitting posture. Invite him to "check in"; observe what's happening inside; and note the thoughts, feelings, and body sensations. Mindful awareness is cultivated by the simple practice of attending to what is present. We make no effort to change what is happening, only to observe. We sometimes call this step "taking inventory." In step 2, gathering, the child directs his attention to the breath. He watches the myriad body sensations associated with each in-breath and each out-breath. Step 3, expanding, is an expansion of the field of awareness around the breath. It begins with awareness of the entire body: sensations, posture, and facial expressions. Next we add awareness of the environment: orientation of the body in the room and a sense of ourselves in relation to others present.

When explaining this practice, the acronym AGE (Awareness, Gathering, Expanding) may be helpful.

Introduce the Three-Minute Breathing Space and verbally guide the group through the initial practice (see handout 4.5). Allow sufficient time to explore each step thoroughly before going on to the next. This may take longer than three minutes. In our experience, the Three-Minute Breathing Space is the preferred practice for many children. It seems to be the one they use most often in their daily lives.

Practice Inquiry

Begin the inquiry by inviting descriptions of the experience. In addition to the usual questions, you might ask, *Are the thoughts, feelings, or body sensations any different after the Three-Minute Breathing Space than what was present beforehand? If so, what changed?* Explore how and why a child might use the Three-Minute Breathing Space in his daily life. In what situations might it be helpful? How could it be integrated into daily activities? You may want to allow a bit more time than usual for this discussion. Finding reasons to cultivate these practices helps each child discover meaning and sustain the motivation to continue them.

Practice: Opening to One Orange

Invite the children to assume a mindful posture. Distribute one orange and a few paper towels to each child. You may introduce the practice by briefly discussing the case of Mark, earlier in this chapter. Emphasize that thoughts, feelings, and body sensations can become personal filters that affect how we experience the world.

> As you hold this object in your hands, I invite you to become
> aware of your posture. Sitting on your mats and taking a moment
> to notice the alignment of your back, neck, and head, simply note
> how the body feels in this moment.

Guide this practice in a way similar to the Raisin Mindfulness activity. The differences here are that this object is larger, its skin can be peeled and explored separately from the object, and its internal structure is more complex. These differences allow for a much longer engagement in the practice of mindful exploration, so this activity might take twenty to twenty-five minutes.

Guide the children as they give mindful attention to exploring the orange with all their senses. Pause between sentences to offer space for exploration and discovery. Guide the child through the process of exploring the outside, peeling the orange, exploring the peel and the internal objects, sectioning the orange, exploring one section, and eating the section with mindful awareness. During the practice, some children might note the presence of distasteful thoughts or feelings (perhaps in tasting the peel). Invite the child to simply explore and observe these experiences as being just thoughts and feelings. Then you may prefer to continue the rest of the activity in silence.

Practice Inquiry

Begin the inquiry by inviting descriptions of the experience:

- *Would anyone like to describe your experiences?*

- *Would anyone like to share what you learned?*

- *Was something different about eating this orange from the way you usually eat?*

In one session, Carla discovered that the inner surface of the orange peel had a velvety texture. John noticed that the skin of the peeled orange was translucent. Biting into a section of the orange, Abby watched her thoughts stray to a recent picnic where she ate an orange much like this one.

Invite an exploration of the idea that thoughts, feelings, and body sensations may change the experience of eating the orange. One lesson to be learned from this practice is that, often, we are not fully aware of our experiences. We may begin to see the differences between eating the orange with awareness and our usual mode of eating. It is common for a child to observe how much stronger the flavors seem or note that this orange tasted different from any other orange he's ever eaten. Some children may discover that attending to the act of eating changes the quality of the experience. During the inquiry, perhaps a child will comment that bringing more awareness to the food and to the act of eating enhanced his enjoyment of the experience. A child will sometimes note that this practice raised his awareness of other experiences previously overlooked.

Another teaching of this inquiry is the recognition that thoughts and feelings may not accurately represent events. For example, we may have a judging thought, *I don't like oranges,* or think, *Oranges are messy and have too many seeds.* We practice noting these thoughts as passing events in the mind. We become open to discovering something new or unique about the one orange that we hold in our hands. We may find that this particular orange really isn't messy, confirm that it does have lots of seeds, or even discover that it has no seeds at all. Thoughts are not the orange. Feelings are not the orange. The orange is perfect just as it is.

During this activity, you may raise awareness of the reciprocal relationship between emotions and food. Eating mindfully may increase our awareness that feelings might influence the felt experience and that our food choices might influence our feelings. You might invite a child to explore what feelings might change if he makes certain food choices. For example, we may react to caffeine or sugar by feeling more anxious, while too much junk food may arouse feelings of sluggishness or negativity. Eating well-balanced meals and healthy snacks may help us feel better and give us greater energy and stamina. We can choose to nourish ourselves with foods that are likely to benefit our physical needs and support our emotional well-being.

Finally, you may invite the group to explore how mindful eating practices can be integrated into daily activities. Practicing mindful eating lets us explore new tastes, discover sensations never before experienced, and cultivate greater presence and awareness. We may become more aware of the flow of thoughts, feelings, and body sensations while we eat. We may realize that these internal events are transient and can change the quality of our experiences. This is one way to connect the idea of slowly eating an orange with letting strong emotions, such as anxiety, come and go as they will.

Life on automatic pilot can be like sleepwalking—we are not awake to what we're doing, feeling, or thinking. Being aware that we are on automatic pilot is mindful awareness. If we experience anxiety about an upcoming event, we can choose simply to observe the thoughts, then note that the thoughts probably color the experience. We can experience any object or event as we experienced the orange, then choose how we respond to the experience. We give ourselves "breathing space" and allow ourselves the freedom to make conscious choices before responding.

Practice: Mindful Yoga Movements

Some yoga postures that work well with children include downward facing dog, cat and cow, butterfly, cobra, and tree poses (see descriptions in table

4 below). Many therapists already have some familiarity with basic yoga postures, but for those who don't, we have provided brief instructions for a few simple postures. The intent of these movements is to practice mindfulness of the body, not to develop yoga skills. You may find it helpful to emphasize the mindful awareness aspect rather than to focus on achieving perfect posture. We urge you to gently discourage any competition between children, if this seems necessary.

Table 4.   Yoga Postures for Children

Downward Facing Dog

1. Stand at one end of the mat with both feet flat, about hip-width apart.
2. Slowly bend at the waist until both hands reach the ground. Knees may be bent if needed to place the hands on the mat. Palms are facing down and about shoulder-width apart.
3. Walk the hands forward (out to about half the height of the child).
4. Raise buttocks in the air, with arms and legs straight, the back straight, and the head hanging down. This posture resembles an upside down "V."
5. Bark like a dog.

Cat and Cow

1. Start by getting down on all fours—on hands and knees on the mat.
2. Arch the back up high, like a cat. At the same time, point the head down and meow or hiss like that cat.
3. Gently let the back fall into a sway downward, belly toward the floor, while lifting the chin and tailbone. Then moo loudly.
4. Repeat, slowly swaying the spine upward and downward, accompanied by the appropriate sound effects. Meowing, hissing, and mooing are encouraged.

Butterfly

1. Start by sitting on the floor with the back pressed against a wall and the soles of the feet together.
2. Take a moment to relax and let the knees sink closer to the floor.
3. Sit up tall, pulling the feet as close to the torso as is comfortable. With both hands, hold the soles of the feet together.

4. Begin to gently "flap" both legs (wings) up and down—like a butterfly flying. Perhaps the butterfly is gathering nectar or flying up high just for the fun of it.

Cobra

1. Lie, stomach down, flat on the mat with legs together and straight behind the torso.
2. Place hands on either side of the chest with elbows pointed upward. Fingers point forward.
3. Push the upper body upward as far as is comfortable with the head and eyes lifted toward the ceiling.
4. Hiss like the cobra.

Tree

1. Start by standing with both legs together and arms straight down at the sides of the body.
2. Slowly slide the bottom of one foot up the inside of the other leg to the calf or thigh. Be careful not to press the sole of the foot against the kneecap.
3. As best you can, keep the knee of the lifted leg pointed out to the side.
4. Gaze at a single, stable point (something that is motionless).
5. When the balance feels stable, slowly lift both arms out to either side, and then stretch them overhead, fingers toward the ceiling, palms together.
6. While making soft wind sounds, let the arms sway back and forth like a tree in the wind.

Practice Inquiry

Invite the children to discuss their experiences of the movement practices:

- *What body sensations did you notice during each movement?*

- *What thoughts and feelings emerged as you practiced bringing attention to the body sensations?*

These movement practices help enhance awareness of body sensations and allow the children an opportunity to stretch their bodies following an extended time seated. At the end of the inquiry, invite each child to put his mat away with mindful awareness, and then return quietly to the circle to conclude the session.

Concluding the Session

Starting with this session, the Three-Minute Breathing Space will be practiced at the beginning and end of every session. Since this is a core practice in MBCT-C, when reviewing the handout, you'll want to make sure every child understands the three steps. In the next sessions, offer verbal guidance as many times as you feel is necessary until each child is comfortable with the practice.

MINDFULNESS IN EVERYDAY LIFE

- Three-Minute Breathing Space

- Mindful Yoga Movements

- Tasting Fruits (distribute the prepared bags of dried fruit)

ADAPTING SESSION 4 FOR INDIVIDUAL THERAPY

Session 4 is easily adapted for individual therapy. Opening to One Orange can be practiced with no modifications. If time becomes an issue, the Mindful Yoga Movements may be introduced with fewer poses. There will be more opportunities later in the program to practice these same movements. It is important that ample time be devoted to the Three-Minute Breathing Space, as this will be the primary mindful breathing practice for the remainder of the program. Children typically enjoy the mindful eating activity and easily engage in the practice inquiry, which is intended to deepen the understanding that bringing greater awareness to ordinary daily activities might enrich or expand their lives.

CHAPTER 9

Sound Experiences

Music is your own experience, your thoughts, your wisdom.

Charlie Parker

We become habituated to the multitude of sounds in our environment. Our limited attentional capacity must block out many sounds just so we can get through our day. Repetitive sounds can become inaudible when they fall into the background of our awareness. Sometimes we may forget to listen at all.

Darren is exhausted and irritable after giving his daughter, Susie, many reminders to finish her chores and homework. Eventually Susie screens out his voice altogether. Darren loses his patience and demands, "Are you hard of hearing?" Susie doesn't answer.

There is nothing wrong with Susie's hearing. She's just not listening. When we choose to listen, we sometimes notice that certain sounds elicit specific thoughts, emotions, and body sensations. When we hear a bird sing, we might think, *Oh, spring is finally here,* and feel joyful. The sound of a garbage truck probably evokes different thoughts. Irritation arises with the thought, *I hate that stupid truck. That awful grinding noise always wakes me up*. Mindful awareness doesn't change the actual sound, nor does it change the thought itself. It can, however, change our relationship to the thought.

Listening with awareness, we attend to what we hear without judgment. Instead of mindlessly reacting on automatic pilot, we just listen to the sounds. We note the thoughts, feelings, and body sensations present in each moment. Our mindful awareness of sounds just as they are may transform previously unpleasant noise into interesting sounds, pitches, rhythms, and frequencies. Sounds are experienced as "just sounds."

SESSION 5 OVERVIEW: MUSIC TO OUR EARS

The same sound often elicits different reactions from different people. Julie hears a dog bark in the distance and has loving thoughts of her affectionate Labrador retriever. Lisa recoils in fear at the same bark, having once been chased by a large dog. John feels sadness, remembering that his dog recently ran away. Each child hears the same sound and yet experiences different emotional reactions—emotions that were aroused not by the sound but by their own thoughts about the sound.

Session 5 focuses on mindfulness of sounds in the receptive mode. Session 6 focuses on mindfulness of sounds in the expressive mode—the expressive creation of music. Music is an example of sounds that, operating mostly outside our conscious awareness, can exert enormous influence. Victor Hugo said, "Music expresses that which cannot be said and on which it is impossible to be silent" (Galewitz, 2001, p. 25). Music can evoke strong images and feelings. Our personal "taste" in music often leads to conditioned judgments about sounds. For many people, the phrase "country music" has certain associations, as does "classical music" or "the blues." Our lives, however, become more limited when we base our choices solely on judgments, labels, or habituated associations.

The goal of session 5 is to practice listening, so that we may learn to hear. We bring awareness to sounds by hearing them just as they are—while knowing that the evoked thoughts, images, feelings, and body sensations are not in the sound. Happy sounds, sad sounds, angry sounds simply don't exist. Those labels consist of our emotional responses, not the actual sounds.

The practice of mindful listening develops awareness of our habituated reactions. The hundredth time we listen to a song, we can choose whether to tune it out altogether or hear it as if for the first time. We learn to see our personal filters and how thoughts and feelings shape our felt experiences. When we hear sounds as "just sounds," we deepen our ability to listen. By listening with mindful intention, we may develop insights into how our filters sometimes contribute to our dissatisfaction.

In session five, the child practices bringing awareness to sounds in her environment. She sees how her own thoughts influence her perceptions of sounds. As she increases her awareness of different sounds around her, she learns more clearly how those sounds may affect thoughts, feelings, and body sensations, and thereby transform the felt experience. When we are more mindful of the outer world, we are more mindful of the inner world. We may feel less desire to move away from difficult emotions and experiences. Instead, we practice just noting what happens in the moment. Listening with mindful awareness, we may find peace and greater acceptance of experiences as they unfold. We observe what is present before choosing how to respond. Cultivating mindful awareness, we may discover that we have more choices in how we respond to events.

Therapy Goals and Essential Questions

- Introduce mindful hearing. Define all sounds as music. Enhance awareness of the natural complexity of musical sounds.

  - What does it mean to listen with mindful awareness?

  - What might we learn about ourselves and our world by listening mindfully?

  - How could mindful listening be helpful in our lives?

- Experience how different sounds may evoke different thoughts, feelings, and body sensations in the same child. Observe that the same sounds may evoke different responses in different children.

  - How might sounds affect thoughts, feelings, and body sensations?

  - How might thoughts, feelings, and body sensations affect what we hear?

Key Points

- When we listen with mindful attention, we become more aware of thoughts, feelings, and body sensations.

- Thoughts, feelings, and body sensations often color how we experience sounds, just as they influence how we perceive other events that happen in our lives.

- With our thoughts, we create individual and unique relationships and experiences.

Session 5 Outline

Preparation

- Use your personal mindfulness practice to prepare for the session.

- Take attendance with the Being Present Board.

- Have children complete the Feely Faces Scale.

- Give brief recap of previous session (tasting mindfully).

- Review agenda for this session.

- Review home practices from previous week.

Mindfulness Practices

- Three-Minute Breathing Space (first practice)

- Do You Hear What I Hear?

- Mindfulness of the Body

- Three-Minute Breathing Space (second practice)

Concluding the Session

- Read the poem: The Door.

- Have children complete the Feely Faces Scale.

- Review session 5 summary.

- Review home practices.

Materials Needed

- CD player or MP3 player with speakers.

- Six to eight different musical selections from various genres, such as rhythm and blues, rock, pop, classical, country, or new age. You may prefer to choose several pieces of music that are likely to be less familiar to the children (for example, Tibetan chanting, African drumming, or Celtic songs).

List of Handouts

5.1 Poem: The Door

5.2 Session 5 Summary: Music to Our Ears

5.3 Home Practices

5.4 Mindful Listening

Mindfulness Practices

Practice: Do You Hear What I Hear?

Today we will explore mindfulness using our sense of hearing. By listening with mindful attention, we have opportunities to make new discoveries and learn more about the people and events around us. As we practice listening, our experiences may be different from what we might expect. Observing our expectations is part of the practice of mindful listening. Listening with mindful awareness, we may hear sounds we have never heard before. We may hear familiar sounds in new ways.

After dimming the lights, invite each child to sit or lie comfortably on a mat and close her eyes, and then say something like this: *"As you listen to the music, I invite you to become aware of any thoughts, feelings, and body sensations that arise."* This part of the practice is done quietly, without discussion or sharing of experiences. Play a short segment (about one minute) from a piece of music. Stop the music and invite the children to create a brief title for the song. Ask them to notice and write down their thoughts, feelings, and body sensations, along with the song title in their notebooks. This procedure is repeated with at least five or six pieces of music. The number of pieces presented may depend on the size of the group. Larger groups are likely to require more time for the practice inquiry, leaving a little less time to play the songs.

Practice Inquiry

You may begin the inquiry by inviting group members to share their experiences of this activity: *What was this experience like for you?* Go back to the first piece of music and ask for volunteers to share thoughts, feelings, and body sensations. It may be helpful to record the children's responses on a blackboard or poster board to emphasize the variety of unique reactions. You may choose to focus on questions that deepen the child's understanding of relationships between thoughts, feelings, and body sensations. Some questions you may ask are:

- *In what ways are thoughts, feelings, and body sensations related to one another?*

- *How are these related to what you hear?*

- *Might what you hear be different if the thoughts or feelings about the sounds change?*

No child will have precisely the same experience of the music. Importantly, the thoughts tend to bring about unique feelings and body sensations in response to the same piece of music. Where a soft lullaby may elicit in Patricia thoughts of a wedding, Alex may imagine a funeral. Patricia feels happy, has a smile on her face, and experiences lightness in her body. Alex feels sad, his muscles tense, and his breathing is fast and shallow. You may wish to contrast these differing experiences to illustrate how our personal interpretations of an event can transform the experience.

- *Do all of us experience the same piece of music in exactly the same way?*

- *Did the same piece of music stir up the same or different images and emotions for each of us?*

- *What made us each have different responses to the same piece of music?*

- *What do we add to the sounds we hear that may create these unique experiences?*

- *Could different thoughts result in having different experiences?*

We usually note that there is no "right" or "wrong" way to experience music—sounds are "just sounds." To anticipate upcoming sessions, you may wish to help each child identify the judgments she may make about any part of the experience and simply label each as a judgment. It's helpful to remind children that judgments of "good" or "bad," or labels, such as the actual name of the song, artist, or genre, don't really describe or capture the full experience. The act of judging or labeling experiences is not "good" or "bad" either; sometimes, these can simply be ways to shorten communications.

Whenever the child digresses in describing her experiences of the music—for example, comparing it to other music she has heard in the past—you may want to gently guide the discussion back to the "here and now" experience.

Invite the children to share their experiences along the second line of inquiry: *How is listening mindfully different from what we do every day?* The children may notice their differing reactions to different types of music. They may also notice a greater capacity to enjoy the musical experience as "just sounds" when they choose to listen with mindful awareness. Greater awareness of the judgments about the music can awaken opportunities for the experience to transform into something fresh and new.

Next, explore how the children might apply this practice: *How can this practice be used in everyday life?* The children may realize that their interpretations of different sounds can affect their emotions and felt experience. Likewise, interpretations of other experiences can influence emotions about those experiences. The children may also realize that different people can experience the same sound in different ways. Realizing that we each create our own realities with our thoughts can be a profound awakening.

Practice: Mindfulness of the Body

Invite the children to lie down on a mat and gently close their eyes. You may prefer to dim the lights. Using the script from session 3, guide the children through a ten- to fifteen-minute practice in cultivating Mindfulness of the Body.

Practice Inquiry

Invite a short discussion of the children's experience with this Mindfulness of the Body practice. You may choose to guide the discussion along these three lines of inquiry:

1.   *What was that experience like for you? What did you notice?*

2.   *How is bringing awareness to the body different from what you do every day?*

3.   *How might this practice be helpful to you in your everyday life?*

Mindfulness of the Body is not an exercise in relaxation, although it may feel quite relaxing. The main purpose is to note how the mind wanders, to observe that thoughts and feelings are related to body sensations, and to practice bringing awareness to body sensations—over and over again. At the end of this activity, children may put the mats away—with mindful awareness of their body movements as they stand up, bend over, reach out, grasp, hold, lift, carry, lower, and place the mat on the pile—and then return to sitting in a circle for the conclusion of the session.

Concluding the Session

By now, children will be familiar with ending each session with a breathing practice, the poetry reading, and the Feely Faces Scale. As the children become more engaged, it can sometimes be hard to remember to allow plenty of time to review the home practices for the coming week. It is important to make sure that each child understands them. At least one home practice will be familiar, while a new one is added each week.

MINDFULNESS IN EVERYDAY LIFE

- Three-Minute Breathing Space
- Mindfulness of the Body
- Mindful Listening

ADAPTING SESSION 5 FOR INDIVIDUAL THERAPY

No specific practice changes are needed for individual therapy in session 5. Generally you will take a more active role with the child during the experiential practices. As you play each segment of music, you may want to write down your own thoughts, feelings, and body sensations. During the practice inquiry, invite the child to share her experiences, and you do the same. During the inquiry, point out when you each had different reactions to the same segment of music. The child learns that her experience of the music is different from yours. Be attentive to the fact that some children will have a tendency to confuse "different" with "better" or "worse." The one-on-one dialogues are intended to share understanding gained from exploring this new way of being in the world. We encourage you not to evaluate or convey any sense of judging whether an experience might be "right" or "wrong."

SESSION 6 OVERVIEW: SOUND EXPRESSIONS

The sounds we make often express how we feel in the moment. We tend to lower our voices when we feel sad and raise our voices when angry. The pace, rhythm, or quantity of our words often changes when we feel anxious or scared.

The aim of session 6 is to continue developing mindful awareness using sounds. In session 5 we learned that sounds in the external world may affect the internal world of thoughts, feelings, and body sensations. This session focuses on the converse of this by demonstrating that events in our inner worlds influence the way we express ourselves. During the expressive sounds activity, each child creates her own piece of music by playing the role of an orchestra conductor. Children rarely have opportunities to make noise, unrestrained and without fear of reprimand, so this activity is generally accepted as novel, fun, and exciting. Note that it also can become rather loud.

As we become more aware of feelings, we begin to notice how the body expresses them. When we feel anxious, muscles may tense, hands shake, or hearts beat faster. We practice mindfulness to become more aware of these experiences—without trying to change them. We move toward honoring and accepting the feelings, no matter how difficult it may be. Mindful acceptance can make it easier to be friends with the feelings. By expressing emotions through sounds, we may better observe the interconnectedness of our inner and outer worlds. Attending to the sounds "out there" with the thoughts and feelings "in here" helps us see how they are related. Giving ourselves permission to slow down, becoming more aware of our experiences, we may hear more clearly and respond to all the events in our lives with greater awareness.

Therapy Goals and Essential Questions

- Introduce mindful expression of sounds. Practice using sounds to express emotions.
  - How can different sounds express how we feel?
  - How do others interpret the sounds we make? The same or different from us?
  - Are sounds other than words important in communicating with others?
- Understand experientially that thoughts affect, and are affected by, feelings and body sensations.
  - How do thoughts, feelings, and body sensations influence how we express ourselves?
  - Can thoughts and feelings lead us to express ourselves to others in ways that we might not intend?

Key Points

- Practicing mindful awareness helps us recognize that how we express ourselves is influenced by thoughts, feelings, and body sensations.

- Thoughts and feelings may change how we interpret events.

- By bringing awareness to thoughts, feelings, and body sensations, we gain freedom to choose more consciously how to express ourselves.

Session 6 Outline

Preparation

- Use your personal mindfulness practice to prepare for the session.

- Take attendance with the Being Present Board.

- Have children complete the Feely Faces Scale.

- Give a brief recap of previous session (mindful listening).

- Review agenda for this session.

- Review home practices from the previous week.

Mindfulness Practices

- Three-Minute Breathing Space (first practice)

- Sounding Out Emotions—Mindfully

- Mindful Yoga Movements

- Three-Minute Breathing Space (second practice)

Concluding the Session

- Read the poem: Hearing.

- Have children complete the Feely Faces Scale.

- Review session 6 summary.

- Review home practices.

Materials Needed

- A variety of small musical instruments, one for each child (for example, drum, tambourine, triangle, maracas). It's not necessary to purchase expensive musical instruments. Everyday household objects can be used (for example, a metal pot with wooden spoon, partially filled water bottle, pet's squeak toy). Sounds also can be produced using the body (such as humming, clapping hands, tapping fingers on a hard or soft object).

- A conductor's baton (a pen, pencil, chopstick, or a small wood stick can be used).

List of Handouts

6.1 Poem: Hearing

6.2 Session 6 Summary: Sound Expressions

6.3 Home Practices

6.4 Unpleasant Sounds Record

Mindfulness Practices

Practice: Sounding Out Emotions—Mindfully

Children can choose to volunteer, or you may invite one child, to be the conductor. Please make sure the children understand that they each will have a turn to be the conductor. Bear in mind that a shy child may prefer not to be the first conductor. Designate the volunteer's position by handing her the conductor's baton, and perhaps even offer a wooden block (or podium) on which to stand.

Today we continue to explore mindfulness using our sense of hearing. We will discover what it's like to express our feelings through music. Each of you will have an opportunity to be the "conductor" of your own symphony—with a little help from your friends. I invite you to take a few moments now to be with your breath. Bringing your attention to the breath, noting the in-breath. Noting the out-breath. (pause) Then checking in with your experiences. What are your thoughts, feelings, and body sensations right now? (pause). Thinking about how different sounds might express different emotions, I invite you to create a short song that expresses what you are thinking and how you are feeling right now.

Invite the conductor to assign one musical instrument to each person, including the therapists. The conductor may also direct the use of other sounds, such as humming, stomping feet, or clapping hands, to enhance her personal concert. In creating her symphony, the conductor may choose to develop her expression of thoughts and feelings by asking the orchestra members to move to different places in the room.

This is your personal symphony, and it is the expression of you and how you're feeling in this moment. Using only your baton to direct the orchestra—without words—create a symphony that expresses your thoughts and feelings right now. For example, you may point to each person, indicating how many beats to play her instrument. You may point to two people when you would like them to play their instruments at the same time. You may choose the particular order of instruments to be played. You may raise your arms to show that you'd like someone to play as loudly as she can. You may lower your arms to show that you'd like someone to play as softly as she can.

Invite all of the children to check in with themselves, becoming aware of their thoughts, feelings, and body sensations as they come together in this creation of music. To some, these symphonies might sound like a confusion of discordant noise. The expectation for a composition to sound harmonious is another judgment, which makes us aware again of the act of automatic judging. The focus is on the child and the group as they share expressions of mindful sound, rather than the subjective quality of the music.

Each child takes a turn in the role of conductor. If a child feels stuck or unsure of how to end her piece, a simple smile or nod of the head by the therapist may be all the encouragement she needs to find a suitable ending.

After each composition, all of the children write down in their notebooks a title for the song just created, along with their thoughts, feelings, and body sensations.

Practice Inquiry

This practice is similar to the receptive listening practice, Do You Hear What I Hear? You may invite each child to share her experiences, including the title of each song and the thoughts, feelings, and body sensations associated with the music. This inquiry can help to clarify the give-and-take relationship between the sounds we make; the sounds we hear; and the thoughts, feelings, and body sensations that influence both.

You may wish to point out that the same sounds often elicit different titles and emotional responses from each person. Jeffrey felt frustrated as he recalled a recent argument with his mother and created a cacophony of sounds by instructing his fellow musicians to play their instruments as loudly as they could all at the same time. He titled his song "Fighting Mad." Jacob, one of the orchestra members, had a completely different experience in response to Jeffrey's song. He felt energized and cheerful, calling Jeffrey's music, "The Carnival." This exercise deepens the understanding gained from the Do You Hear What I Hear? activity in session 5.

The same symphony of sounds usually evokes different thoughts, feelings, and body sensations in each listener. This insight can be an important perspective for the anxious child. Adopting an attitude of inquisitive curiosity, you may ask something like:

- *How is it that several people had an entirely different experience of the same song?*

- *Do different thoughts and feelings contribute to our creating different song titles?*

- *How is it that we don't have the same thoughts and feelings when we hear the same thing?*

- *Are the thoughts, feelings, and body sensations related to our past experiences, to our current emotions, or to both?*

- *In what ways do these things influence how we experience the world?*

The main purpose of the inquiry is to understand that our experiences (of the music) are influenced by our subjective interpretations. We may be better able to express ourselves when we are aware of thoughts, feelings, and body sensations. Once the children have a basic understanding of these ideas, the dialogue can be expanded to explore how practicing mindful expression of sounds might be applied to everyday life. For example, you may wish to help them understand that different people may hear the same spoken words very differently, although they hear the same sounds.

Practice: Mindful Yoga Movements

Invite the children to select a mat and find a space on the floor. Yoga postures were introduced in session 4, and the children will have some familiarity with them. Guide the children through several poses as they continue to cultivate mindful awareness of the breath and the body.

Practice Inquiry

Invite the children to discuss their experiences of the Mindful Yoga Movements practice. After the children have a chance to reflect on their experiences, invite them to practice awareness of body movements as they put away the mats and return to be seated in the circle.

Concluding the Session

A child might still be excited at the end of the session after the exuberant and often loud expressions of sound. This is a wonderful opportunity to practice the Three-Minute Breathing Space to help the child reconnect with the present moment and return to a quieter mode of being.

MINDFULNESS IN EVERYDAY LIFE

- Three-Minute Breathing Space
- Mindful Yoga Movements
- Unpleasant Sounds

ADAPTING SESSION 6 FOR INDIVIDUAL THERAPY

In individual therapy, the Sounding Out Emotions—Mindfully activity poses a small challenge. Without the group, a conductor must work with a smaller, two-person, orchestra. For this reason, we offer a modified activity to practice the mindful expression of sounds in an individual therapy. You still will need a few musical instruments from which the child can choose.

Practice: Sounding Out Emotions—Mindfully (adapted for individual therapy)

In this activity, we will see how different sounds might express the thoughts and feelings present in the moment. We may sigh to express relief, groan to express despair, laugh to express amusement, or scream to express anger or fear.

Invite the child to remember a specific time when she felt angry. If the child has difficulty thinking about a specific incident, you might say, *Think about the last time you were really angry. Maybe you were accused of starting a fight, even though you were innocent. Maybe your friend cancelled your plans at the last minute.* Encourage the child to write down the specific event in her notebook along with the associated thoughts, feelings, and body sensations. Then invite her to express her thoughts and feelings through sounds, without words. She may choose to use different instruments or make sounds of her own (such as tapping, stomping, growling). She can also instruct you in what sounds to create that might enhance her own. If the child has trouble starting, it can sometimes be helpful for you to provide an initial demonstration.

After both you and the child have had the opportunity to express feelings of anger with sounds, invite the exploration of thoughts and body sensations that may be related to the feelings. For example, even though you and the child may have experienced similar feelings, the thoughts and body sensations may have been quite different. Furthermore, you may have chosen different ways to express those feelings, using different instruments and different sounds. Once the child understands the practice, repeat using other emotions (for example, happiness, anxiety, sadness, or fear). You and the child may alternate, each creating sounds and writing down in your notebooks the precipitating event, the emotions, and associated thoughts and body sensations.

> *Okay, now we shall do the same practice, but this time we might choose to express feelings of happiness. For example, you may remember the time that you made a card for your friend's birthday. You have just given it to her and are watching the delighted smile on her face. You're thrilled to be sharing this happy moment with your friend.*

For sadness, you might say:

> *Imagine that your best friend called and shared the news that she's moving to another part of the country. You feel very sad. You are thinking about how much you'll miss her.*

For worry, you might say:

> *Pretend that you're at school and you just realized that your science project is due today. You completely forgot about it. You are worrying about how to tell your teacher that you will need to turn in your project late.*

You can use these scenarios or similar ones if the child has difficulty remembering her own experiences. This activity will generally be more effective if it is personally relevant, so you may prefer to help the child think of a real-life scenario from her recent past.

Practice Inquiry

After both you and the child have "sounded out" feelings of anger, happiness, anxiety, sadness, or fear, you may want to explore the associated thoughts and body sensations. For anger, the child may have chosen to stomp her feet loudly, while you may have beaten on the drum at a frantic pace. The child may have felt her throat tighten, while you noticed that your breathing was faster and deeper. Sharing these different experiences can reinforce the main point of the session: the expression of sounds may reflect internal experiences. With the intention to practice mindful awareness, we become more conscious of the sounds that we create in expressing ourselves.

CHAPTER 10

Seeing Clearly

I Don't Take Criticism Well

I don't take criticism well,
Or evaluations, instructions, or directions,
You know the kind,
Helpful comments for my own good,
By anyone,
Not even myself.

William Menza (2007)

Humans are creatures of habit—we naturally seek orderly ways to structure our lives. In doing this, we tend to develop expectations of what we see, habituate to seeing things in a certain way—and then stop paying attention. The world is seen through a filter of prior beliefs and expectations. This can be helpful when we don't need to pay close attention to routine activities. I walk down a familiar hallway without looking at the floor with every step. I have expectations that the floor is flat and smooth. My expectations are reasonably accurate to the reality—until I step on the toy left behind by a forgetful child.

Session 7 focuses on enhancing concentration using visualization techniques. Session 8 helps children experience changes that may occur when everyday acts are performed with intention and awareness. The child will practice seeing with his "mind's eye" and learn to look at familiar objects in new ways. We help him understand that images created in the mind may not be completely accurate to reality—what we see sometimes becomes distorted when filtered through thoughts or feelings. This is an essential first step in an experiential understanding of how judgmental thinking might make it more difficult to be aware and present in one's life.

Practicing mindful seeing involves attending to the things we see and accepting them just as they are. Acceptance helps us let go of conditioned beliefs, judgments, expectations, or commentaries about what is seen. With mindful awareness, we note the presence of these internal experiences, which may distort how we interpret the realities around us. We may notice that we push away or hold on to particular thoughts and emotions. The practice of noting instead of judging can result in a mind state that promotes compassionate acceptance of ourselves and events in our lives.

SESSION 7 OVERVIEW: PRACTICE LOOKING

When we mindfully observe what is present in our world, we pay attention as best we can to what we see. As with other senses, it is easy to leap to judgments. We may see a "beautiful" bouquet of flowers or an "ugly" factory building, but do we actually look at the features, shapes, colors, movements, and other details of the objects? As we practice mindful seeing, we learn to become more aware of the judgments that may bias what we see. We practice seeing objects simply as patterns of color, shape, and movement—just as they are. We may see more than just the things we want or expect to see.

The aim of this session is to increase mindful awareness by looking with intention. We shift from automatic pilot and learn to see familiar objects as if for the first time. We can become more aware of our judgments—whether we like or dislike what we see—by noting what we are seeing, thinking, and feeling. Of course, judging thoughts will come up. This happens to everyone.

We simply note the act of judging and gently return our awareness to the colors, lines, shapes, movements, and features of the object itself.

Therapy Goals and Essential Questions

- Introduce mindful seeing in order to enhance concentration and attention. Practice looking clearly to experience what might change as we become more aware.

  - What does it mean to look with mindful awareness?

  - How is it different from what we do every day?

- Learn to differentiate between judging and noting. Observe that cognitive and emotional responses may be different when judging an experience rather than noting it. Deepen the understanding that judging may transform a felt experience.

  - Does adding judgments to the events around us make our lives easier or more difficult?

  - What can we learn about caring for our emotions by practicing mindful seeing?

- Our experiences are formed from a combination of things, including what we see (the actual object) plus the cognitive interpretations we make (labels or judgments) about what we see.

- We often make automatic judgments without really seeing what's right in front of us. Noting and judging seem to have an inverse relationship to one another. When we simply note what is happening, the influence of judging may decrease.

- If we simply observe rather than judge, our felt experiences may change. We can observe our thoughts and feelings as well as events or situations in our lives.

Session 7 Outline

Preparation

- Conduct your own personal mindfulness preparation.
- Take attendance with the Being Present Board.
- Have children complete the Feely Faces Scale.
- Give brief recap of previous session (expressing mindful sounds).
- Review the agenda for this session.
- Review the home practices from the previous week.

Mindfulness Practices

- Three-Minute Breathing Space (first practice)
- Visualizing with Clarity
- Mindful Yoga Movements
- Seeing What Is in the Mind's Eye
- Three-Minute Breathing Space (second practice)

Concluding the Session

- . Read the poem: Looking.
- Have children complete the Feely Faces Scale.
- Review session 7 summary.
- Review home practices.

Materials Needed

- Drawing paper
- Crayons, colored pencils, or felt-tip pens

List of Handouts

Mindfulness Practices

Practice: Visualizing with Clarity

Each child may choose to sit or lie down on a mat. After dimming the lights, invite the children to relax in a comfortable position and close their eyes.

Today we explore mindful awareness using our sense of sight. By looking with mindful attention, we have opportunities to see the people and events around us more clearly. We may see things in ways that might be different from what we are used to. Many of the things we "see" are really inside our heads. So we'll begin by practicing looking very closely at what is going on in our heads. We may see things we have never seen before. We may also see familiar things in new and different ways.

Create a verbal description of a pleasant scene. This may be an image of an afternoon at the beach, a walk in a sunlit park, a picnic, or any other familiar scene. Verbally sketch the scene without offering too much detail. Invite the children to fill in the details using the "mind's eye." As best you can, create the scene descriptively, without using words that may convey judgments. Speaking in the present tense can facilitate the visualization:

You see yourself walking along a path in a park. There are trees all around you. The sun is shining and you hear other children playing not far away.

You will want to invite the children to use the "mind's eye" to "see" the scene as vividly as possible and encourage them to "see" each detail with clarity and precision, including the sounds, smells, tastes, and physical sensations of being in the experience. Maintain the visualization for about five minutes. Then invite each child to write down in his notebook a brief description of the scene, along with the thoughts, feelings, and body sensations that he experienced.

Practice Inquiry

Invite the children to describe the details of the visualized scene. Elicit the thoughts, feelings, and body sensations that were present. When children report very different images, you may explore other factors that might have influenced what they "saw." The aim is to help the children understand that adding thoughts and judgments about the event may change how the event itself is perceived.

- *What thoughts, feelings, and body sensations arose while you imagined this scene?*

- *How is seeing with your "mind's eye" different from seeing with your real eyes?*

- *What parts of the image were the most vivid or clear? Were those elements related to specific memories?*

- *Were there elements from the verbal description that you chose not to "see" too clearly? If so, what might those be? Were any memories or feelings triggered by those elements?*

- *How might thoughts and feelings change what we actually see?*

Practice: Mindful Yoga Movements

Invite the children to practice five to ten minutes of mindful yoga movements (for example, cobra, tree, cat and cow, downward facing dog). Refer to chapter 8, session 4 (table 4) for a description of the poses. After mindfully putting the mats away, practice a few minutes of slow walking, followed by one minute of fast walking. We suggest that the movement practices be done in silence. You may invite the children to be mindful of their movements in specific body parts. For example, you may ask them to bring attention to the movement of the feet and ankles as they walk, the shifting of body weight as each foot is lifted and moved forward, the tightening and relaxing of the calf muscles. We encourage you to participate along with the children. The practice inquiry following this exercise can be kept brief.

Practice: Seeing What Is in the Mind's Eye

After distributing drawing materials, you may introduce the activity by saying: *We invite you to look into your mind's eye and draw a picture of the phone you use most often. Include every detail as accurately as you can, as best as you can remember.*

You may substitute any other fairly complex item that has a high degree of familiarity to the children, such as a computer, television, or gaming device. Encourage the children to create a clear, detailed reproduction of the object rather than focus on artistic quality. Allow ten to fifteen minutes for drawing. After the drawings are complete, invite each child to take his picture home and mindfully compare the picture to the actual phone. We offer some questions that he may consider while doing so. These questions also guide the home practice review at the beginning of session 8.

- *What details did you see most clearly in your mind's eye while you were drawing your picture?*

- *Do those details hold any special meaning for you?*

- *What details did you not see? What might be different about those details?*

- *Did the mind's eye "see" some parts as being in a different place, or a different size, shape, or color, than they really are?*

- *Did you add details that aren't really there?*

- *Do we have to look closely and pay attention in order to know or to remember what we see?*

- *How often do we look right at something without really seeing it?*

- *What helps us to remember seeing some things and forget seeing other things?*

- *What thoughts or feelings about this familiar object might have influenced what you drew?*

Practice Inquiry

You may wish to explore the experience of practicing mindful awareness while drawing the pictures. Elicit descriptions of the drawing experience. Gently note judgments or evaluations, either of the experience or the artistic quality of the drawing.

When you draw mindfully, you are present right here, right now. All that exists is you and your drawing—being present together. Perhaps your breath slows down. Your arm and leg muscles may relax. Maybe even a deep feeling of satisfaction arises. This is what is happening right now, and it's perfect just the way it is.

We generally comment that the picture may be different in some ways from the actual phone, and that's perfectly okay. Questions like these can facilitate the inquiry:

- *What thoughts and feelings arose while you drew your picture?*

- *What body sensations did you observe?*

- *Did your thoughts and feelings change in any way while you drew? If so, how?*

- *Were there times when you were not aware of thoughts, feelings, or body sensations at all?*

Concluding the Session

This session, like the others, ends with a breathing practice, the shared poetry reading, and the Feely Faces Scale. Continue to summarize the theme of each session and review each practice for the coming week. The Stressful Events recording is similar to the Pleasant Events recording (session 3) and the Unpleasant Sounds recording (session 6). The aim of these practices is to understand that judging helps define an event as "wanted" or "unwanted." How an event is perceived and evaluated may shift, simply by bringing awareness to the presence of judgments. The child may experience how judgments influence his felt experiences.

MINDFULNESS IN EVERYDAY LIFE

- Three-Minute Breathing Space
- Seeing the Little Details
- Stressful Events

SESSION 8 OVERVIEW: STRENGTHENING THE MUSCLE OF ATTENTION

In this session, the children will learn to focus and redirect their attention with intention, clarity, and awareness. They are invited to become more mindful of their environment—at home, in school, in the park, on the school bus. When a child says, "I never noticed before that…," he is choosing to see with mindful awareness, be it the color of the kitchen chair that he sits in every day or the texture of the lamp shade in his bedroom. A child learns to slow down and really see the world.

The aim of this session is to further develop mindful awareness to the world around us. Our world is marvelous and complex. As we strengthen the muscle of attention, we learn to see the world with greater clarity and awareness. We learn that thoughts and feelings often influence speech and actions, and may come between us and the experience. We learn to see choice points—moments in which we can make conscious choices—to help us respond to events in our lives. We may discover even more choice points when we look with mindful awareness and see events as they are.

Therapy Goals and Essential Questions

- Continue to develop mindful awareness through seeing. Exercise our ability to shift attention with purpose and intention.
  - What might change when we shift our attention to see something in a new or different way?

- How does our experience of the world change when we shift our attention from one part of our surroundings to another?

- Deepen the understanding that "mind chatter" (for example, judging thoughts) can influence what is seen. Become more aware of judgments that may change how we relate to thoughts and feelings.

  - Do thoughts and feelings affect what we see and how we behave?

  - How might changing our relationship to thoughts and feelings make our experiences more stressful? Or less stressful?

- Introduce "choice points," which are moments that present opportunities to make mindful choices. Practice looking carefully at the present moment in order to choose how to respond to situations or events.

  - How might looking more mindfully at the world around us increase opportunities to make helpful choices?

  - In what ways can practicing mindful awareness help us see our choice points?

Key Points

- What we actually see is a combination of our perceptions of an object plus our interpretations (labels or judgments) about that object.

- Seeing and noting what we see are different from judging what we see.

- We can redirect our attention in ways that change the quality of our experiences.

- We can choose how to respond to thoughts and feelings.

- We can't control most of the events in our lives. We can, however, choose how to respond to them.

Session 8 Outline

Preparation

- Conduct your own personal mindfulness preparation.
- Take attendance with the Being Present Board.
- Have children complete the Feely Faces Scale.
- Give brief recap of previous session (practice looking).
- Review the agenda for this session.
- Review the home practices from the previous week.

Mindfulness Practices

- Three-Minute Breathing Space (first practice)
- Seeing Through Illusions
- Moving Mindfully
- Seeing What Is Not There
- Three-Minute Breathing Space (second practice)

Concluding the Session

- Read the poem: Choices.
- Have children complete the Feely Faces Scale.
- Review session 8 summary.
- Review home practices.

Materials Needed

- At least five or six optical illusions (each printed large enough for the whole group to see at one time). Many different optical illusions can be downloaded from the Internet. Several website addresses appear in appendix A.

- A set of wooden or plastic blocks. You will use them to construct a three-dimensional structure with a variety of shapes, angles, and interior (negative) spaces. This should be constructed before the session and placed where the children can see it, without its obstructing the other session activities. Placing it on a small table at the side of the room works well. The children will draw only the interior (or negative) spaces rather than the object itself, so we recommend including a number of these negative spaces. (For more details, refer to the Seeing What Is Not There practice later in this chapter.)

- Drawing paper.

- Crayons, colored pencils or felt-tip pens.

List of Handouts

8.1 Poem: Choices

8.2 Session 8 Summary: Strengthening the Muscle of Attention

8.3 Home Practices

8.4 Practice Looking Record

Mindfulness Practices

Practice: Seeing Through Illusions

How often do we look closely and see clearly? We often miss small but important details, because our attention is focused on thoughts in our heads—anticipating the future, remembering the past, or not paying attention at all. When we choose to look with mindful awareness, we may discover a clearer, more focused way of seeing. Practicing mindful awareness, we simply observe what is, and so may develop greater acceptance of ourselves and our experiences.

Choice points are those moments in which we can make choices. When we look with mindful attention, we may see choices that we didn't know were there. We may see previously unnoticed things that help us make those choices. When we look very closely, we may see many choice points. But—we must look at the present, not the past or future. The present is the only moment in which choice points occur.

Today we continue to explore mindful seeing. Start by asking the children not to discuss what is seen, only to look with mindful attention and then quietly write down in their notebooks whatever they see. Then show the group the first optical illusion. Allow the children to observe the image for about thirty to sixty seconds while inviting them to write down what they saw. Then present the next illusion. After each image has been seen once and the children have written down what was seen, show each illusion a second time and elicit verbal descriptions of what was observed. For example, one image that may be used is called "Duck and Rabbit." Some children initially will have seen the duck figure while others will have seen the rabbit. You can help each to see the other figure.

When all children can see both figures, invite them to shift their attention back and forth—first to see one figure and then the other. Explore the experience of shifting attention at will. Invite the children to try to see both figures at the same time and explore how the effort to do so changes the quality of the experience. The children may learn that it is not possible to see both figures at the same time. They may learn that they can choose what they see simply by redirecting their attention.

Practice Inquiry

This inquiry is intended to draw out the understanding that shifting attention can change the quality or nature of the experience. During this discussion, elicit descriptions of the experience of willfully shifting attention and how this may change what is seen. What else might have contributed to different children initially seeing the images in different ways? Explore how thoughts and feelings might influence what is seen.

Shifting attention to see different things may help a child learn that he has choices in how he relates to his experiences. He can choose to attend to different elements of his experiences or not to attend at all. He can develop conscious intentions to be more present. He can notice when he functions on "automatic pilot" and then choose to bring more awareness to the activities in the moment.

Practice: Moving Mindfully

Spend three to five minutes practicing mindful stretching, similar to the Mindfully Moooving Slooowly practice (chapter 7, session 2), giving the same attention to body sensations as with the yoga postures. For example, you might suggest that the children practice moving their bodies with mindful awareness, first by moving as if they were a flower unfolding, then a tall tree swaying in the wind, then a butterfly, then a bird. It's not necessary to use the floor mats for this stretching exercise. The practice inquiry can be a brief exploration of the sensory experience itself.

Practice: Seeing What Is Not There

Mindful seeing is the practice of looking at the ordinary with awareness. We practice seeing and accepting our experiences just as they are. Expecting things to be different from the way they are may exacerbate our worries and decrease happiness and satisfaction with life as it is. Mindful awareness may help us more easily accept and let go of strong thoughts and feelings, such as anxiety, anger, or sadness. We may learn to be friends with our most difficult feelings by using mindful attention to see them clearly. As we practice mindful seeing, we note the thoughts and feelings that arise. We allow the thoughts and feelings to come and go. Over and over again, we bring attention back to what we see in this moment. Mindful seeing is a practice in mindful living.

This activity further develops mindful attention, looking at an object as if never before seen. Beforehand, you will create a three-dimensional structure from blocks or other objects. It should have a number of interior angles and interior open spaces (negative space). Common household objects in uncommon configurations can create unusual perspectives and interior spaces. We recommend that the structure be abstract and somewhat complex, at or just below eye level when the children are sitting, and large enough that all children can comfortably see it from where they sit.

Invite the children to sit around the structure so that each views it from a unique perspective. Distribute drawing materials. Embodying an inquiring and exploratory attitude, ask the children to look at the structure in a new way. Spend a few minutes simply observing the structure with mindful awareness before inviting them to draw what they see. As their minds get lost in thoughts or attention becomes distracted, you may remind them to bring their attention back to seeing the structure. Allow ten to fifteen minutes for the experience of mindful drawing.

Invite the children to see the structure as patterns of color, shape, space, and light rather than to identify components by label or function. You might invite them to draw, say, only the spaces between and around the structure, only the straight lines and omit any curved line, or only the parts that include a particular color or texture. This might lead to a mindful exploration of seeing a part versus seeing the whole. Each child has seen a different and unique perspective of the same structure. You might lead a mindful discussion of how our point of view changes what we see. You may remind the children to bring their attention back to observing when they become aware that they have slipped into thinking about what is being seen (making inferences). The children learn that direct observations may be mingled with subjective thoughts, feelings, and body sensations.

Practice Inquiry

Nearly everything in our world is unique and ever changing. To see better in the present moment, we practice seeing the wealth of details of this one structure. Start by eliciting descriptive (objective) observations, perhaps after reviewing the distinction between judging and noting. After the descriptions are shared, each child may be encouraged to describe the thoughts, feelings, and body sensations that arose while he was looking at and drawing the object. Associations, memories, beliefs, or expectations can gently be identified as such. You may choose to introduce the words "subjective" and "objective" and invite the children to reflect on how these words might relate to the distinction between judging and noting.

- **Subjective.** Based on or influenced by personal feelings or opinions. From within the observer; not from the external environment. Lacking external reality or substance.

- **Objective.** Based on observed facts. Not influenced by personal feelings or opinions. Relating to a material object, actual existence, or external reality.

The children may want to explore the distinction between making descriptive observations and discussing thoughts, feelings, and body sensations. What was it like to be limited initially to sharing only objective observations?

Is the object somehow different when thoughts and feelings aren't included? Elicit an understanding that noting an object is not the same as judging it. You are deepening the understanding that the words we choose to describe experiences may influence what we experience.

Continue to discuss choice points. Choice points are simply moments in which a choice can be made. Choice points only occur in the present moment. By giving mindful attention to the present, more choice points may be seen. It may be helpful to relate the concepts of subjective and objective to choice points. Events are objective. Thoughts and feelings are subjective. Only rarely can we choose the thoughts and feelings, but we can choose how to respond to them. We can choose which thoughts and feelings to listen to or even which to believe. We can choose our words and many of our behaviors. Mindful seeing can help us to see more choices.

Concluding the Session

This session is focused on seeing clearly and making conscious choices, so you will offer the children a choice in the home practices for the coming week. They are invited to practice any mindful awareness activity of their choosing. They will also be asked to practice the Three-Minute Breathing Space twice daily and to look at a familiar environment (their classroom) in a new way.

MINDFULNESS IN EVERYDAY LIFE

- Three-Minute Breathing Space
- Choosing to Be Aware
- Seeing Five New Things

ADAPTING SESSIONS 7 AND 8 FOR INDIVIDUAL THERAPY

Sessions 7 and 8 may be completed in sixty-minute individual therapy sessions in a number of ways. Thoughts, feelings, and body sensations from the guided imagery practice may be expressed verbally in dialogue with you instead of in writing. The visualization and drawing activities can be shortened by about half (that is, five minutes instead of ten). The optical illusion activity can be conducted in one round instead of two, with you providing immediate feedback and guiding the practice of shifting attention between images. You may also choose to use fewer images. You may wish to shorten the mindful movement practice if necessary. We prefer to shorten this practice rather than exclude it altogether.

CHAPTER 11

Being Touched by Mindfulness

If you have fear of some pain or suffering, you should examine whether there is anything you can do about it. If you can, there is no need to worry about it; if you cannot do anything, then there is also no need to worry.

His Holiness the 14th Dalai Lama

At times, our survival may depend on our sense of touch. We learn to associate certain objects or situations with thoughts of danger. As young children, we hear, "Stay away from the stove; you may get burned," and "Don't touch that knife; you may cut yourself." Judgments like these are essential, but may also contribute to our tendency to judge most of our experiences.

Judgments permeate experiences and often influence behaviors and emotions. Negative judgments may pull us away from objects that feel slimy, like snails or worms. Positive judgments may pull us toward objects that feel soft, like furry kittens or cashmere sweaters. With repetition, these judgments can become conditioned. Conditioned associations may be so strong that the body reacts to the judgment alone, even without making contact with the object itself. We may get "goose bumps" in anticipation of jumping into a pool of cold water or wince at the remembered pain of a stubbed toe. We may experience body sensations as if they were happening in the moment, even when they are not. Conditioned associations may further exert a strong influence on behaviors and emotions. For example, a child with social anxiety often experiences heart palpitations at the mere thought of entering a room full of strangers.

By judging our experiences, we may miss opportunities to cultivate awareness. Judging may interfere with our capacity to open fully to an experience. Once we decide that we "know" something, it is easy to disengage from it. We may decide that the weather is nice today. This is a judgment. But do we then pay attention to the warmth of sunshine against our skin or the cool breeze across our faces? How might the experience of washing dishes be transformed if we brought awareness to each vibrant sensory experience? We might find pleasure in the slippery sensations of the soap, the cool hardness of the plate, and the flowing warmth of the water. Contrast this experience to our usual preoccupation with judging thoughts: *This is so boring* or *I hate washing dishes.*

Mindful touching allows us to experience objects as a collection of tactile sensations. Enhanced awareness of the sensations may also enhance awareness of the judgments that often accompany the sensations. Becoming more aware of labeling sensations as good or bad, pleasant or unpleasant may increase awareness of how those judgments might contribute to our felt experiences, and even change its nature.

The mindful touching practice in session 9 helps a child become more aware of textures and other physical sensations. Becoming more aware of the stream of sensations and judgments, we may become more aware of our choice points. Touching the world with mindful awareness, we also cultivate compassionate acceptance. We may choose to observe whatever arises, simply noting those urges to move toward pleasant sensations and away from unpleasant ones. We may discover that we can often choose how to respond—or choose not to respond at all.

SESSION 9 OVERVIEW: TOUCHING THE WORLD WITH MINDFULNESS

Thoughts influence perceptions. As a child, you may have played a Halloween party game that involves reaching into a box to feel "gruesome body parts." You might have put your hand into a bowl of "eyeballs," which proved to be peeled grapes floating in water. You might have felt a "mummy's ear" (dried apricot), the "tongue of a prehistoric creature" (oily banana peel), or "goblin brains" (a bowl of cold, cooked spaghetti). You might have felt sick, scared, or disgusted. Yet the simple sensation of grapes or spaghetti is unlikely to elicit a strong emotional reaction. How often do we react to the conditioned associations rather than the actual events? As with other senses, thoughts, beliefs, and expectations may influence our felt experience of touch.

The aim of session 9 is to become more aware of the myriad judging thoughts about the things we touch every day. We practice bringing awareness to physical sensations, while noting the thoughts and feelings that emerge about those sensations. Practicing mindful touching can enhance awareness of our personal "filters" and how thoughts and feelings influence our felt experiences. Awareness of the present moment brings more awareness of choice points and a greater sense of acceptance in our lives.

Therapy Goals and Essential Questions

- Introduce mindfulness of touch. Practice mindful attention to tactile sensations. Observe that we often categorize and label experiences. Cultivate awareness of our judgments and how those judgments influence our perceptions of the things we touch.

  - What does it mean to touch with mindful awareness? Could our labels and judgments somehow change the nature of the experience?

  - What might change if we simply noted what we're touching instead of judging it?

- Deepen the understanding that judging may interfere with seeing the choices we have.

  - How might judging our experiences interfere with seeing some of our choice points?

  - Could practicing mindful awareness of sensations help us learn to see more choice points?

  - How might we use this understanding to cope with anxiety and other strong emotions more effectively?

Key Points

- We have little control over many things that happen around us, but we often have choices in how to respond. When we learn to stay present with an experience rather than judge it, we may become aware of more choice points.

- Choice points exist only in the present moment. Greater awareness of this moment may let us see more choice points and have more freedom in how we respond.

Session 9 Outline

Preparation

- Use your personal mindfulness practice to prepare for the session.

- Take attendance with the Being Present Board.

- Have children complete the Feely Faces Scale.

- Give a brief recap of previous session (mindful seeing).

- Review the agenda for this session.

- Review the home practice from the previous week.

Mindfulness Practices

- Three-Minute Breathing Space (first practice)
- Being in Touch
- Mindfulness of the Body
- Three-Minute Breathing Space (second practice)

Concluding the Session

- Read the poem: Touch.
- Have children complete the Feely Faces Scale.
- Review session 9 summary.
- Review home practices.

Materials Needed

- Many small objects with a variety of textures (for example, hairbrush, plastic bubble wrap, pinecone, pumice stone, velvet, silk, fake fur, cotton balls, toy ball, Silly Putty, toothbrush, apple, pretend play food, and so on). Collect one or more objects for each child in the group. It's helpful to use unusual objects that may be more difficult to identify by touch alone. For example, pumice feels like a rough stone, but weighs less than most stones.

- If washing facilities are available, objects that might elicit stronger emotional responses may be used (such as Vaseline, peeled grapes, cold cooked spaghetti, gelatin).

- Strip of cloth or eye shades to use as a blindfold.

List of Handouts

9.1 Poem: Touch

9.2 Session 9 Summary: Touching the World with Mindfulness

9.3 Home Practices

9.4 Mindful Touching Record

Mindfulness Practices

Practice: Being in Touch

Today we will have opportunities to explore mindfulness using our sense of touch. As we practice touching objects with mindful awareness, we may sometimes discover that the experience is not quite what we expected. When we are fully present with our experience, we may become more aware of our judgments about them. Mindful awareness raises the possibility of learning something fresh and new in every moment. This is how we may further cultivate mindful awareness.

To begin this activity, invite a volunteer to the front of the room. The other children will sit in a semicircle facing that child. You may wish to remind them that everyone will have a turn. The volunteer may choose to be blindfolded or hold her hands behind her back. For the former, place a blindfold over the child's eyes and invite her to hold her palms up and in front of her. For the latter, the child turns her back toward the group with her palms up and behind her. The other children should be seated so that they can see the object she will be holding. Invite all the children to assume a mindful posture. Then hand the blindfolded child a single object and consider saying something like: "*Holding this object in your hands, I invite you to explore it with your sense of touch. As best you can, describe this object without naming it or making judgments about what you are touching.*"

It is important that the child clearly understand that identifying or naming the object is not the aim of this activity. The other group members act as "participant-observers" to help identify when descriptions become judgments. For example, if the blindfolded child responds, "It feels nice," or "I don't like it," the observers may wish to provide feedback that those statements are not descriptive but rather are personal judgments about the object. Judging words are subjective: good, bad, pleasant, unpleasant, nice, disgusting, wonderful, gross. Descriptive words are objective: cold, warm, hot, sharp, smooth, rough, prickly, pointy, hard, soft, wet, dry, sticky, slimy, spongy, furry, or fuzzy. If the blindfolded child has difficulty coming up with descriptors, invite the other children to ask prompting questions:

- *Is the shape regular or irregular?*

- *How heavy is it?*

- *How warm or cold is it?*

- *Is the surface smooth or bumpy?*

After the child who is touching the object has described it as thoroughly as she can, invite the participant-observers to add descriptions of whatever they observed. These observations likely will include qualities of the object not accessible to the blindfolded child, such as its colors or a design printed on its surface. Finally, the child is invited to take off the blindfold and visually inspect the object. Rotate positions until each child has an opportunity to practice mindful touching at least once, using different objects each time.

Practice Inquiry

Invite and facilitate a group discussion of the practice:

- *What was it like to explore the object using only your sense of touch?*

- *Did describing the object affect how you experienced it?*

- *How might this be different from what you do every day?*

- *Did anyone notice how easy it was for us to misjudge something when we can only be mindful in one sense at a time? Might we do the same misjudging when we are on automatic pilot? Or even when cultivating awareness of all our senses?*

- *Did anyone discover some of your own automatic judgments—ones that might seem familiar—while you were touching these things?*

A child becomes more fully present with her experiences just by becoming aware of her automatic habit of judging them as "good" or "bad." In practicing Being in Touch, she may also learn that no one sense by itself can provide complete information about an experience—mindful seeing can provide information not accessible through touch alone. No one sense can ever tell us all there is to know about an object, and yet we commonly formulate judgments based on similarly incomplete information.

One object we use in our sessions is a pretend-play food—a piece of flexible rubber shaped like a green lettuce leaf. Amanda, exploring the object with her sense of touch, described it as "cold, light, and rubbery with a rough, uneven surface." Aidan, one of the participant-observers, looked at the object and exclaimed, "That must taste disgusting!" This event provided another opportunity to differentiate between describing and judging. Another child then asked Aidan, "How do you know it tastes disgusting? Have you ever tasted it before?" Events like this become rich opportunities to observe how immediate our reactions often are, and how quick we are to judge an experience as positive or negative.

The group then encouraged Aidan to describe the object with his sense of sight, to which he responded, "Green, flat, and fits in the palm of your hand." Later Aidan had the opportunity to take the object in his hands and experience it as "just an object." Indulging his childlike curiosity, Aidan also tasted it, to discover that rubbery lettuce has barely any taste at all. (For hygiene, of course, you will wish to wash everything thoroughly.)

After all children have opportunities to share their experiences, invite the group to explore how this practice might apply in everyday life. At any moment, a child may choose to bring awareness to her experiences in that moment. When feelings of anxiety, sadness, fear, or anger arise, she may discover that she can choose simply to observe and note the experience, without labeling it as good or bad and without trying to change it. Children may discover that, sometimes, it's perfectly okay just to let emotions be present without needing to do anything at all. As these experiences are repeated, the child may begin to recognize more choice points and discover that she can choose how to respond to stressful events. Children can and do make conscious choices, responding with intention and mindful awareness.

Practice: Mindfulness of the Body

The physical component of session 9 is a ten-minute mindfulness of the body practice. By now, children in some groups may be comfortable extending this practice up to fifteen minutes. Invite the children to take a mat, lie down, and gently close their eyes. Dim the lights and then guide the children through the practice. A script for this practice is in chapter 7, session 3.

Practice Inquiry

Invite the children to discuss their experience of the practice:

*   *What thoughts, feelings, or body sensations did you observe during the mindfulness of the body practice?*

*   *What happened to the awareness of body sensations when thoughts wandered off?*

*   *How might practicing keeping your attention focused on the body be helpful in everyday life?*

As we've discussed, the aim of this practice is to enhance awareness of body sensations and return attention back to the body sensations whenever the mind wanders. Following the inquiry, you may invite the children to put away their mats with mindful intention and then take their seats in a circle for the conclusion of the session.

Concluding the Session

By now, all the children will be familiar with the end-of-session procedures. Some children may even take it upon themselves to ring the bells of mindfulness, guide the Three-Minute Breathing Space, distribute handouts, and begin the poetry reading. These behaviors empower the child and are certainly to be encouraged. It's up to the therapist, however, to ensure that each child clearly understand the home practices for the upcoming week.

MINDFULNESS IN EVERYDAY LIFE

*   Three-Minute Breathing Space
*   Mindfulness of the Body
*   Mindful Touching

ADAPTING SESSION 9 FOR INDIVIDUAL THERAPY

No modifications to the session structure are required to adapt session 9 for individual therapy. During the Being in Touch practice, you may wish to provide an initial demonstration. Put on the blindfold, choose one object from the bag, and then describe the object. Invite the child to pick an object from the bag and explore it with mindful touching. Should the child express judgments, gently help her determine if they were judging or describing words. For example, ask if an outer-space creature would understand the sensation of "yucky." Encourage the child simply to describe the objects, as best she can. Judging thoughts are inevitable, and simply enhancing awareness of judgments is the aim of this practice. You may choose to explore how experiences might feel different if the judgments were separated from the object itself. You may explore multiple objects, perhaps alternating with the child in the role of participant-observer.

CHAPTER 12

Making Sense of Scents

River of Feelings

The river of feelings,
Flows night and day,
Without end.

Sit on the side
and watch,
Or be carried away,
and drowned.

This is how it is.
Feelings are not a problem,
As they constantly change.

William Menza (2005)

The world is saturated with scents. The sense of smell is our most primitive sensory mode and acts on parts of the brain responsible for our most basic instincts—fear, hunger, and attraction. We seem to react to smells more instinctively and viscerally than we do to other senses. When we smell something new, we typically make an immediate, often habituated judgment of whether or not we like it. To experience smells while maintaining awareness of the associated thoughts and feelings may be the most challenging of the sensory-based mindfulness practices.

Smells are often associated strongly with specific emotions—typically the emotion present when the smell was first experienced. Heather smells baking cookies and remembers happy afternoons in her grandmother's kitchen. She associates the smell of disinfectant with the hospital where her tonsils were removed. Our unique experiences create unique contextual associations, so the same smell can elicit different emotions for different people. Smells can also trigger different forms of cognitive processing. For example, smells stimulate memories ("Smelling that seashell reminds me of our trip to the ocean"), comparisons ("That smells just like lemons"), determinations ("The milk smells sour, so it must be spoiled"), and judgments ("Those dirty clothes smell terrible"). The mind becomes very thoughtful about olfactory sensations.

Curiously, though, describing scents is very difficult. Many words exist to describe sensations from other senses, but smells seem to defy descriptive language. We don't have a smell-specific vocabulary, except within a few specialized industries such as perfume making and wine tasting. Consequently we borrow words from other senses. Mint leaves can smell "cool," camphor might smell "sharp," the ocean may smell "salty," and an attic can smell "dark." We make associations and comparisons, saying that "this" smells "like that." Most of all, we seem to make judgments. Chocolate smells good. Rotten eggs smell horrible. Judgments arise quickly, and are often strong, unconscious, and resistant to change.

This tendency toward rapid judgments makes mindful smelling an advanced practice. Judgments add layers of interpretations, cognitive elaborations, and emotional responses to the sensory experience. Activities in mindful smelling may illustrate for the child the habitual, often unconscious judgments of his experiences. We simply bring greater awareness to the complete sensory experience while noting the myriad reactive judgments that often emerge.

SESSION 10 OVERVIEW: WHAT THE NOSE KNOWS

We are learning that judgments can affect how we experience our lives. When we make a judgment that we like something, we may want to move closer to it, want more of it, or want it to last longer. For example, we may judge that roses smell good. Even with something that smells as nice as roses, we are not always happy. We may worry that the roses won't last very long, or be jealous that someone else has more roses than we do. When we judge that we don't like something, we may move away from it, want less of it, or want it to go away. When we are served boiled spinach and judge that it smells bad, we may wrinkle our nose and push the plate away. We often can't control much in our lives, and sometimes we might have to eat spinach. Spinach isn't bothered by how it smells. Spinach is just spinach.

When we practice mindful smelling, we experience just how easy it is to make quick judgments without being aware of what we're doing. Thereafter, we may lose awareness of the experience just as it is. We may start to believe the judgments more than the actual experience. Judging can make small worries seem like big ones, thereby increasing our unhappiness. Mindful smelling helps us bring more awareness to the judgments that we normally use to make sense of the smells around us. Instead of smelling something as "nice" or "nasty," we learn to note the judgments and smell the scents—just as they are.

The aim of this session is to bring greater awareness to the judgments we make and understand how those judgments may affect our lives. We cannot choose many of our experiences, but we usually can choose how we respond to them. Practicing mindful awareness helps us to see more choice points, which are available only in the present moment. The shift from automatic pilot to mindful awareness helps us smell familiar things as if for the first time. We practice neither liking nor disliking our experiences. This is what it means to practice mindful smelling.

Therapy Goals and Essential Questions

- Practice observing how quickly we tend to judge the things we smell. Enhance awareness that those judgments frequently influence our experiences.

  - How can practicing mindful smelling help us become more aware of all the judgments we make about the world around us?

  - How do all those judgments affect how we feel and how we act?

- Learn that we have choices in how we respond to our experiences. Cultivating mindful awareness may help us see more choice points.

  - How can practicing mindful awareness help us be more aware of the choice points available to us?

  - How might we use this skill to respond to the events in our lives without being pushed and pulled by judgments and feelings that arise?

Key Points

- What we smell is actually a combination of the scent plus our judgments about the scent. Smelling something and judging the smell are two different activities.

- We often react to events by moving toward the ones we judge positively and by moving away from those we judge negatively. In the long run, neither reaction reduces anxiety or increases happiness.

- Judging may interfere with seeing clearly what is present in each moment.

- We don't have control over many events, but we can choose how we respond to them.

Session 10 Outline

Preparation

- Use your personal mindfulness practice to prepare for the session.
- Take attendance with the Being Present Board.
- Have children complete the Feely Faces Scale.
- Give brief recap of previous session (mindful touching).
- Review the agenda for this session.
- Review the home practices from the previous week.

Mindfulness Practices

- Three-Minute Breathing Space (first practice)
- Judging Stinks!
- Mindful Yoga Movements
- Three-Minute Breathing Space (second practice)

Concluding the Session

- Read the handout: Things We Can Learn from a Dog.
- Read and discuss the handout: To Be or Not to Be.
- Have children complete the Feely Faces Scale.
- Review session 10 summary.
- Review home practices.

Materials Needed

- An assortment of scents. Prepare at least eight to ten samples of different scents before the session. Place each scent separately in a small container or tightly sealed plastic bag. Saturating cotton balls with liquids will retain the scent longer. Bolder scents are generally

more effective than subtle ones. To facilitate clear negative and .
positive judgments, choose scents that evoke wrinkled noses or
big smiles. However, be aware of allergies a child may have to specific scents. For example, some children are allergic to the smell
of ammonia. We recommend that you. always ask parents about
any allergies or other reactions to certain smells during the initial
interview or parent orientation session, and then choose the scents
with care.

- Examples of scents that work well: camphor; vinegar; vanilla or pep-
permint extract; mashed strawberries; boiled eggs; a cut lemon or
lime; chocolate; hot pepper sauce; chopped onions or garlic; moist
dirt; pungent cheeses; pine needles; ground coffee; tuna fish; per-
fumes; scented candles, soaps, or lotions; dried or fresh.crushed
herbs; or flowers, such as roses, honeysuckle, or jasmine.

List of Handouts

10.1 Handout: To Be or Not to Be

10.2 Session 10 Summary: What the Nose Knows

10.3 Home Practices

10.4 Mindful Smelling Record

10.5 Things We Can Learn from a Dog

Mindfulness Practices

Practice: Judging Stinks!

*The world around us is full of scents of all kinds. We don't often
stop to notice how many different smells there are and how they
might affect our experiences. For example, when we smell cotton
candy, we may feel happy. Smelling a garbage truck, we might
wrinkle our noses. We can be quick to judge the things we smell,
sometimes not even realizing that we are judging them. When
we judge something as "good," we might feel happy, or when we*

judge it as "bad," we might feel unhappy. Judgments sometimes get in the way of seeing clearly what is really happening in this moment. When we start believing the judgments, we may miss seeing some of our choice points. When we are very anxious or unhappy, we might feel that we have no choices at all. With greater awareness, we may see more choice points.

Inviting the children to sit in a circle, start by passing around one scent container. Ask the children to open the container, smell what's inside, then— without identifying or naming the scent—offer one word to describe what he smells. Invite each child to explore mindfully smelling the scent while noting his thoughts, feelings, and body sensations, particularly noting any judgments that may arise. Table 5 (below) lists a number of words that can be used to describe different scents. If a child offers a word that names the scent, judges it, or compares it to something else, the other children may help that child identify words that are more descriptive or less judgmental. You may ask something like, *Does this word help someone who has never before smelled it to understand the experience?* Then repeat with the next scent. You may wish to help the children develop their vocabulary of describing words by listing them on a blackboard or poster during the activity and practice inquiry.

Table 5. Adjectives That Can Be Used to Describe Smells

acrid	cloudy	fiery	meaty	rancid	spicy
airy	cold	flowery	minty	raw	stale
aromatic	complex	fragrant	moist	salty	strong
ashy	cool	fresh	moldy	sharp	subtle
bitter	crisp	fruity	musty	smoky	sweaty
bland	damp	grassy	natural	smooth	sweet
bold	dark	heavy	papery	soapy	unnatural
burnt	dry	hot	pungent	soft	wet
clean	dull	light	putrid	sour	wild
clear	faint	loud	quiet	sparkly	wispy

Practice Inquiry

Begin the inquiry by inviting each child to describe his experience of smelling the various scents. Questions you might ask include these:

- *How might we describe two smells, such as two different flowers, so that a listener could understand that they are different?*

- *Did you observe any judging thoughts arise as you smelled each scent? Was the judgment the same throughout the entire experience, or did it change as you continued to practice mindful smelling?*

- *Did the emotional experience change when the judgment changed? If so, how?*

- *Could you see when a judgment might be arising by the wrinkled nose or the smile of another child? Did anyone notice perhaps that the smile went along with moving toward the scent and the wrinkled nose went along with moving farther away from it?*

- *Could those movements toward experiences we judge as "good" and away from those we judge as "bad" affect how we respond to the events of our lives?*

- *What memories or associations were evoked by the smells?*

- *How might focusing on the memories make us less aware of the present experience?*

- *How might thoughts and judgments about the smell get in the way of seeing some of our choice points?*

This activity is challenging and can engage a child's attention quite intensely. Emotional responses to the various scents may be very strong. We work toward helping the child understand that judgments and emotional reactivity can change the nature of his experience. With younger or less cognitively developed children, it may be sufficient to increase awareness that judging thoughts and strong feelings may interfere with seeing choice points. You may wish to focus part of the dialogue on the child's freedom to choose his own behavioral response. We prefer to avoid language that might imply that mindful awareness can (or should) be used to regulate his thoughts, stifle his emotions, or control other people and events in his life.

Smells may elicit memories so strong that it becomes challenging for the child to practice mindful smelling, or even to have much awareness of the current experience at all. If a particular scent evokes memories of a stressful event, the child may experience a sudden increase in anxiety. Should this occur, you may have an opportunity for a potentially powerful clinical intervention. Practicing mindful awareness in such moments can provide a kind of intrapsychic exposure therapy. Helping the child stay present with intense anxiety or fear can be facilitated by first practicing the Three-Minute Breathing Space (together) and then encouraging the child to mindfully describe his thoughts, feelings, and body sensations. Your own skill at staying present, connected, and conveying compassion for the child's experience supports the child's cultivation of mindful awareness. Arising from your own practice, your compassionate presence can go a long way toward deepening a child's understanding that thoughts and feelings influence what he experiences. The child may learn that he can stay present with strong emotions and suffer no ill effects. This insight can foster increased self-confidence and a greater ability to tolerate distressing emotions.

Practice: Mindful Yoga Movements

Practice mindful yoga postures or slow movements for about ten minutes. Detailed instructions are provided in chapter 8, session 4 (table 4).

Concluding the Session

End the session by reading the handouts, completing the Feely Faces Scale, and reviewing the home practices for the upcoming week. This session concludes the sensory-focused practices. You may wish to let the group know this and introduce the idea of integrating mindfulness across all the senses to bring greater awareness into everyday life. This integration will be the aim of sessions 11 and 12.

MINDFULNESS IN EVERYDAY LIFE

- Three-Minute Breathing Space
- Mindful Yoga Movements
- Mindful Smelling

ADAPTING SESSION 10 FOR INDIVIDUAL THERAPY

The mindful smelling activity is easily conducted with one child in individual therapy. The therapist participates more interactively with the child than is necessary in group sessions. With one child, mindfully describing each scent and facilitating the practice inquiry takes less time than in a group format. The session may be shortened by twenty minutes or more. The mindful yoga movement practices can be used without modifications.

CHAPTER 13

Mindfulness as a Way of Life

In Stillness

The perfection of the moment is realized.
The innate beauty of existence shines forth.
The veil of illusion is lifted.
I am free. I am aware. I am.

Scott Jeffrey (2009)

Regardless of our individual situations or life circumstances, none of us can avoid living our own lives. During the program, we help children understand that bringing greater awareness to their lives is always possible, in any context or circumstance. As the popular phrase says, "Wherever you go, there you are" (also the title of a book about mindfulness meditation by Jon Kabat-Zinn). We believe that efforts to be elsewhere are futile and tend to increase suffering. Mindfulness is practiced by bringing awareness to whatever is happening in the present moment—over and over again.

MBCT-C is intended to deepen a child's understanding that mindful awareness is available in every moment. Each of us has boundless opportunities to practice presence, awareness, and compassion. Every interaction with another person is an opportunity to practice mindful speech and behavior. Every situation offers the choice to live with greater clarity and awareness. Every thought, feeling, and body sensation helps us awaken to the experiences happening in this moment. We learn to relate to our thoughts in a different and perhaps more compassionate way. Mindfulness represents a different way of being in the world—a way of being with immeasurable possibilities, any of which may promote profound, life-altering changes.

SESSION 11 OVERVIEW: LIFE IS NOT A REHEARSAL

Session 11 is intended to integrate and consolidate understanding gained from lessons taught in earlier sessions. We will revisit a few practices with perhaps a greater presence of mind and continue to explore our commitment to the daily cultivation of mindfulness.

We have practiced bringing awareness to tastes and smells, to music and sounds, and to touch. Perhaps we are learning to perceive with greater clarity. We have practiced grounding ourselves in the present moment using the breath and the body. Perhaps we have integrated the Three-Minute Breathing Space and other practices into our daily activities. We have practiced seeing that thoughts are just thoughts. We may have learned to be more accepting of our thoughts and feelings. We have learned that judging the world can interfere with seeing our choice points. Perhaps we have become more mindful in choosing how we respond. We have also explored many differences between living on automatic pilot and bringing mindful awareness to our experiences, and hopefully learned how practicing mindfulness can let us live with greater peace and happiness. In life, challenges are inevitable. We hope to face and accept those challenges by bringing more awareness and compassion into our lives.

Therapy Goals and Essential Questions

- Enhance principles of mindfulness with continued practice. Understand that thoughts and emotions are not facts. Thoughts are just thoughts. Emotions are just emotions.
  - Since thoughts are not facts, why should we believe anxious thoughts any more than we believe other thoughts?
  - Since emotions are not facts, do we need to get carried away by them?
  - How might we continue to bring greater awareness to our lives and to understand our experiences with greater clarity and compassion?
- Integrate mindfulness across the senses.
  - In what ways might we practice being more mindful using our combined senses?
  - We've learned that bringing awareness to thoughts, feelings, and body sensations may help us cope with strong emotions. In what other areas of our lives might cultivating mindfulness be helpful?

Key Points

- Mindfulness is always an ongoing option in everyday life. Every moment offers us another opportunity to practice.
- We can cultivate mindful awareness using the breath, the body, and all of our senses.

Session 11 Outline

Preparation

- Use your personal mindfulness practice to prepare for the session.
- Take attendance with the Being Present Board.
- Have children complete the Feely Faces Scale.
- Give brief recap of previous session (mindful smelling).
- Review agenda for this session.
- Review home practices from the previous week.

Mindfulness Practices

- Three-Minute Breathing Space (first practice)
- Thoughts Are Not Facts
- Feelings Are Not Facts Either
- Raisin Mindfulness
- Mindfulness Is...
- Three-Minute Breathing Space (second practice)

Concluding the Session

- Read the poem: Slow Dance.
- Have children complete the Feely Faces Scale.
- Review session 11 summary.
- Review home practices.
- Plan graduation party.

Materials Needed

- Chalkboard, whiteboard, or poster-sized easel paper for writing activity.

- Raisins, one small bowl, and a spoon to distribute the raisins.

- Copies of template for back cover of the book *Mindfulness in Everyday Life* (appendix C). One for each child and therapist.

- Crayons, colored pencils, or felt-tip markers.

- One #10 envelope for each child.

List of Handouts

11.1 Poem: Slow Dance

11.2 Session 11 Summary: Life Is Not a Rehearsal

11.3 Home Practices

11.4 Letter to My Self

Mindfulness Practices

Practice: Thoughts Are Not Facts

A child now understands that thoughts can be experienced as discrete events in the field of awareness. She can watch thousands of thoughts emerge and disappear every day. She may have experienced how thoughts can influence feelings and body sensations. She may understand that thoughts might not reflect reality. She sometimes may make mindful choices rather than react on automatic pilot. She may now be more aware that she has choices.

The following activity, borrowed from MBCT (Segal, Williams, & Teasdale, 2002, p. 244) and used by permission, reinforces decentering from thoughts by deepening the understanding that beliefs and expectations are often inaccurate. You may begin by inviting the children to gather a mat, their notebook, and pencil, then settle themselves comfortably. Read the four-sentence story shown next (in bold) one sentence at a time. Pause after each sentence and invite the children to write down what they think the story is about. If a child has difficulty understanding the directions, it may be helpful for you to ask the prompt question for that sentence. After each child has written down her current understanding of the story, advance to the next sentence. After each child has written down her understandings from all four sentences, read the entire story again. Finally invite the children to share the descriptions they wrote.

> *John was on his way to school.*

Prompt question: *Who is John? As best you can, describe John and what you believe he is doing.*

> *He was worried about the math lesson.*

Prompt question: *Describe more about John based on what you just learned. What do you think is about to happen?*

> *He was not sure he could control the class again today.*

Prompt question: *Does this change your picture of John? Who do you think John is now? What might be about to happen?*

> *It was not part of a janitor's duty.*

Prompt question: *What is your description of John now?*

Practice Inquiry

Dot-pictures created from too little information are filled in with inferences, beliefs, and expectations—which may not be accurate and continually shift as more information emerges. The initial mental image is usually of John as a school-aged boy. By the end of the story, the image of John has transformed from a young student to an adult math teacher to a school janitor. This practice helps a child understand that we sometimes create inaccurate pictures of reality based on limited information. We augment these inaccurate pictures with our own beliefs and expectations. Thoughts are often inaccurate. They influence emotions, change our perceptions of reality, and affect how we act and behave.

During the practice inquiry, you might explore how the children could apply what they just learned to their own lives. One important question to ask is *How could learning that thoughts are not always accurate help you deal with strong anxiety when it arises?* If a child finds it hard to connect the lesson to her own life, ask her what she might tell herself when she feels anxious, perhaps about an upcoming exam or another anxiety-provoking situation. Test anxiety is common. The thoughts elicited are frequently pessimistic and fatalistic: *I'm going to fail, I'm terrible at math,* or *I'm stupid.* Anxious children often anticipate negative, global, sometimes catastrophic outcomes while making overly critical self-attributions. Help them to understand that thoughts may become self-fulfilling prophecies by exploring how such thoughts might affect their performance on the exam. Intense test anxiety can and does interfere with a child's concentration. Additional problems arise when a child fails to separate the event from her expectations about it. She has forgotten that thoughts are just thoughts and she has choices. To reinforce this idea, you might ask something like this:

> *Andrea believes that a test is an opportunity to demonstrate what she has learned. Mike thinks a test is an evil experiment designed to show how stupid he is. They both have studied and know the material equally well. Who do you think is likely to be more anxious or nervous about the upcoming test—Andrea or Mike? Could Mike's thoughts affect his concentration or otherwise make it harder for him to do his best? Might Andrea's thoughts affect her feelings and test performance in other ways?*

Practice: Feelings Are Not Facts Either

This activity provides another way to explore relationships between thoughts and feelings. Children will imagine being in different emotional states to observe how their interpretations change. They may better understand that emotional states can influence thoughts and perceptual experiences.

First, introduce the activity as a practice of seeing thoughts and feelings more clearly:

> *Listen carefully to this story. Try to picture it as vividly as you can, putting yourself into the middle of the story, as best you can. See and feel it as if it is happening to you right now.*

First Story: Anger Imagined

> *You are at school and feeling really angry because you just had an argument with a good friend.* [Pause to let the children imagine the scene and note the thoughts and related emotions.] *Then you see another friend, named Jessie, who runs away from you, saying,*

"I'm too busy to stop and talk." What might you think about Jessie and Jessie's behavior?

Invite each child to visualize the experience clearly and then write down her thoughts and related feelings in her notebook. Then repeat the same instructions before reading the second story.

Second Story: Happiness Imagined

You are at school and feeling really happy because you've just been included in an after-school activity by a group of children who normally exclude you. [Pause to let the children imagine the scene and note the thoughts and related emotions.] *Then you see your friend, Jessie, who runs away from you, saying, "I'm too busy to stop and talk." What might you think about Jessie and Jessie's behavior?*

Again, allow the children a few minutes to record their thoughts, feelings, and body sensations in their notebooks.

Practice Inquiry

The start of each story is different and meant to induce different emotions. The ending is the same. Interpretations of Jessie's behavior are commonly related to the child's imagined emotional state. Following the first story, thoughts may reflect negative interpretations and are often more self-referential or global; for example, *Jessie must be mad at me too* or *Everybody hates me.* Explore how these thoughts might affect the child's emotions and behaviors. Following the second story, interpretations are generally more benign; for example, *Jessie must be late for something important. I'll call her later to make sure she's okay.* These thoughts tend to be more neutral or positive, with greater focus on the other person. Exploring these changing interpretations may help the child better understand that her emotions influence how she thinks, perceives, and responds to events. Anxious, sad, or angry moods tend to generate pessimistic thinking. Happier moods are likely to promote more optimistic thoughts. Neither mood nor their related thoughts are facts.

Some children (we hope) will separate the emotional state from the interpretation of the event. For example, following the first story, a child might offer the thought, *Jessie was probably just in a hurry. I'll talk to her later.* Should this happen, you may want to explore further what strategies the child used to see more clearly the actual event or to be less influenced by the initial emotional state. This exploration may help other children better understand that emotions do not need to interfere with their ability to see clearly.

Practice: Raisin Mindfulness

Children reexperience the Raisin Mindfulness practice. This practice provided an early introduction to mindfulness (chapter 7, session 2). It set the foundation for experiential learning by offering a different way of relating to the ordinary act of eating. Revisiting Raisin Mindfulness here may demonstrate some of the positive changes that can result from living with greater awareness and consolidate insights gained over the past ten weeks.

Practice Inquiry

Inviting the children to share their experiences, you may find that their depth of understanding will be markedly different from in session 2. The child who disliked raisins may still dislike them but may relate to the experience of eating one quite differently. The taste may not seem so bothersome, and she may notice the desire to push the experience away without actually doing so. The child who liked raisins may slow down to better experience the entire spectrum of perceptions and sensations moment by moment. She may observe an impulse to eat it quickly and note thoughts of wanting to eat as many as she can. Practicing Raisin Mindfulness gives her an opportunity to become more conscious of the desire for more, especially for those things that are judged pleasurable. Ongoing practice lets us see more of the inclinations, impulses, aversions, urges, longings, cravings, and desires that impel so many of our behaviors. The capacity to relate to these intrapsychic experiences as such may be the essential component of decentering. Experiencing thoughts, feelings, and body sensations for what they are grants the freedom to choose our words and behaviors.

Practice: Mindfulness Is...

This activity returns us to where we started. In session 1, the children personalized the front covers of their notebooks with words or images of what mindfulness meant to them. Now they have the opportunity to decorate the back covers of their notebooks with their current understanding of mindfulness. To begin this practice, distribute drawing materials and copies of the back cover templates of *Mindfulness in Everyday Life*. The words "Mindfulness is..." are printed on what will become the back cover of each child's book. We suggest that she first meditate a few minutes on what mindfulness means to her. Then invite the child to complete this sentence with words or pictures: "In my everyday life, mindfulness is..." We urge you to create the back cover for your own book. Being involved and engaged in this creative activity in parallel with the children can support a process of shared discovery.

Practice Inquiry

Some children will want to show their notebook covers to the group and describe what mindfulness means to them. It can be fascinating for the children to look at their drawings from the first session and compare them to their drawings now.

At the beginning of one group, a twelve-year-old boy, whom we'll call Mario, decorated his notebook cover with an assortment of disconnected shapes, with no particular theme, and wrote his name in block letters several times using red and blue crayons. Eleven weeks later, we watched with amazement as the same child slowly and thoughtfully decorated his back cover with a red heart, with the word "life" placed in the center. Mario carefully, spaciously surrounded the heart with each of these words written in a different color: "attention," "love," "forgiveness," "justice," "share," "relaxation," "knowledge," "peace," and "freedom." Filled with awe, we watched and wondered how meaningful it was for him that he began with "attention" and ended with "freedom." Leading into (or radiating out of) "life," Mario connected each word to the center of the heart. In eleven weeks, Mario apparently had developed a remarkably insightful appreciation of mindfulness and its many life-affirming gifts. We sometimes don't have opportunities to see how deeply the work of therapy might affect our young clients. Mario's artwork attested to the potential of mindful awareness practices to inspire meaningful changes. It was an extraordinary experience to witness this evidence of insight and transformation. He also expressed feeling less anxious and angry as the program progressed, and his parents reported a significant reduction in behavioral issues at home. Unknowingly, Mario had given us a very special gift.

Denise McMorrow Mahone, 2011

These covers are an artist's reproduction of drawings created by a twelve-year-old boy who participated in the program. The child's name has been changed to protect his privacy.

Concluding the Session

During this session, the children have opportunities to integrate mindfulness across the senses, revisit some key practices from earlier sessions, and reflect on their experiences. Following the now-familiar Three-Minute Breathing Space, poetry reading, review of home practices, and completion of the Feely Faces Scale, children are also invited to share in planning the graduation party that will be held during session 12.

HOME PRACTICES

As you approach the end of the program, you may wish to discuss the upcoming transition from guided weekly group sessions to a self-directed daily practice that the child maintains for herself. The next home practice activity is a bit different from those assigned in earlier sessions. It is intended to support the child's motivation and desire to continue these practices. In addition to practicing the Three-Minute Breathing Space at least twice each day, each child is asked to reflect on her experiences in the program and write a Letter to My Self describing what she has learned and how it may have influenced her life. You will need to collect the letters, and then mail them back to each child three months later. As you review this week's home practice, distribute mailing envelopes for each child to address to herself. The home practice for this session (handout 11.3) suggests a number of questions to help inspire the writing. We provide a form on which to write the letter (handout 11.4).

In session 12, you can invite the children—if they choose—to share their letters with the rest of the group. Some may choose to keep their letters private, and this choice is perfectly okay. The letters serve to explore what mindfulness means to each child and to cultivate these practices in their daily lives. It is not hard to be mindful, but it can be hard to remember to be mindful. Three months later, these letters may be a reminder of insights inspired by this new way of being in the world.

You may wish to spend some time helping the children understand why the letter could be important to them. We discovered that nearly every child gives a great deal of thoughtful consideration and attention to writing her letter. If a child should arrive empty handed the following week, you may offer encouragement, writing materials, and time at the beginning of the session for that child to write her letter if she chooses.

GRADUATION PARTY PLANNING

Invite the children to consider the graduation party that will be held during the next and last session. What kind of foods would they like? Drinks? Music? What activities might they enjoy? Typically, we collectively develop a modest list of preferred foods, drinks, supplies, and activities. The group members can be responsible for bringing what is needed, potluck style. Because we work with children from lower-income families, we typically offer to bring the main food item (for example, pizza or sandwiches). The purpose of the party is threefold: to mark the child's "graduation" from MBCT-C, to create a space for yourself and the children to celebrate this shared journey, and to say farewell.

MINDFULNESS IN EVERYDAY LIFE

- Three-Minute Breathing Space
- Letter to My Self

ADAPTING SESSION 11 FOR INDIVIDUAL THERAPY

For the child in individual therapy, if time is not sufficient for both visualization activities (Thoughts Are Not Facts and Feelings Are Not Facts Either), you may choose to do just the first one. As usual, you play a more interactive role, helping the child relate her understanding of the activity to her own life. Allow approximately ten minutes for the Raisin Mindfulness practice and approximately fifteen minutes to draw the back covers of the book *Mindfulness in Everyday Life*. In planning for a smaller graduation party, you will want to collaborate in choosing a few contributions of food and drink, perhaps again offering to bring the more expensive items.

SESSION 12 OVERVIEW: LIVING WITH PRESENCE, COMPASSION, AND AWARENESS

In this final session, there is likely to be a different energy in the room. Children may arrive with their party supplies, feeling a mixture of excitement and sadness. In this session, they will celebrate this unique journey and experience with their now-familiar friends, and then say farewell.

Session 12 is divided into two parts with different aims for each. The first half is devoted to group practice and dialogue. Children may share their Letters to My Self and discuss their experiences in the group. They may reflect on the past twelve weeks and consider what future role these practices might play in their lives. They may have learned that mindful awareness practices can help them see choices and respond with presence and compassion. This awareness doesn't need to end just because the group is ending.

Awareness in our lives takes only commitment and attention—moment by moment. We expect that most children will have learned that the benefits well repay the investments of time and attention.

In twelve weeks of shared exploration and practice, the bonds forged within a group can become quite strong. The second half of the session celebrates the children's "graduation" from the program, honors the ongoing cultivation of mindful awareness, and allows you and the children to say good-bye.

Therapy Goals and Essential Questions

- Support the ongoing nurturing of mindful awareness, bringing more presence to our lives and compassion to ourselves and all those who share this remarkable world.

    - How do we continue to cultivate mindful awareness in our daily lives?

    - What are the benefits of continuing to cultivate mindfulness?

    - What are some potential problems or pitfalls that we might consider?

    - How might we address those potential problems or pitfalls with more skillfulness?

- Explore personal experiences of the program.

    - What have we learned from practicing mindful awareness in our everyday lives?

    - What might we do to continue to build on what we've learned?

- Celebrate the shared journey and bring closure to the group.

Key Points

- Practicing mindfulness may enrich our experiences and be helpful to us in living our lives.

- We can choose to live with greater presence in any moment, interaction, or situation in which we find ourselves.

- Bringing greater awareness to our lives is a personal choice and doesn't depend on anyone but ourselves.

- We can choose to see our choice points clearly and respond with mindful awareness.

- Living with awareness requires commitment, compassion, and continued daily practice.

Session 12 Outline

Preparation

- Use your personal mindfulness practice to prepare for the session.

- Take attendance with the Being Present Board.

- Have children complete the Feely Faces Scale.

- Give a brief recap of the previous session (integrating mindfulness).

- Review the agenda for this session.

- Review home practice from the previous week: Letter to My Self.

Mindfulness Practices and Activities

- Three-Minute Breathing Space (first practice)

- Exploring Everyday Mindfulness

- Program Evaluation (optional)
- Three-Minute Breathing Space (second practice)
- Graduation Ceremony
- Graduation Party!
- Three-Minute Breathing Space (third practice)

Concluding the Session

- Read the handout: Little Gidding.
- Have children complete the Feely Faces Scale.
- Review Session 12 Summary: Living with Presence, Compassion, and Awareness.
- Practice Three-Minute Breathing Space (third practice).
- Exchange farewells.

Materials Needed

- Graduation certificates or certificates of completion for each child
- Prepared farewell letter for each child (handout 12.3 is a sample letter)
- [optional] Small symbolic remembrance of participation for each child (for example, a glass bead, a special key or coin, a marble, or a polished stone)
- CD player or MP3 player with speakers and music (if music for the graduation party was requested)

List of Handouts

12.1 Little Gidding

12.2 Living with Presence, Compassion, and Awareness

12.3 Letter from Therapist to Child

12.4 Daily Practice Calendar

Program Evaluation Questionnaire (optional)

Mindfulness Practices

Exploring Everyday Mindfulness

Exploring Everyday Mindfulness is a group discussion. It gives children an opportunity to reflect on and put words to their experiences of the past twelve weeks. One session 11 home practice for each child was to write a Letter to My Self, describing what she may have learned about mindful awareness and her experiences in the program. You may open the discussion by inviting children to share their letters, thoughts, or reflections with the group, or by sharing some of your own thoughts. Sharing letters is not mandatory. Many children will choose to share their letters with enthusiasm. A few may choose not to. We advocate each child's making mindful choices, which includes choices about participating in any program activity. We haven't yet seen this happen, but if the entire group seems to have difficulty sharing their letters, you may choose to ask questions from the session 11 home practice sheet to facilitate the discussion.

The meaning of mindfulness is always personal and unique to each of us. We would like to share some examples from our experiences with MBCT-C groups. What follows are actual quotes from child participants. Some children explore themes of greater equanimity:

- "Mindfulness to me is thinking moment to moment. It is basically life. For example, eating, touching, smelling, listening, science, and analyzing."

- "Mindfulness means being more aware of my actions and knowing when I am angry so I can stop it from going too far."

- "Mindfulness means to learn how to calm down when you're mad, stressed, or worried."

- "Mindfulness means to love and to share."

- "Mindfulness means...to be relaxed and to express yourself."

- "Mindfulness means a lot to me because it taught me a lot of stuff like not to let things get in your way when you can be doing something better and not to always be distracted."

Children also discuss how bringing awareness to their experiences helped them relate to their emotions in a different way:

- "Mindfulness has showed me to control my anger. And not get angry when being teased. I practice my breathing exercise. It helps me cool down and think what can happen before I get in trouble."

- "When I am angry or sad I always need to breathe ten times each day. I learned that when I get anxious, I need to breathe ten times."

- "I don't talk back at my teachers or get mad as much as I did in the past. Mindfulness helped me not talk back to the teachers."

- "I think that it has helped me a lot at home. It has helped me by being more calm and the way I react…At home now I like to express my feelings to my mom or sister. It made my life easier."

- "I have learned that people don't have to worry about so much stuff…I will take deep breaths to calm down."

- "The skills that I learned during this program were how to be relaxed, patient, and calm."

Children observe that what they learned may be used to support their academic tasks:

- "It has made me have more confidence in myself. Lately I have not been nervous or scared of my citywide test. Long ago I used to be, but not anymore."

- "Mindfulness has helped me in school to concentrate more."

- "Before I take a test, I breathe three minutes or more."

Many children have commented on the power of the group to cultivate compassionate self-acceptance. For a child with emotional difficulties, it is common for her to feel like an outcast or that she is the only one who experiences such severe anxieties. Participating in a supportive group can bring about profound feelings of acceptance. Although every group is unique, group cohesiveness is cultivated when a tone of self-compassion and kindness toward others is established early. This atmosphere arises naturally when the therapists embody mindfulness, as it emerges from their own practice. An anxious child can learn that she is a valued member of the group. In this environment, she can freely speak about her experiences and be listened to with courtesy and attention:

- "I never in my life heard [of] a program of mindfulness, but I'm glad I was a part of this group. I felt happy that I can share my thoughts with people like my real friends, that I'm not the only one that goes through their difficulties in life."

- "I learned that I could participate with the others [in the group]. Because I used to be shy, but now I know how to share my ideas without being shy."

- "Being part of this group makes [me] feel like we are one big family."

- "My experience of the group was good because now I get less angry. So the group did help me, and I like the group and the teachers. I felt like I was part of a group."

- "It has taught me how to relax and be mindful. I think I was very lucky to enter this program. I just made seven new friends. I really love this program. I wish we could have at least had twenty sessions."

After sharing experiences of the program, you may want to explore how the children might continue cultivating mindful awareness in their daily lives. We try to convey the idea that this session does not mean the end of what was learned in the program. As the poet T. S. Eliot suggested, what is called the beginning may, in fact, be the ending, and that which ends inevitably becomes the start of a new beginning. Children likely will generate their own ideas about how to continue their practices, and find interesting and unique ways to integrate mindfulness into their lives. For example, they may (with parental permission) post a favorite poem on their bedroom walls. They may choose to practice the Three-Minute Breathing Space at a specific time each day, perhaps lying in bed in the morning or before beginning their schoolwork each evening. They might commit to eating one meal each day with mindful awareness. Some children have opted to make a Worry Warts Wastebasket for their homes.

Sustaining these practices can be challenging. With consistency and continuity, the rewards become evident. Segal, Williams, and Teasdale (2002) emphasize the "everydayness" of practice and recommend maintaining a brief daily practice instead of a longer but less frequent practice. They suggest that resolutions are difficult to adopt unless linked to a positive reason. The key, they emphasize, is to anchor the practice in something for which the individual cares deeply.

Inviting each child to consider why she might like to maintain a daily practice can help her understand the relationship of these practices to her everyday life. One child may associate mindfulness with less test anxiety and better academic achievement. Another may have found that mindful attention improves her social relationships. If a child expresses her motivation in a negative manner (for example, "to stay out of trouble"), you may want to encourage her to reframe it in the positive (for example, "to get along better with my family and teachers").

We consistently promote a strength-based approach that helps the child harness her existing strengths to enrich her own life. Helping each child identify personal reasons to continue these practices serves this purpose. You may want to invite the group to record their motivations in their *Mindfulness in Everyday Life* books. Handout 12.2 (Living with Presence, Compassion, and Awareness) has space at the bottom to record this.

Important procedural note: Remember to collect the children's letters and preaddressed envelopes. We have found it best to collect them at the end of the Exploring Everyday Mindfulness discussion. Mark your calendar to mail the letters back to the children in three months along with your own follow-up letter (see sample letter, handout F.1). Daily practice record forms (handout 12.4) may be distributed at the end of session 12. You may also want to enclose another daily practice record form (handout F.2) along with the three-month follow-up letter.

Program Evaluation

When our work with a child or group comes to an end, we like to explore the child's experiences in therapy and what changes, if any, she has seen in herself. Changes may be evident. The child may act less nervous in conversations, engage less often in worried ruminations, attend school more regularly, or do better academically. For more subtle changes, you likely will need to ask the child directly.

The groups we conduct are also for research, so we ask parents and children to complete a program evaluation and questionnaire (appendix D). You may or may not wish to collect this information. Completing the questionnaire takes about ten minutes. It includes ten statements that are rated on a five-point scale (from strongly disagree to strongly agree), and ten sentence-completion items (for example, "The most [or least] helpful part of the program is...”). The last section of the questionnaire provides an opportunity to evaluate the specific practices.

Graduation Ceremony

We enjoy closing the first part of the final session by inviting the children to gather once again in a circle to practice the Three-Minute Breathing Space. We provide a sample letter from the therapist to the child that may be read aloud if you wish (handout 12.3). We feel that giving each child a letter of farewell helps bring closure to the program and allows you to share your own reflections in your own words. Every group is different and inevitably will teach you new things.

Next, you may distribute the certificates of completion and, if you have chosen to do so, give a small token to each child. We give each child who participates in our groups a small polished stone. This token may remind her of lessons learned over the past twelve weeks or come to represent the shared group experience. It may symbolize the beginning of a life journey for one child. For another, it may serve as a reminder to consider her innate strengths or her life choices with compassion and mindful awareness. We guide the children in a short practice—explore the token with all of their senses, and perhaps in doing so, discover personal meaning.

I invite you to take this object in the palm of your hand, exploring it with your eyes; noticing its shape, its colors, and its textures; looking at it...seeing clearly. Are the colors uniform throughout? Practice touching the object with mindfulness: feeling its weight in the palm of your hand; holding it—feeling the textures under your fingertips; feeling the smoothness, the coolness, the roundedness. Noting the thoughts and feelings that are present right now and then returning your attention to exploring the object. You may choose to explore this object with all your senses. Let this object be a reminder of all of your hard work over the past twelve weeks. It can represent the skills you have cultivated and will continue to have, even as this group comes to an end. Please accept it as a symbol of the friendships you have made, to remember the other children who have accompanied you on this journey. When you hold this object in your hands, remember that mindfulness is available in every moment and your breath is always with you.

Graduation Party!

After the graduation, it's time to celebrate. You should allow at least thirty minutes for the party. Sharing food and drink is a time-honored way of celebrating nearly everything, and MBCT-C is no exception. Invite the children to eat or drink with mindful awareness of the experience. Each group is likely to choose different celebratory activities. For example, younger children may choose to play board games, while older children might prefer to dance or listen to music. We encourage you to conclude the party and bring the program to an end by, again, sitting in a circle and sharing in a mindful awareness practice once more—the Three-Minute Breathing Space. Invite the children to gather their belongings (including their *Mindfulness in Everyday Life* books) and then bid them farewell.

ADAPTING SESSION 12 FOR INDIVIDUAL THERAPY

The agenda for a child in individual therapy in session 12 is the same as for a group. You will want to encourage the child to reflect on her experiences in the program, read the letter she wrote, and explore ways to maintain the practice of mindfulness in her daily life. She may complete a program evaluation and receive a graduation certificate, letter from the therapist, and small keepsake of the program. The therapist and child can also celebrate her graduation from the program by sharing food and a fun activity.

PARENT REVIEW SESSION

A few weeks before session 12, you will need to advise parents of a date and time to attend the parent review session. It seems to be helpful to host this group session within a week or two of the program's end. If a parent is unable to attend the session or prefers to speak with the therapist privately, you may instead choose to schedule an individual session. For the child in individual therapy, you may prefer to meet with the parents, with or without the child present, but following a similar review session format. The parent review session provides opportunities for parents to share their experiences of the program. Since they are expected to play an active role in the home practices, parents are instrumental in supporting the child's continued practice. This meeting also allows parents an opportunity to deepen their own understanding of mindfulness.

This session is somewhat different from the Introduction to Mindfulness orientation session, which is more structured. The review session is mostly a group discussion, having three main purposes. First, you and the parents can discuss your experiences of the program, giving and receiving feedback about its effectiveness. Everyone is invited to offer specific recommendations. Second, parents may explore ways to support the child's continued practice (and sometimes their own practice as well). Third, the session can provide closure for parents and give them an opportunity to say farewell. We choose to begin and end this session by practicing the Three-Minute Breathing Space. You may wish to invite parents to complete an evaluation questionnaire (appendix D). This information may be helpful to you in conducting your next groups or used as research data.

We generally begin the dialogue by inviting parents to describe their experiences. One mother in our program was clearly moved by the changes she had witnessed, not only in her daughter but also within herself. She shared with us, "Programs such as these motivate me to be a better mother... I know it was a good and safe environment, because every week my daughter looked forward to the next session." Parents have been generally enthusiastic about the small group format. Some have shared how their child benefited by having supportive, socially interactive experiences with other children struggling with similar issues. Some parents noted that the group interactions helped their child feel more secure and confident when participating in academic or social activities.

It is also important to solicit feedback about aspects of the program that may not have worked so well. Some parents may not have noticed any reductions in anxiety or desired behavioral changes in their children. It is always important to explore this further. To our surprise, the main "negative" feedback we have received so far has been that children and parents wanted the program to last longer than twelve weeks. We do encourage all participants to continue and suggest that, with ongoing practice, the skills learned in MBCT-C will likely develop and deepen. MBCT-C may help children embark on an important journey, but it's up to each child to continue this journey on her own with her newfound awareness and commitment to daily practice.

You may want to explore ways that parents can support their child's home practices, and perhaps their own. One parent told us that both she and her son put a colored "flower face" on the ceiling over their own beds to remind themselves to practice Mindful Breathing Lying Down. Another parent encouraged her child to carry the stone received at session 12, touching it when she felt anxious or worried. One family made a weekly commitment to practice mindful eating of a shared meal together. Whichever practices the parents and child choose, it can be important to reiterate that consistent daily practices, even if brief, are more likely to be helpful than longer, less frequent practices.

CLOSING THOUGHTS

As therapists, we always hope that the children who participate in MBCT-C will continue to bring greater awareness to their lives. We also hope they will be inspired to explore their experiences with curiosity and compassion. At times they will. Other times they won't. Knowing and accepting this is part of our own practice. We let go of the desire to force changes upon those we wish to serve. Each of us is ultimately responsible for our own life. Mindfulness practices are not the only path to happiness, and they may not always be comfortable or even accessible to some. We may harness the inherent power of mindfulness by embodying it ourselves, but we can never impel anyone else to bring greater awareness to their lives. We only hope that what we share will enrich the lives of the children and parents with whom we work. We simply continue, as best we can, to embody mindfulness with compassion and gratitude.

PART 3

MBCT-C in Perspective

CHAPTER 14

The Past and Future of MBCT-C

If I have ever made any valuable discoveries, it has been due more to patient attention than to any other talent.

Sir Isaac Newton, mathematician and physicist

After publishing our initial research findings (Lee, Semple, Rosa, & Miller, 2008; Semple, Reid, & Miller, 2005; Semple, Lee, Rosa, & Miller, 2010), we discovered a tremendous interest in using mindfulness-based psychotherapies with children. We received numerous requests from clinicians and researchers around the world asking for a thorough and detailed description of the "nuts and bolts" of MBCT-C. We wrote this book in response to all those inquiries.

As clinical psychologists, we are trained to evaluate critically the potential effectiveness of any clinical intervention we use. The phrase "what works for whom?" is practically a mantra in psychotherapy research. This chapter provides an informal discussion of the research on MBCT-C, a look at some other work being done with children in this area, and a consideration of some possible future directions for MBCT-C.

LOOKING BACKWARD: MBCT-C RESEARCH AND EVALUATION

Here we review our main published findings in "non–research scientist" language. Detailed analyses of our research studies appear elsewhere and are listed in appendix A.

Initial Pilot Study

Our initial step in the development of MBCT-C was an open trial to examine the feasibility and acceptability of a brief mindfulness-based training program with children (Semple, Reid, & Miller, 2005). We conducted a small pilot study at an elementary-school-based clinic in New York City. Children seven and eight years old were referred to us by the school psychologist for exhibiting high levels of anxiety. Some referred children also had anxiety-related academic problems. We conducted group sessions with five children on-site at the school clinic. One-hour sessions were held once a week for six weeks. Each session focused on mindful awareness in a specific sensory mode, using techniques adapted from the MBSR and MBCT programs for adults (described in chapter 4).

The pilot program was acceptable to these young children and feasible to implement in a school-clinic setting. Every child showed improvements in at least one of three areas: academic performance, anxiety or depression symptoms, and conduct or behavioral problems. The children expressed pleasure in being part of the group, and most wanted the group to continue. One child complained that the sessions were "only" once a week.

Initially we felt that these children understood the intent of the mindful awareness practices and learned ways to integrate them into their daily lives. A careful clinical evaluation of each videotaped session, however, raised some doubts. Most children seemed to regard the practices as games. Although we did, and still do, encourage a playful approach to learning, we saw little translation of the practices into their everyday lives. The main activity they wanted to continue was the Worry Warts Wastebasket. Writing down their worries and putting them in the basket was undoubtedly helpful to these children. Nevertheless, we did not intend it to be the primary learned intervention in a mindfulness-based model of therapy for anxiety.

Lessons Learned from the Pilot Study

Reviewing the videotapes, we came to believe that the children's undeveloped cognitive abilities were the primary obstacle to comprehending this particular mindfulness-based approach. In Piaget's (1962) theory of cognitive development, children in the pilot study straddled the preoperational stage (approximately two to seven years) and the concrete operational stage (approximately seven to twelve years). At this age, children may have limited ability to understand the concept of mindful awareness. Possible cognitive factors include *egocentrism*, or the inability to understand that others may not experience the world in the same way; *centration*, or a tendency to focus on one detail to the neglect of other important components; difficulty considering past and future time; and inability to make "if-then" causal inferences. Our observations suggested that our mindfulness training with children this young became a "pretend" game, having little relevance or connection to their daily lives. Although mindfulness is not conceptualized as a function of higher-order thinking, certain cognitive abilities may be necessary before a child can comprehend mindfulness concepts or meaningfully engage in the practices.

We hypothesized that essential cognitive functions include an ability to comprehend multiple perspectives; an attentional orientation to the experiences of others; an ability to distinguish past, present, and future thinking; and being able to make causal inferences. This analysis led us to work with older children. We revised the program to be age appropriate for nine- to twelve-year-olds. Children of this age are nearing the end of Piaget's concrete operations stage and entering the formal operations stage, which is marked by the development of abstract reasoning skills. We considered three reasons why this age range might be better suited for the teaching and comprehension of mindfulness.

First, the level of cognitive development may facilitate an increased flexibility and receptive openness to new experiences. The child can now adopt different perspectives beyond the egocentrism of the preoperational child. A key aim in MBCT-C is to help children become more aware of their personal filters, see the role of thoughts and emotions in creating those filters, understand that others may have different filters, and so see that others may have radically different interpretations of the same event.

Second, the mean age of onset for anxiety disorders is eleven years old (Kessler et al., 2005). Childhood anxiety is the primary predictor of depression and anxiety in adolescence and adulthood (Kessler & Greenberg, 2002). Targeting our treatment to preadolescent children allows the intervention to occur before anxiety symptoms become more pronounced and potentially more impairing.

Finally, we wished to reach children before they faced the sometimes intense challenges of adolescence. In this "last breath" before adolescence, children have opportunities to develop their resiliency and coping skills. Cultivating mindful awareness may help preteens strengthen their emotional equanimity in preparation for challenges unique to the adolescent stage of development.

Randomized Controlled Trial of MBCT-C

We applied what we learned in the pilot study to the development of a child-friendly mindfulness program. Our experiences of psychotherapy with children informed many specific interventions of MBCT-C, while our personal mindfulness practices guided the conceptualization and implementation. We tested the revised program at a university-based mental health clinic, which provided psychological and educational services to the surrounding community in Harlem and Spanish Harlem, New York City. Children were recruited from the clinic's remedial reading program. Most children did not have a diagnosable anxiety disorder but showed some anxiety symptoms, generally related to below-grade-level reading skills and stress about passing the citywide reading exam.

Twenty-five children, aged nine to thirteen, mostly fourth through sixth graders, were randomly divided into four therapy groups, each of which lasted twelve weeks. Most children were ethnic minorities (60 percent Latino, 24 percent African American) from low-income, inner-city neighborhoods. These randomized controlled trials are briefly summarized here; details are reported elsewhere (Lee et al., 2008; Semple et al., 2010).

FEASIBILITY AND ACCEPTABILITY OF MBCT-C

This mindfulness-based approach was eagerly embraced by the parents. Nearly three-quarters of invited parents gave permission for their children to participate, far exceeding our expectations. To our surprise, we also were approached by other parents who asked if their children might participate. We discovered that some parents had described MBCT-C, session by session, to other parents in the clinic waiting room.

With children, the acceptability of a given therapy is vital. Unlike adults, children usually do not refer themselves for treatment. An unwilling child without any real interest or sense of involvement is unlikely to show clinical improvement. Several analyses have found that cognitive-behavioral therapies (CBT) are not completely effective for nearly half of all children (In-Albon & Schneider, 2007; James, Soler, & Weatherall, 2005). We hypothesized that the "school-like" quality of some CBT programs might be a barrier to engaging some children. We wished instead to create an environment where each child was a full and free collaborator in a shared process.

We appear to have reached this aim. We had a remarkably high attendance rate (over 90 percent), low dropout rate (20 percent), and overwhelmingly positive ratings on the program evaluations. We concluded that MBCT-C was highly acceptable to these children.

EFFECTIVENESS OF MBCT-C

We also evaluated the clinical effectiveness of MBCT-C. Children who completed the program showed significant reductions in attention problems. Those improvements were maintained at three months after the intervention. We also found a strong relationship between attention problems and behavior problems. Reductions in attention problems accounted for nearly half the reductions in behavior problems. We also found trends for the entire group showing overall reductions in anxiety symptoms and behavior problems. Those improvements were statistically significant for the few children who reported clinically elevated levels of anxiety at pretest. We concluded that MBCT-C was a feasible, acceptable, and promising intervention to reduce attention problems, behavior problems, and childhood anxiety.

LOOKING FORWARD: THE POTENTIAL OF MBCT-C

Today is an exciting time for mindfulness-based therapies and research. So many advances have been made in the past decade that many no longer consider mindfulness-based approaches as "alternative" therapies. We don't know what the future holds, but we would like to consider a few promising directions.

The Challenge of Measuring Mindfulness

Appropriate assessment instruments are critical to investigate different facets of mindfulness and its relation to other psychological constructs (Baer, Smith, Hopkins, Krietemeyer, & Toney, 2006). Mindfulness and certain forms of attention seem to be related. We used the attention subscale of the Child Behavior Checklist (Achenbach, 1991) in our research. It is a relatively gross measure of attention problems and subject to reporting biases. Parent and teacher reports cannot directly assess attention; they only infer disruptions of attention from overt behaviors. Other attention measures seem impractical for general use. For example, without a large computer lab, it's not possible to use psychophysiological assessments such as the Attention Network Test (ANT; Rueda et al., 2004) or Test of Variables of Attention (TOVA; L. M. Greenberg & Waldman, 1993) with groups of children. Physiological measures associated with attention (for example, heart rate variability) and brain imaging require expertise and expensive equipment.

What remains are self-report measures. Established self-report measures of mindfulness for adults include the Mindful Attention Awareness Scale (MAAS; Brown & Ryan, 2003), the Kentucky Inventory of Mindfulness Skills (KIMS; Baer, Smith, & Allen, 2004), the Toronto Mindfulness Scale (TMS; Lau et al., 2006), the Freiberg Mindfulness Inventory (FMI; Walach, Buchheld, Buttenmüller, Kleinknecht, & Schmidt, 2006), and the Five Facet Mindfulness Questionnaire (FFMQ; Baer et al., 2008). An adolescent version of the MAAS is under evaluation (Brown, West, Loverich, & Biegel, in press). At this writing, only one validated measure of mindful awareness for children has been developed, the Child and Adolescent Mindfulness

Measure (Greco, Smith, & Baer, in press), which is a brief self-report questionnaire. The development and validation of additional child mindfulness measures is an urgent research priority.

Continuing to Evaluate MBCT-C for Childhood Anxiety

We wrote this book, in part, to make the MBCT-C protocol available to researchers interested in conducting clinical trials. The children in our initial studies were representative of inner-city children with academic problems. The subset of children with clinically elevated anxiety did show statistically significant reductions in symptoms. This finding highlights the importance of evaluating MBCT-C with larger samples of children with clinical anxiety. We have much more to learn about the acceptability, feasibility, and effectiveness of MBCT-C with varying diagnoses and populations. We extend an open invitation to clinical researchers who have their own mindfulness meditation practices to conduct controlled randomized clinical trials of MBCT-C. This book provides the means to do so, using evidence-based research standards with a manualized protocol.

Adapting MBCT-C to Treat Childhood Depression

MBCT-C for childhood depression is another potentially promising line of research. Segal, Williams, and Teasdale (2002) developed MBCT for adults who experience recurrent episodes of major depression. They present a compelling rationale, theoretical mechanisms, and empirical evidence for MBCT in this population. Cognitive theory suggests that anxiety is related to worried thoughts about the future, while depression is characterized more by ruminative thinking about the past.

Adapting MBCT-C for the treatment of childhood depression would focus on past-oriented thinking. Similar to MBCT, the practice inquiries might focus on helping the child recognize depressive thinking patterns before they become entrenched, learn to see the variety of choices available in the present moment, and then respond with greater awareness. We believe that MBCT-C could be adapted easily to focus on childhood depression.

Teaching Parents and Teachers to Teach Mindfulness

Gains made in therapy are more likely to be maintained when supported across school and home environments. We believe that effective MBCT-C therapists must practice cultivating mindful awareness in their own lives. We do not know if this is also true of parents and teachers, though we expect that it would be helpful in cultivating an environment in which mindful awareness practices are valued. At present, there is little research on parent or teacher training to support mindfulness-based clinical interventions. This is rapidly changing, however, and a growing number of mindfulness-based initiatives designed for home and school settings are being developed.

Taking MBCT-C to School

There are now a number of mindfulness-based programs available in the schools, including Inner Kids in southern California (Greenland, 2010) and the Stress Management and Relaxation Techniques in Education (SMART in Education) program of the Impact Foundation in Colorado. Programs that serve at-risk youth include the Lineage Project in New York City and the Mind Body Awareness Project in northern California (Suttie, 2007). Mindful Schools, a community outreach program based in Oakland, California, offers in-class mindfulness training to teachers and students. The Mindfulness in Education Network is a professional organization that offers informational resources to develop and implement mindfulness-based programs in educational settings. The Omega Institute sponsors workshops and conferences that include practical guidance for teachers and administrators interested in integrating mindfulness practices into classrooms (D. Rechtschaffen, personal communication, June 1, 2010). Information about each of these programs is available in appendix A.

For elementary school students, mindful awareness practices may support the development of social-emotional competencies, particularly those related to self-awareness and interpersonal conflict resolution (Hannesdottir & Ollendick, 2007; Wisner, Jones & Gwin, 2010). The Inner Resilience Program in New York City was developed by Linda Lantieri to integrate social and emotional learning with contemplative practices (Lantieri & Goleman, 2008).

Transforming MBCT-C into a mindfulness-based education program would require that four key considerations be addressed. First, the clinical focus of MBCT-C would be expanded to fit a broader population of children. Second, the program would be restructured into shorter sessions that fit a typical school day. Third, mindfulness training would need to be provided for teachers who may not have prior experience with mindfulness practices. Fourth, the involuntary nature of a child's participation in the classroom would need to be reconciled with a central tenant of MBCT-C—that we have freedom to choose our behaviors. Clinical research can inform educators in making these changes as they create classroom environments to support the cultivation of awareness, social-emotional resiliency, and compassion (Ritchhart & Perkins, 2000).

Bringing MBCT-C Home

We do not believe that a home-based MBCT-C program is appropriate as the primary intervention for a child exhibiting clinical anxiety or depression. We strongly recommend that these children be referred for therapy with a licensed mental health professional. Home-based support of MBCT-C can supplement a child's ongoing work in individual or group therapy.

The MBCT-C model could be modified easily to serve children not in need of therapy. Mindful parenting principles may address the interpersonal dynamic between the parent and the child (Duncan, Coatsworth & Greenberg, 2009; Sawyer Cohen & Semple, 2009). Shared time can be an occasion for parent and child to cultivate the practice of mindful awareness together. They could practice increasing awareness of thoughts, feelings, and body sensations while engaging in the sensory-based activities. The ordinary activities of family life also provide rich opportunities to integrate mindfulness into the daily rhythm of the home.

MINDFULNESS-BASED THERAPY AS A CLINICAL INTERVENTION: UNANSWERED QUESTIONS

In 2000, as we began the development of MBCT-C, the landscape of clinical psychology was changing. Now, academic interest has grown enormously. In the past decade, more than 800 professional journal articles, over 230 book chapters, and over 100 books about mindfulness-based psychotherapies have been published.

Psychotherapy has made many valuable advances in this time. A multitude of questions remain unanswered: What exactly is it we're doing? How can we best teach mindful awareness in a clinical setting? We do know that anxiety disorders in children and adolescents are an enormous and growing problem. Most children who struggle with anxiety are left undiagnosed and untreated. One long-term challenge will be to find more effective ways to disseminate mindfulness-based interventions to populations in need.

Evidence for the effectiveness of mindfulness-based interventions for a variety of disorders is strong and growing. There are increasing numbers of qualified therapists and available training opportunities. Our current challenges, however, are to continue our research and evaluation of mindfulness-based cognitive therapy for specific anxiety disorders, learn more about the change mechanisms that may underlie the clinical effectiveness of this approach, and remember to practice mindful awareness in our own lives.

Epilogue

We close this book by reflecting upon where we began. The dialectic between acceptance and change helps us stay mindful of what it means to be a therapist. By the end of therapy, we hope and expect to see changes. If we see beneficial changes, we usually conclude that the therapy was successful. If not, we may question its effectiveness. Paradoxically, mindfulness-based therapies seek to create change by accepting things just as they are. As we said at the beginning, we hope to transform nonacceptance into acceptance.

Acceptance and change appear to be paradoxical, but this is an illusion. Desiring change carries an assumption that something is not quite right. Acceptance carries an assumption that things are perfect just as they are. And yet, undeniably (and unavoidably), circumstances arise that are not to our liking. We accept this as well. Acceptance and change, like yin and yang, only appear to be opposites; actually, they are interconnected, complementary processes. We, and the children we serve, can foster the changes we seek simply by accepting ourselves and our experiences just as they are. Though simple in theory, in reality this is an ongoing practice.

Cultivating acceptance allows therapeutic change to become a process of growth and development. The child may experience events that arise, view her interactions with others, and understand the situations in which she finds herself, all in subtly different ways. The external world may be viewed more kindly and with a heightened sense of curiosity, wonder, and delight. She may become better attuned to the internal world—the rich, ever-changing nowscape of thoughts, feelings, and body sensations. She may discover how to befriend her thoughts and emotions, permitting them to come and go, not wishing them to be other than they are. She may develop emotional resiliency, focused attention, and a greater sense of equanimity, while discovering internal peace and the rich landscape of choice points available to her.

As this process unfolds, you may rediscover the power of mindfulness as a way of life, just as you encourage this understanding for the children you serve. We hope that your personal journey inspires them. We hope, too, that in sharing these explorations of mindfulness with kindness, curiosity, compassion, and acceptance, every one of us discovers the profound and lasting happiness that can emerge as we commit to living our lives with greater awareness.

Namasté,

Randye and Jennifer

Information and Resources

MINDFULNESS AND PSYCHOTHERAPY

Books

Baer, R. A. (Ed.). (2006). *Mindfulness-based treatment approaches: Clinician's guide to evidence base and applications.* Burlington, MA: Elsevier/Academic Press.

Didonna, F. (Ed.). (2009). *Clinical handbook of mindfulness.* New York: Springer.

Fontana, D., & Slack, I. (1997). *Teaching meditation to children.* Shaftesbury, UK: Element Books.

Germer, C. K., Siegel, R. D., & Fulton, P. R. (2005). *Mindfulness and psychotherapy.* New York: Guilford Press.

Greco, L. A., & Hayes, S. C. (Eds.). (2008). *Acceptance and mindfulness treatments for children and adolescents: A practitioner's guide.* Oakland, CA: New Context/New Harbinger Publications.

Greenland, Susan K. (2010). *The mindful child: How to help your kid manage stress and become happier, kinder, and more compassionate.* New York: Free Press.

Kabat-Zinn, J. (1990). *Full catastrophe living.* New York: Bantam Doubleday Dell.

Kabat-Zinn, J. (1994). *Wherever you go, there you are: Mindfulness meditation for everyday life.* New York: Hyperion.

Kabat-Zinn, J. (2005). *Coming to our senses: Healing ourselves and the world through mindfulness.* New York: Hyperion.

Segal, Z. V., Williams, J. M. G., & Teasdale, J. D. (2002). *Mindfulness-based cognitive therapy for depression: A new approach to preventing relapse.* New York: Guilford Press.

Williams, J. M. G., Teasdale, J. D., Segal, Z. V., & Kabat-Zinn, J. (2007). *The mindful way through depression: Freeing yourself from chronic unhappiness.* New York: Guilford Press.

MINDFULNESS-BASED COGNITIVE THERAPY FOR CHILDREN

Articles

Lee, J., Semple, R. J., Rosa, D., & Miller, L. (2008). Mindfulness-based cognitive therapy for children: Results of a pilot study. *Journal of Cognitive Psychotherapy, 22,* 15–28. doi:10.1891/0889.8391.22.1.15

Semple, R. J., Lee, J., Rosa, D., & Miller, L. F. (2009). A randomized trial of mindfulness-based cognitive therapy for children: Promoting mindful attention to enhance social-emotional resiliency in children. *Journal of Child and Family Studies, 19,* 218–229. doi 10.1007/s10826-009-9301-y

Semple, R. J., Reid, E. F. G, & Miller, L. (2005). Treating anxiety with mindfulness: An open trial of mindfulness training for anxious children. *Journal of Cognitive Psychotherapy, 19,* 379–392. doi:10.1891/jcop.2005.19.4.379

Book Chapters

Semple, R. J., & Lee, J. (2008). Treating anxiety with mindfulness: Mindfulness-based cognitive therapy for children. In L. A. Greco & S. C. Hayes (Eds.), *Acceptance and mindfulness interventions for children, adolescents, and families* (pp. 94–134). Oakland, CA: Context Press/New Harbinger Publications.

Semple, R. J., Lee, J., & Miller, L. F. (2006). Mindfulness-based cognitive therapy for children. In R. A. Baer (Ed.), *Mindfulness-based treatment approaches: Clinician's guide to evidence base and applications* (pp. 143–166). Burlington, MA: Academic Press. doi:10.1016/B978-012088519-0/50008-3

MINDFULNESS-BASED SCHOOL AND COMMUNITY PROGRAMS

Inner Kids

Los Angeles, CA

Website: susankaisergreenland.com/inner-kids.html

The Inner Kids program, developed in 2001 by Susan Kaiser Greenland, is designed for schoolchildren in pre-K through sixth grade. The program focuses on cultivating mindful awareness through introspective practices within a secular framework. The website offers a general overview of the program, methods of instruction, and information about ongoing research.

The Inner Resilience Program

40 Exchange Place, Suite 1111
New York, NY 10005
Phone: (212) 509-0022
Fax: (212) 509-1095

Website: www.innerresilience-tidescenter.org

E-mail: info@innerresilience-tidescenter.org

The Inner Resilience Program (IRP) is a project of the Tides Center. Founded in 2002 by Linda Lantieri, IRP integrates mindfulness-based approaches to help foster healthy learning environments for students and teachers. *Building Resilience from the Inside Out* is a school-based curriculum integrated into the regular school day by trained teachers. Other programs offered include parent workshops, professional workshops, and residential retreats for educators. The IRP website provides information about the history of IRP and a list of research publications.

The Lineage Project in New York City

Phone: (718) 408-1492

Website: lineageproject.org

Founded by Soren Gordhamer, the Lineage Project serves at-risk and incarcerated youth in collaboration with local community-based organizations, schools, and New York city and state detention facilities. Through mindful awareness practices, children and adolescents learn to manage stress, develop self-awareness, and commit to nonviolent, compassionate engagement with their communities. Program information, downloadable research articles about at-risk youth, and other resources are available on the website.

The Mind Body Awareness Project

111 Fairmount Avenue, Suite 508
Oakland, CA 94611
Phone: (415) 824-2048

Website: www.mbaproject.org

E-mail: info@mbaproject.org

The Mind Body Awareness (MBA) Project brings mindful awareness practices to at-risk and incarcerated youth in northern California. The MBA Project is a ten-module rehabilitation program that promotes mindful awareness, impulse regulation, emotional intelligence, empathy, and forgiveness. The core aim of MBA is to "inspire and awaken the intrinsic value of young people" by helping at-risk youth reconsider pathways to violent or self-destructive behaviors, and make wiser, better choices.

Mindful Schools

P.O. Box 22944
Oakland, CA 94609

Phone: (510) 653-0317, ext. 105

Website: mindfulschools.org

E-mail: info@mindfulschools.org

Mindful Schools is a community outreach program that offers mindful awareness training to teachers and students. The program focuses on enhancing attention, empathy, and conflict resolution among students to foster a calm, positive learning environment.

Omega Institute

Omega Institute
150 Lake Drive
Rhinebeck, NY 12572

Phone: (877) 944-2002

Fax: (845) 266-3769

Website: eomega.org

E-mail: registration@eomega.org

The Omega Institute sponsors an annual Mindfulness and Education Conference, as well as other retreats, workshops, and training activities throughout the year. The conference offers practical guidance for teachers and administrators interested in bringing mindful awareness practices into classrooms.

The IMPACT Foundation

264 Quari Street
Aurora, CO 80011
Phone: (303) 317-5767

Website: theimpactfoundation.org

E-mail: information@theimpactfoundation.org

The IMPACT Foundation sponsors the Stress Management and Relaxation Techniques in Education (SMART) program. SMART is an eight-week "teacher renewal" curriculum. The curriculum was designed specifically for K–12 teachers and administrators to develop personal skills in concentration, emotional awareness, and empathy in order to support a positive classroom environment.

ONLINE COMMUNITIES

Mindfulness Together

Website: mindfulnesstogether.net

Mindfulness Together is a social network hosted by Susan Kaiser Greenland, author of *The Mindful Child* and founder of the Inner Kids program. The purpose of this online community is to share information and resources about mindful awareness with children and their families.

Mindfulness in Education Network

Website: www.mindfuled.org

The Mindfulness in Education Network (MiEN) is a professional organization whose purpose is to facilitate dialogue among educators, administrators, parents, and students to promote contemplative practices in educational settings. MiEN hosts a LISTSERV for members to share ideas and best practices.

OTHER RESOURCES

Mindfulness-Based Cognitive Therapy (MBCT)

Websites: mbct.com; mbct.co.uk

E-mail: info@mbct.com

These websites are hosted by the developers of MBCT: Zindel Segal, Mark Williams, and John Teasdale. Here you will find information ranging from the practical aspects of MBCT to its theoretical basis, development, and effectiveness. Information about worldwide training resources for clinicians is offered with links to those sites. References for key research papers about MBCT are also provided, with some papers available for download.

Mindfulness-Based Stress Reduction (MBSR)

Center for Mindfulness in Medicine, Health Care, and Society
University of Massachusetts Medical School
55 Lake Avenue North
Worcester, MA 01655

Phone: (508) 856-2656

Fax: (508) 856-1977

Website: umassmed.edu/Content.aspx?id=41252

E-mail: mindfulness@umassmed.edu

The Center for Mindfulness in Medicine, Health Care, and Society (CFM) at the University of Massachusetts Medical Center provides ongoing MBSR and teacher-training programs, and sponsors an annual professional conference. The CFM website also offers lectures, resources, and a searchable database of MBSR programs worldwide.

University of California at San Diego Center for Mindfulness

Moores UCSD Cancer Center
3855 Health Science Drive, #0658
La Jolla, CA 92093-0658

Phone: (858) 822-6868

Fax: (858) 822-3449

Website: mindfulness.ucsd.edu

E-mail: shickman@ucsd.edu

The UCSD Center for Mindfulness offers an extensive program of clinical care, professional training, education, research, and outreach intended to further the practice and integration of mindfulness in health care and education. The website offers downloadable audio files of meditations, poetry, and printable handouts used in the MBSR program.

Meditation Cushions and Supplies for Children

DharmaCrafts, Inc. (DharmaKids)

dharmacrafts.com/106xCC/DharmaKids.html

Still Sitting Meditation Supply

www.stillsitting.com/sitting-on/small-zafu.html

Ziji

www.ziji.com/Meditation-Supplies-Meditation-for-Kids-Children's-Meditation-Cushions/c3_126_158/index.html

Optical Illusions for Session 8

A Collection of Optical Illusions for Kids

www.newopticalillusions.com/illusions/kids-optical-illusions

Cool Optical Illusions

www.coolopticalillusions.com

Illusion-Optical.com

www.illusion-optical.com

National Institute of Environmental Health Sciences

kids.niehs.nih.gov/illusion/illusions.htm

Table of Contents for *Mindfulness in Everyday Life* Notebook

Section 2: Session Summaries

Section 3: Home Practices

Section 4: Poems, Stories, and Other Materials

Section 5: Experiencing Mindful Awareness

Blank lined paper

BACK COVER: MINDFULNESS IS...

MBCT-C Session Handouts

Mindfulness-Based Cognitive Therapy for Children

What Is Mindfulness?

Mindfulness means paying attention in a particular way;
on purpose, in the present moment, and nonjudgmentally.
— Jon Kabat-Zinn

The aim of this program is to cultivate attention and develop greater moment-to-moment awareness in our lives. Practicing mindfulness helps us transform stressful situations by relating to them differently. We can become more aware of events, situations, ourselves, and other people in our lives. We can see more clearly how thoughts and feelings influence our experiences. We can develop mindful awareness of thoughts, feelings, and body sensations as they arise in the present. As we become more aware of ourselves and the world around us, we often can choose to respond to stressful events with greater clarity and emotional equanimity.

What Is Mindfulness-Based Cognitive Therapy for Children?

Mindfulness-Based Cognitive Therapy for Children (MBCT-C) is a twelve-week program for the management of anxiety. The techniques of MBCT-C include simple breathing practices, body awareness, and mindfulness in the five senses. MBCT-C helps children become aware of how anxiety symptoms may be expressed in thoughts, feelings, body sensations, and behaviors.

MBCT-C adapts adult mindful awareness practices for use with children. It was adapted from two mindfulness programs for adults, both of which are supported by many years of research: mindfulness-based stress reduction and mindfulness-based cognitive therapy (for adults).

> **Mindfulness-Based Stress Reduction** (MBSR) was developed in 1979 by Jon Kabat-Zinn and colleagues at the University of Massachusetts Stress Reduction Clinic, the oldest and largest hospital-based stress reduction clinic in the world. MBSR is effective for various physical and psychological disorders. The program lasts eight weeks and requires daily home practice.

> **Mindfulness-Based Cognitive Therapy** (MBCT) was developed by Zindel Segal, Mark Williams, and John Teasdale. MBCT is an approach to prevent the relapse of depression. It helps adults see their usual patterns of thinking more clearly and identify connections between negative moods and negative thinking. It attempts to break the cycle of negative thoughts and moods that can sometimes spiral into depressive relapse. This program also lasts eight weeks and requires daily home practice.

How Does Mindfulness Work?

Research has shown that mindfulness practices can help reduce symptoms of anxiety for children. With practice, children can learn to stay in the present and not ruminate about the past or worry about the future. With greater awareness, they may become aware of more choices in how to respond to stressful events. This creates greater freedom to choose to disengage from unhelpful *automatic pilot* reactions. In MBCT-C, children develop a mindful relationship to all their thoughts and feelings—including anxious thoughts and feelings. Children often learn that they can handle stressful situations with greater ease and skillfulness when they bring awareness to the present moment.

Can Mindfulness Help My Child?

If you feel the answer is yes to any of these questions, MBCT-C may be helpful to your child.

- Does your child experience frequent anxiety or excessive worry?
- Does your child have difficulty concentrating or paying attention?
- Is your child frequently tense, restless, or irritable?
- When your child is nervous, does he or she tend to worry or ruminate about many things?
- Does your child become nervous or worried in response to minor uncertain events?
- Does your child sometimes experience anxious body sensations, such as headaches, nausea, difficulty breathing, dizziness or shakiness, chest pain, or heart palpitations?
- Does your child worry about dying or "going crazy" when he or she feels anxious?
- Does your child fear or avoid situations in which he or she is nervous, such as social settings, crowds, elevators, or small spaces?
- Is your child excessively anxious about going to school or being home alone?
- Does your child express marked distress when separated from you?
- Does your child have sleep disturbances or nightmares?
- Does your child practice ritualized or repetitive behaviors to "ward off" anxious feelings?

Additional Information

There are many different forms and practices of mindfulness meditation. The MBCT-C program described here uses a Westernized form of "insight meditation." You may find it helpful to explore opportunities to learn more about this tradition or find a teacher or therapist who specializes in this approach separately or in combination with cognitive therapy.

Suggested Readings about MBSR and MBCT

Kabat-Zinn, J. (1994). *Wherever you go, there you are: Mindfulness meditation in everyday life.* New York: Hyperion Books.

Kabat-Zinn, M., & Kabat-Zinn, J. (1998). *Everyday blessings: The inner work of mindful parenting.* New York: Hyperion Books.

Williams, M., Teasdale, J., Segal, Z., & Kabat-Zinn, J. (2007). *The mindful way through depression: Freeing yourself from chronic unhappiness.* New York: Guilford Press

Parents' Home Practice Record

Date	What mindful awareness activity did you practice?	What did you observe about the experience?

Handout C   Mindfulness Defined

Mindfulness means

paying attention

in a particular way:

on purpose,

in the present moment,

and

nonjudgmentally.

—Jon Kabat-Zinn

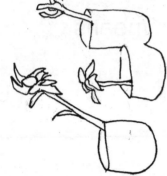

Handout D   Guidelines for Mindful Behavior

Guidelines

for

Mindful Behavior

1. We choose to act and speak to other people with care and kindness.

2. We can remember not to talk when another person is talking.

3. We can remember to raise a hand to share our ideas with the group.

4. We agree not to talk during mindful awareness practices so as not to disturb others.

5. We agree that if anyone does not wish to take part in an activity, one person at a time may sit in the **Quiet Space**.

Handout E

How do I feel right now?

Feely Faces Scale

	week 1	week 2	week 3	week 4	week 5	week 6	week 7	week 8	week 9	week 10	week 11	week 12
	1	1	1	1	1	1	1	1	1	1	1	1
	2	2	2	2	2	2	2	2	2	2	2	2
	3	3	3	3	3	3	3	3	3	3	3	3
	4	4	4	4	4	4	4	4	4	4	4	4
	5	5	5	5	5	5	5	5	5	5	5	5
	6	6	6	6	6	6	6	6	6	6	6	6
	7	7	7	7	7	7	7	7	7	7	7	7

SLOW...

mindfulness
in progress

Mindfulness
in
Everyday Life

Created by:

_____

Mindfulness is...

Handout 1.1   Mindful Breathing Is the Best Practice

MINDFUL BREATHING

Is *THE BEST PRACTICE*

Mindful breathing

goes like this,

Just sit and

feel your breath

As it goes

in and out,

Be each breath.

No future, no past.

No thoughts,

No to do,

Only to be,

Paradise.

William Menza

(2001)

Handout 1.2   Session 1 Summary: Being on Automatic Pilot

In everyday situations, we can sometimes go for hours on *automatic pilot*, not fully aware of what we are doing or what is happening. We may never notice that our thoughts are miles away. We might think about the past so much that we forget where we are—right here in the present. We might become sad or angry at what's already happened. Other times we might be so busy trying to see what will happen next that we completely miss what is happening now. The future may feel scary or uncertain, and we may feel worried or anxious. All that thinking and worrying can cause us to miss what is happening right now. When we are on *automatic pilot*, we may react without thinking instead of mindfully choosing how we wish to respond to events.

The aim of MBCT-C is to practice bringing mindful awareness to our thoughts, feelings, body sensations, and all of our senses. Our eyes, ears, fingers, mouths, and noses bring us a wealth of information. When we practice living with mindful awareness, rather than on *automatic pilot*, we can respond to other people and the events in our lives with greater choice. This is why we practice mindfulness.

Handout 1.3   Session 1 Home Practices

- **Mindful Breathing Lying Down.** Place a flower face on the ceiling or wall by your bed so that you can see it when you wake up. This is your reminder to practice Mindful Breathing Lying Down every morning for the next week. Before you get out of bed, enjoy a few moments of practice in bringing awareness to the breath. Slowly breathe in three times and breathe out three times while keeping a gentle smile on your face. You are practicing being aware of each in-breath and each out-breath. Rest, then breathe three more times with awareness of each breath.

- **Mindful Breathing Sitting Up.** Start by assuming a mindful posture. Sitting on the floor, you may sit with your legs crossed and hands resting on your thighs. Sitting in a chair, you may put both feet flat on the ground a few inches apart. Practice bringing awareness to the breath and the movements of your belly as you breathe in and out. Whenever you note that thoughts have wandered off, gently bring your attention back to the breath. Bringing your awareness to each breath, breathe in three times and breathe out three times. Rest, then breathe three more times with awareness of each breath. *Use the Breathing Practice Record to note your experiences.*

- **Living with Awareness.** Practice bringing mindful awareness to one daily activity. You may place a flower face where it can remind you to bring attention to that activity. For example, you might place a flower face on your bathroom mirror as a reminder to bring awareness to brushing your teeth. You may choose to bring mindful awareness to getting dressed, eating breakfast, making your bed, walking to school, taking out the garbage, doing the dishes, or anything else that you do most days. Pick one activity—the same activity every day—and as best you can, practice being mindfully aware of what you are doing *as you do it.*

Handout 1.3   Session 1 Home Practices

Handout 1.4   Session 1 Mindful Breathing Record

Name: _____   Date: _____

Mindful Breathing Record

Record each time you practice bringing mindful awareness to the breath.

	Describe how you felt when you practiced Mindful Breathing. What were you thinking? Did you notice when your attention wandered? What happened when you noticed that your attention had wandered? Did you discover something about your breath that you never knew?
Sunday	
Monday	
Tuesday	
Wednesday	
Thursday	
Friday	
Saturday	

Handout 1.5   **Mindfulness Is Cultivating Attention**

Mindfulness Is Cultivating Attention

Ken McLeod
(adapted with permission)

In mindfulness, we cultivate attention.

We can compare the development of attention to the cultivation of a plant. We can't control how quickly a plant grows or how it grows. We can't tell a plant what to do or how to grow. We can't make it put leaves out here and form buds there. How the plant grows is up to the plant. We simply put a seed in soil and provide water, food, and sunlight. In other words, we simply bring together the conditions for the seed to sprout and for the shoot to grow into a plant. If we try to force the process by trying to pull the plant upward to make it grow faster, we destroy it. If we give the sprout too much food, we may burn the roots, too much sunlight and it dies, too much water and the plant drowns. All we can do is to provide the best conditions for its growth, and it will grow in its own way, on its own time. Then the plant will flower and bear fruit.

We have the seed of attention within us already. We simply provide conditions for attention to develop. The practice of mindfulness is the practice of providing those conditions. This is how we cultivate attention, just as we would a plant or tree.

The conditions to develop attention begin with our posture. We sit straight, balanced, still, not too stiff or too relaxed. Other conditions are found in how we breathe, naturally, without using the breath to speak. With our minds, we watch the breath, or to put it another way, we simply feel ourselves breathing.

To cultivate attention, we can rely on one basic principle: return again and again to what is already there. Our bodies know how to sit straight. Our breath knows how to flow naturally. Our minds and our hearts already know how to rest. In this practice, we simply allow them to do that. Whenever there is a disturbance, we return to what is already there.

Handout 2.1 **Flight from the Shadow**

Flight from the Shadow

There was a man who was so disturbed by the sight of his own shadow

and so displeased with his own footsteps

that he determined to get rid of both.

The method he hit upon was to run away from them.

So he got up and ran.

But every time he put his foot down, there was another step,

while his shadow kept up with him without the slightest difficulty.

He attributed his failure to the fact that he was not running fast enough.

So he ran faster and faster,

without stopping,

until he finally dropped dead.

He failed to realize that if he merely stepped into the shade,

his shadow would vanish,

and if he sat down and stayed still,

there would be no more footsteps.

—Parable of wisdom attributed to Chuang Tzu

Handout 2.2   Session 2 Summary: Being Mindful Is Simple, but It Is Not Easy!

Practicing mindfulness means bringing our awareness to what's happening in this moment—and accepting all of our moments. It's not hard to be mindful. But we've already learned that it can be hard to be mindful all the time or even most of the time. Although it's not hard to *be mindful*, it can be hard to *remember* to be mindful. It takes a lot of practice. Over the coming weeks, we will discover new and exciting ways to remember to practice mindfulness.

Being mindful means being *aware of* and *accepting of* what is happening in this moment. Sometimes the barriers to being mindful are inside us. We might think something is not good enough. We might judge that an experience is "not right" in some way. All those judgments may get in the way of being present with our experiences. Other times, our experience is not what we want. We might feel sad, scared, or angry because we want things to be different. We might also feel bad when we think about things that have already happened or worry about things in the future that haven't even happened.

When we judge the present, or hold on to past or future events in our heads, we are not fully aware of what is happening in this moment. This lack of awareness may cause us to react before we see what is really going on. Instead we can bring greater awareness to whatever situation we find ourselves in—without judging it or wanting it to be different. Mindful awareness helps us see more clearly the way things are now—without having to do anything about it at all. Then we might see more choices in how to respond.

Handout 2.3   **Session 2 Home Practices**

- **Living with Awareness.** Practice bringing mindful awareness to one daily activity. You may place a flower face where it can remind you to bring attention to that activity. For example, you might place a flower face on your bathroom mirror as a reminder to be more mindful of brushing your teeth. You may choose to be mindful of getting dressed, eating breakfast, making your bed, walking to school, taking out the garbage, doing the dishes, or anything else that you do most days. Pick one activity—the same activity every day—and as best you can, practice being mindfully aware of what you are doing *as you do it*. You may enjoy choosing a different activity than the one you practiced last week.

- **Mindful Breathing.** Sitting on a firm surface, assume a mindful posture. Practice bringing your attention to the breath and the movements of the belly as you breathe in and breathe out. Gently bring attention back to the breath whenever you notice that your thoughts have wandered. Practice bringing awareness to each breath, breathing in three times and breathing out three times. Relax for a moment and then begin again. Practice mindful breathing for a few minutes every day this week.

- **Mindful Eating.** Practice mindfully eating the objects in your bag in the same way we ate the raisins in the session. Explore these objects with your sense of sight, smell, hearing, touch, and taste. Practice eating only one or two of the objects each day with awareness. As best you can, explore them sloooowly with all your attention. Each one of these objects is unique (the only one of its kind). See if you can discover something new or different about each one. *Note your observations and what you learned on the Mindful Eating Record.*

Handout 2.4   **Session 2 Mindful Eating Record**

Name: _____   Date: _____

Mindful Eating Record

Record each time you practice mindfully eating one of the objects in your bag.

	I'm exploring each of these objects with my fingers, eyes, nose, ears, and mouth. Practicing mindful awareness, I may discover something new, exciting, or different about each object. What are my thoughts and feelings as I eat these objects? When did I notice that my attention wandered? What discoveries have I made by eating with mindful awareness?
Sunday	
Monday	
Tuesday	
Wednesday	
Thursday	
Friday	
Saturday	

Handout 2.5   Practicing Mindful Awareness

- **The Importance of Practice.** Together we'll be working to change habits that have been around for a long time. Some habits may not be very helpful and can sometimes add to our worries or fears. Changes may happen when we form an intention to learn new skills. The way to learn mindfulness is to practice every day. The home practices take about ten or fifteen minutes most days for the next twelve weeks. Mindful awareness practices are simple and pleasant to do. We know that it can be hard to find time in our busy lives. Forming the intention to spend time each day practicing these exercises is important. This is what it means to have mindful intentions.

- **The Importance of Patience.** As best we can, we practice each of the mindfulness activities in sessions and at home with awareness. Little by little, with patience and practice, changes may appear. In some ways, this is like learning to hit a baseball. We must first learn how to hold the bat, how to stand, and how to move our bodies. After that, we learn to swing the bat, carefully watch the ball, and then—practice, practice, practice! With practice and patience, we begin to see changes. In the same way, we ask you to take part in the sessions and do the home practices with patience—even if you may not see changes right away.

- **Facing Difficulties.** Taking part in the sessions and home practices can help you feel more aware and in charge of your own life. These practices can make life more interesting and fulfilling. But it also means facing *everything* that is present in our lives, even when it might be hard or unpleasant. Being present with difficult thoughts and feelings—even making friends with them—can help you cope with fear, worry, anger, and sadness. When you bring more awareness to the thoughts and feelings, you may be better able to deal with them before they grow too strong. Over the coming weeks, we will practice gentle ways to stay present with difficult thoughts and feelings. We will all help each other in this practice.

Handout 2.6   **Instructions for Mindful Breathing**

Start by sitting on a firm chair or on the floor with your bottom supported by a cushion. If you use a chair, sit with your back straight and place both feet flat on the floor. Adjust the chair or cushion until you are comfortable and feel firmly supported. If you wish, you may close your eyes or gaze softly at a spot on the floor about three feet in front of you.

Practice bringing awareness to your body, perhaps starting by noting the sensations on your skin, watching the sensations where your body touches the floor, the chair, or cushion. Practice looking inside too—at the sensations inside your body. Spend a few minutes exploring body sensations, not trying to change what is there—just watching what the body experiences. Then shift your awareness to sensations in the belly as you breathe in and out. You may wish to place your hand on the lower belly to feel the breath more deeply. As best you can, bring awareness to the sensations in the belly as the air comes in and goes out. Observe the pauses between each in-breath and out-breath. We are just letting the breath do what it does best— breathing in and breathing out, just noting it, not trying to control it. Soon the mind may wander away—carried away by thoughts or daydreams. That's okay; it's simply what minds do. As best you can, just note that your attention has wandered, and gently bring attention back to the breath. Continue to watch each in-breath and out-breath. The wanderings of the mind are just more opportunities to bring mindful awareness to your experiences. Continue practicing for about three minutes, or longer if you wish, reminding yourself from time to time that the aim is simply to be aware of the experience in each moment. Each time you notice that the mind has wandered, gently return awareness to the breath.

Handout 3.1   **Have You Ever Gotten a Thought?**

Have You Ever Gotten a Thought?

Have you ever gotten a thought
That would not leave you alone?

No matter what you did,
It kept coming back,
Like a bad dream,
A haunting ghost,
Demanding your attention,
Taking possession of your mind.

Maybe all she wants is to be held
Tenderly, as a mother would
Her sick or troubled child,
And lullabied to sleep.

Breathe in the fear, confusion,
Hurt and pain,
Breathe out understanding
kindness, warm sunshine, lightness
To set him free.

William Menza
(2007)

Handout 3.2   Session 3 Summary: Who Am I?

Thoughts sometimes can carry us away. We call this being on *automatic pilot*. By bringing more awareness to thoughts, feelings, and body sensations, we may notice things that we have not seen before. By practicing mindfulness, we may get carried away by thoughts less often.

The same event can bring about many different thoughts and feelings. For example, the way we understand an experience can change depending on how we feel. Have you ever gotten mad at a good friend and had negative thoughts that changed as soon as you made up? We may not even be aware of the thoughts, but they can have a powerful effect on our emotions. Thoughts can and do change over time. *Thoughts are not facts.*

In this session, we learned that thoughts sometimes affect how we feel and how we react to everyday events. We also learned that we can be aware of the thoughts without always believing them. We practice watching the breath as we learn to bring greater awareness to thoughts, feelings, and body sensations. When we see more clearly, we may discover ways to choose our words and behaviors with more skill and compassion. *We do not have to react as if we were on automatic pilot. We can respond with mindful awareness.*

Handout 3.3   Session 3 Home Practices

- *Mindful Breathing.* Practice two or three times every day. Bringing awareness to the breath may help you become better friends with thoughts, feelings, and body sensations—in this moment—without having to do anything at all. Sometimes practicing along with another activity that we do every day can help us remember. For example, you might practice Mindful Breathing while riding the school bus each day. You may also find it pleasant to begin and end your day this way.

- *Mindfulness of the Body.* Begin by lying comfortably on your back on a flat surface. You may wish to put a pillow under your head. Relax and rest your arms loosely by your sides with your legs slightly apart. Stretch out so that your body is lying in a straight line. You may even give your body permission to close its eyes. We practice bringing awareness to the body sensations—simply noting what sensations are present. Practicing Mindfulness of the Body is a moment-by-moment awareness. As you breathe in and breathe out, as best you can, practice focusing the attention on one part of the body at a time. Note how thoughts and feelings keep coming and going even as you focus attention on the body. Each time the mind wanders, we have more opportunities to practice bringing attention back to our bodies. Complete the practice by listening to the silence and stillness in the body. Whenever you feel ready, bring awareness back to the body as a whole. Begin to move your hands and feet. You might touch your face or rock from side to side before opening your eyes. Practice Mindfulness of the Body for five minutes (or more) every day.

- Complete the *Pleasant Events Record* by bringing awareness to one pleasant event every day. Practice noting the thoughts, feelings, and body sensations that come along with the pleasant event that you choose to be mindful of. *Afterward, record the thoughts, feelings, and body sensations on the Pleasant Events Record.*

Handout 3.4   Session 3 Pleasant Events Record

Name: _____   Week of: _____

Pleasant Events Record

You are practicing mindful awareness of a pleasant event when it is happening. The questions here are to help focus attention on the details of the event as it happens. Remember to write down your thoughts, feelings, and body sensations on this form.

What was the event?	What body sensations did you notice during this event?	What thoughts and feelings did you note at the time?	What are your thoughts now as you record the experience?
Example: *Walking home after school, I stopped to listen to a bird sing.*	*Light feeling across my face, shoulders dropped, smile at corner of mouth.*	*Happy, relaxed. I thought, The bird sounds so cheerful, and it's nice to be outside on this sunny day.*	*It was a small thing, but I'm glad I noticed it because it made my day more pleasant.*
Sunday			
Monday			
Tuesday			

What was the event?	What body sensations did you notice during this event?	What thoughts and feelings did you note at the time?	What are your thoughts now as you record the experience?
Wednesday			
Thursday			
Friday			
Saturday			

Handout 3.5   Breathing

Breathing

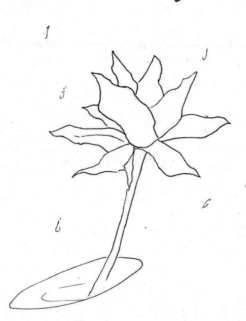

Breathing in,
I see myself as a flower.
I am the freshness
of a dewdrop.

Breathing out,
my eyes have become flowers.
Please look at me.
I am looking
with the eyes of love.

Breathing in,
I am a mountain,
imperturbable,
still,
alive,
vigorous.

Breathing out,
I feel solid.
The waves of emotion
can never carry me away.

Breathing in,
I am still water.
I reflect the sky
faithfully.
Look, I have a full moon
within my heart,
the refreshing moon of the
bodhisattva.

Breathing out,
I offer the perfect reflection
of my mirror-mind.

Handout 3.6 Who Am I?

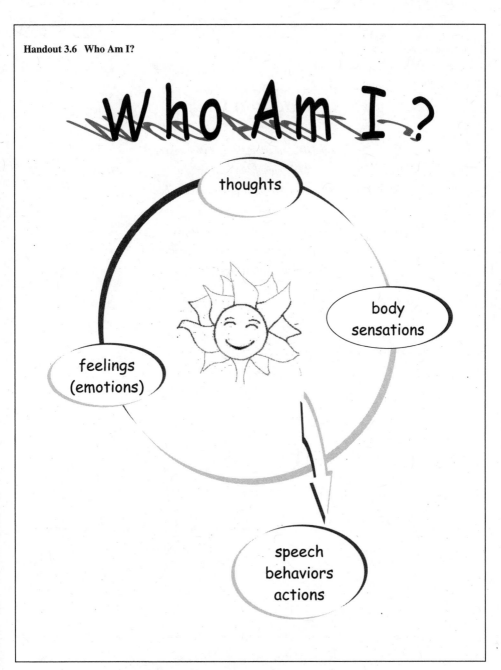

Ode to a Grape

Round like a marble, fleshy, bitter, and cool,

My tongue bounces it around,

Like a dolphin playing with a beach ball.

I bite down ever so softly.

A slight, sweet essence emerges.

Ah…a prelude of what's to come.

One more rally around the tongue.

It's the moment of truth.

Syrupy juices explode in all directions.

My teeth converge on a cool, slippery core.

What delightful sweetness!

But wait, the bitter, leathery skin is back.

The sweet, juicy center unites with the bitter wrapping.

A moment of harmony and balance unfolds.

The world makes sense again.

Scott Jeffrey (2009)

Handout 4.2   Session 4 Summary: A Taste of Mindfulness

It's easy to spend much of our lives on *automatic pilot.* A lot of the time we may not be fully aware of what's happening or even what we're saying or doing. We may eat a snack and not remember what we ate. Bringing attention to *automatic pilot* helps us become more aware of thoughts, feelings, and body sensations just as they are in each moment—moment by moment.

When we tune in to the thoughts, feelings, and body sensations, we may discover new and different ways to experience all kinds of events—whether it's eating something we don't particularly like or doing something that we like a lot. With practice, we may begin to see more clearly and learn to live with more awareness and compassion. We may learn to deal better with challenging situations, such as getting along with a person who is difficult or taking exams at school. We might notice a thought like, *I'll never pass this test.* We may note that the thought brings up feelings of anxiety or worry. We may feel tense body sensations or notice that our breathing changed. Thoughts sometimes can have very powerful effects on how we feel or how we speak to others. Thoughts can even change our behaviors.

Once we learn simply to note all those thoughts in the mind, we may discover that thousands of thoughts come and go all the time. We may be able to step back from the thoughts a little bit—and not get so caught up in those *automatic pilot* kinds of thoughts. Mindful awareness can help us see other things that might be happening in the moment.

Handout 4.3   Session 4 Home Practices

- *Three-Minute Breathing Space.* Practice this activity at least once or twice each day. Practicing being with your breath every day can bring greater awareness and presence without your having to do anything at all.

- *Mindful Yoga Movements.* Practice this activity twice (or more if you wish) during the week. You may practice some of the postures we learned in class (cobra, tree, butterfly, cat and cow, downward facing dog) or even make up some of your own. As you move, practice bringing awareness to the movements in the body. Are you noting sensations in your body that you have never before been aware of? Mindful Yoga Movements is a practice of becoming more aware of thoughts and feelings as well as body sensations.

- *Tasting Fruits.* Practice bringing awareness to the present moment by noting thoughts, feelings, and body sensations while mindfully eating one or two pieces of dried fruit each day. Practice noting the thoughts and feelings that come up as you really taste each bite of fruit. *On the Tasting Fruits Record, write down the thoughts, feelings, and body sensations you noticed while exploring each experience.*

Handout 4.4   Session 4 Tasting Fruits Record

Name: _____   Week of: _____

Tasting Fruits Record

As I practice bringing mindful awareness to tasting different fruits, I may discover new and interesting things. During this week, I have become more aware of these experiences.

Description of Fruit (color, pattern, size, shape)	Tastes and Sensations	Thoughts	Feelings	Body Sensations
Example: Dark red, freckled with a few brown spots.	*The cranberry tastes sweet but also a little tart. It feels cool and is kind of chewy.*	*Eating the cranberry reminds me of a hot summer day.*	*I feel happy.*	*My mouth is watering, and I feel calm and warm inside.*
Sunday				
Monday				
Tuesday				
Wednesday				
Thursday				
Friday				
Saturday				

Handout 4.5   **Three-Minute Breathing Space**

Three-Minute Breathing Space

Awareness

Bring yourself into the present moment by deliberately adopting an erect and dignified posture. If possible, close your eyes. Then ask:

What is my experience right now...in thoughts...in feelings...and in bodily sensations?

Acknowledge and register your experience, even if it is unwanted.

Gathering

Then, gently redirect full attention to breathing, to each inbreath and to each outbreath as they follow, one after the other.

Your breath can function as an anchor to bring you into the present and help you tune into a state of awareness and stillness.

Expanding

Expand the field of your awareness around your breathing, so that it includes a sense of the body as a whole, your posture, and facial expression.

The breathing space provides a way to step out of automatic pilot mode and reconnect with the present moment.

The key skill in using MBCT is to maintain awareness in the moment.

Nothing else.

Handout 5.1   The Door

The Door

My neighbor's musical instrument

of choice is the door.

At first, I thought it a major nuisance,

and then I saw it was really part

of a kind of percussion sonata—

and then the aggravation dissolved.

Now I observe how skillful this

soloist is

in his entrance and exit.

—Aharon Shabtai (1939)

Handout 5.2   Session 5 Summary: Music to Our Ears

Different sounds can sometimes bring up many different thoughts,
feelings, and body sensations. For example, listening to a lullaby, imagine that
you first think loving thoughts about your baby brother but then remember that this morning he
accidentally broke your favorite video game. With mindful awareness, perhaps you might notice
that the feelings start out warm and loving, but then the feelings become upset or frustrated as

you watch the thoughts say, *I really liked that game, and now I can't play it
anymore. That's not fair!* You may feel your breathing change or become
aware of tightness in your belly. If you feel really angry, you might even feel
the urge to shout or stomp around the room. And all of these thoughts, feelings,
and body sensations can be going on while you are still listening to the lullaby!

When we listen with mindful awareness, we practice bringing attention to the things we
hear. We practice letting go of names, labels, or categories as best we can. Instead of hearing a
piece of music as a lullaby that reminds you of your little brother, we invite you to hear sounds
simply as patterns of musical notes, pitch, tone, rhythm, and volume. Whenever you become
aware that your attention has wandered, gently bring it back to the experience of hearing.

The aim of this session is to help us learn that thoughts can affect how we feel and that
how we feel can affect what we think or do. We start by becoming more aware of how we
experience and react to different sounds. By noting thoughts, feelings, and body sensations while
listening to music, we can become more aware of our personal "filters" that can change the
simple experience of listening.

Handout 5.3   Session 5 Home Practices

- *Three-Minute Breathing Space.* Practice this activity at least twice each day, or more if you wish. Bringing awareness to the breath can help us stay present as we cultivate awareness of thoughts, feelings, and body sensations.

- *Mindfulness of the Body.* Practice this once each day. Lie on your back on a firm, flat surface, rather than on a mattress or pillow. Keep your arms loose by your sides and your legs slightly apart. Stretch out so that your body is in a straight line while keeping a half smile on your face. As you breathe in and breathe out, practice watching the breath. Allow your body to relax—as if it were as soft and flowing as a piece of silk hanging in the breeze to dry. Practice noting body sensations while keeping part of your attention on the breath. Practice Mindfulness of the Body for about ten minutes. Note how thoughts and feelings keep coming and going even while bringing awareness to the breath and body sensations.

- *Mindful Listening.* Find a place to sit (either indoors or outdoors). Assume a mindful position and practice Mindful Listening by bringing awareness to the sounds around you. You may be in a noisy cafeteria or a quiet park. No matter where you are, you can tune in to the thoughts, feelings, and body sensations that arise when you listen to sounds with mindful attention. As best you can, simply note when judging thoughts become part of the experience. Practice Mindful Listening for about five minutes, at three different times during the week. *Record the thoughts, feelings, and body sensations afterward on the Mindful Listening Record.*

Handout 5.4   Session 5 Mindful Listening Record

Name: _____   Week of: _____

Mindful Listening Record

Find a place to sit (indoors or outdoors). As best you can, practice being mindful of the sounds around you. Listen carefully with full attention. Use these questions to observe how you respond to sounds.

Day	Describe where you are sitting. Describe the day.	What sounds did you choose to listen to?	What are the thoughts as you listen to the sounds of the world around you?	What are the feelings?	How did the body feel during this experience?
Example: *Monday*	*On my balcony, looking at the street below. The sun is shining and there is a cool breeze.*	*A child's laughter as she walks down the street with her mother; a bicycle bell as it passes by; a puppy barking.*	*Why is the child laughing? Where are they going? The puppy is so cute. I really want a puppy.*	*I'm happy that other people are enjoying this beautiful day too. It's peaceful sitting out here by myself.*	*I feel the breeze on my cheeks and warm sun on my skin. I feel relaxed and a little sleepy too.*

Handout 6.1   Hearing

Hearing

Our ears, which swallow sound,

Can whisper to our fears

Of squeaking doors, the pound

Of hurricanes upon the roof,

The brutal anger of a thunderstorm.

But also they can set our hearts alight

To dance to flutes and drums,

To sway with violins and saxophones.

There is both love and disdain

In this sonic rain. Don't complain.

The world is what it is.

Our ears, shaped and whorled

Deliver it unfurled.

—Jan Sand

Handout 6.2   Session 6 Summary: Sound Expressions

Different sounds evoke different thoughts, feelings, and body sensations. When we experience different feelings, we may create different sounds. For example, if we feel happy, we might laugh and loudly sing a cheerful tune. If we feel sad, we might cry or sing a soft, slow song. What is it that makes one sound happy and another sad?

When we listen with all our attention to the sounds around us, we may become aware of thoughts, feelings, and body sensations. All those thoughts and feelings may affect how we experience the sounds we hear and the sounds we ourselves create. Bringing attention to the sensations in our bodies can also help us become more aware of the "chatter" of thoughts in the mind. We begin to see that thoughts, feelings, and body sensations are related to each other in many ways—and that they often change how we experience our lives. Thoughts may label the sounds as happy or sad and so define the quality of the listening experience. Bringing greater awareness to our lives, we may discover more choices as we respond to our experiences.

We may even decide not to respond to them at all.

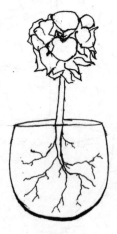

Handout 6.3   Session 6 Home Practices

- *Three-Minute Breathing Space.* Practice this activity at least twice each day, or more if you wish. Bringing awareness to the breath may help us become more aware of thoughts, feelings, and body sensations.

- *Mindful Yoga Movements.* Practice the movement exercises we did in class (downward facing dog, cat and cow, butterfly, cobra, tree) or even make up some of your own. You may practice moving with awareness for ten to fifteen minutes or more, three times this week. As you move, bring your awareness to the small and large movements in your body. Are you aware of different and new body sensations? Thoughts may wander as you practice Mindful Yoga Movements. When you become aware that this is happening, just practice noting that the thoughts are wandering. Then gently bring attention back to the body movements. When you become aware of feelings, simply practice noting that the feelings are there and then return your attention to the body sensations.

- *Unpleasant Sounds.* During the next week, practice becoming more aware of three different "unpleasant" sounds—that is, sounds that you earlier may have called unpleasant, before you began listening to sounds with mindful awareness. As we practice mindfulness of sounds, we can simply note the thoughts, feelings, and body sensations that are present while we listen. What is it that makes the sound unpleasant? Is it because the sound hurts your ears or because thoughts have defined the sound as "unpleasant"? Practice bringing greater awareness to sounds while noting the thoughts, feelings, and body sensations that are present. *Afterward, record your experiences on the Unpleasant Sounds Record.*

Handout 6.4   Session 6 Unpleasant Sounds Record

Name: _____   Week of: _____

Unpleasant Sounds Record

You are practicing mindful awareness of an unpleasant sound while it is happening.
These questions may help you focus attention on the details of the event.

Day	Describe where you are and what is happening.	What sounds did you become mindful of?	What were the thoughts and feelings as you listened to the sounds around you?	How did the body feel during this experience?	How might the thoughts affect how I feel?
Example: *Thursday*	*At night, lying in my bed. Outside it's raining heavily with lightning and thunder.*	*Rain pounding against the window. Whistling of the wind. Every few minutes, there is a loud clap of thunder.*	*I don't like thunderstorms; they feel creepy to me. What if the roof blows off? I feel kind of worried and scared.*	*My belly hurt. Teeth were clenched. Curled up in a ball with my fingers in my ears and my eyes closed tightly.*	*The thunder booms are really loud, but so are the fireworks that I like. All these scary thoughts might be making me more afraid.*

Handout 7.1   Looking

Looking

Once when I read the funnies
I took my little magnifying glass
and looked too close.
    Forms became colors and colors
        were just arrays of dots
    and between the dots I saw the rough bleak
        storyless legend of the pulp paper
        empty as the winter moon
                and I dreaded it.
            I had looked right through,
            when I wanted a universe
                that sustains
        looker and looking and the seen
            forever, detail after detail
        never ending. And all I had found
            was between. But between
                had its own song:
Find it in the space between—
it is just as empty as it seems
but this blankness is your mother.

Robert Kelly (1995)

Handout 7.2   Session 7 Summary: Practice Looking

We sometimes get used to seeing a *beautiful* bed of roses, a *pretty* sunset, a *fantastic* view of the mountains, or that *cute* little kitten. We also may get in the habit of seeing *ugly* trash, a *disgusting* snake, or that *nasty* spinach. When we are on *automatic pilot*, judging thoughts often get confused with the things we see. Without even knowing it, we tend to make judgments about many of our experiences. We may even believe the judgments and ignore the actual experiences.

When bringing mindful awareness to the things we see around us, we simply pay attention to what is really there, as best we can. With practice, we sometimes see through those judging thoughts. Instead of seeing a *pretty* flower or an *ugly* car, we practice seeing the flower or the car as patterns of colors and shapes and movement—just as they are. Whenever we notice that the mind has wandered or when we find ourselves thinking about what we are looking at, we again practice gently bringing attention back to what is present in this moment.

The aim of this session is to continue cultivating mindfulness by practicing bringing awareness to what we see. Colors, shapes, lights, and movements surround us at every moment. As we shift out of *automatic pilot*, we may see familiar objects as if for the first time. When thoughts and feelings don't color what we are looking at, we may see more clearly. We can choose to let go of deciding if we like or dislike our experiences, and be more comfortable with what is happening right now. When becoming aware that thoughts and feelings are present, we simply note them and then practice bringing attention back to what we are seeing.

We practice mindful looking so that we might learn to see with greater clarity and compassion.

Handout 7.3   Session 7 Home Practices

- *Three-Minute Breathing Space.* Practice this activity at least twice each day, or more if you wish. Bringing awareness to the breath can help us see when we are on *automatic pilot*. We practice by bringing our awareness to thoughts, feelings, and body sensations in this moment.

- *Seeing the Little Details.* Bring home the picture that you drew in the group. Compare the picture to the real object. Fill in the parts that you might have seen differently in your mind's eye. Note whatever details you did not see clearly. When you were drawing, did you see some parts as being in a different place or being a different shape or color than they are? Do thoughts and feelings affect what we see? Why do we see some things in the mind's eye and not others?

- *Stressful Events.* Practice bringing mindful awareness to an event that you might feel is challenging for you. Pick three different events on three different days. We can use this practice to become more aware of thoughts, feelings, and body sensations that come up when these events happen. What is it that makes the event a stressful one for you? *Afterward, record the thoughts, feelings, and body sensations on the Stressful Events Record.*

Handout 7.4   Session 7 Stressful Events Record

Name: _____   Week of: _____

Stressful Events Record

Practice bringing mindful awareness to a stressful event when it is happening.
These questions may help you focus attention better to see the details of the event.

Date	What was the event?	What were the body sensations?	What were the feelings?	What were the thoughts?	What did I do? What happened afterward?
Example: Tuesday	Argued with my best friend.	Tight feeling in my chest. My face felt hot. Started to feel a little sick to my stomach.	I was angry when my friend yelled at me, and then I felt very sad.	This is so silly. We are friends. Why are we arguing?	I breathed deeply three times, and then I didn't feel as angry as I was before. I didn't yell back because I felt calmer.

Handout 8.1   Choices

Choices

Every situation has thousands
   But we wear blinders
      Which cause our view to narrow
         So our perceptions are wrong.

         The way to see open and free
          Is to be in the here and now only.

    Who can know the future?
  The past is only a fantasy of memories.

It's one step at a time, one day at a time
         With all its wonder of being alive.

   To see the sun, the stars,
    To feel this breath,
       To be kind,   *To do no harm,*
                 To be smiling
                    To a thousand possibilities.

                    William Menza
                    (2000)

Handout 8.2   Session 8 Summary: Strengthening the Muscle of Attention

When we look with intention, we simply pay attention to what we see as best we can. Shifting out of *automatic pilot*, we practice looking at familiar objects as if we've never seen them before. With practice, we may see most things more clearly. We may notice that what we "see" might be different from what is really there. Thoughts and feelings about the object are there too. So we might look at a flower or a tree and see a *pretty* flower or an *ugly* tree. Mindfulness practices can help us learn to see the flower or the tree just as it is. *Pretty* and *ugly* are judging thoughts about the flower or the tree. Thoughts are in us, and not part of the flower or the tree. This is why we practice looking. We look at the object, and we look at the thoughts, feelings, and body sensations. Whenever we notice that the mind has wandered or we have started thinking *about* what is being seen, we bring our attention back to *seeing*.

Mindful seeing practices help us learn to see more clearly all the different thoughts that pass through our minds. We may see when thoughts and feelings make it harder to deal with events that we don't have any control over. When we bring greater awareness to those thoughts and feelings, it's sometimes easier to be okay with whatever is actually happening. When we become aware that a judging thought is present, we simply practice kindness toward ourselves by noting the thought, and then bring our attention back to what we see.

The aim of this session is to continue cultivating mindful awareness of all the things we see around us and inside us. As we strengthen the muscle of attention, we may learn to see with greater clarity and awareness. Seeing clearly, we may see more *choice points*. Choice points can feel like moments of freedom, because they are the moments at which choices can be made. With clarity and compassion, we may discover wonderful opportunities to make mindful choices in how we respond to the events of our lives.

Handout 8.3   Session 8 Home Practices

- ***Three-Minute Breathing Space.*** Practice this activity at least twice each day, or more if you wish. Mindful breathing may help us become more aware of thoughts, feelings, and body sensations.

- ***Choosing to Be Aware.*** Each day next week, you may choose any other mindful awareness practice you wish. For example, you may choose to practice mindful yoga movements, bring more awareness to eating your dinner, or practice mindful walking while going to school. Practice noting the thoughts that arise while you are practicing. Observe when you might be *noting* and when you might be *judging*. Do these feel like different experiences? If you were to choose a different thought, how might the experience change?

- ***Seeing Five New Things.*** This activity may help you become more aware of your surroundings. Practice Seeing Five New Things in your classroom at school. Write down five things that you noticed by bringing your attention to the room—things that you have never noticed before. Perhaps you might see a telephone hanging on the back wall of the room that you never noticed was there. Or maybe you looked closely at your teacher's chair for the first time. What interesting things might be hanging on the walls around you? What color is the ceiling of your classroom? What discoveries have you made by practicing mindful seeing? *Note on the Seeing Five New Things Record each time you do this activity.*

Handout 8.4   **Session 8 Seeing Five New Things Record**

Every day at school, I sit in the same classroom. Once I practice bringing awareness to all the things around me, I may begin to notice many things that I have never before noticed. During this week, I have discovered these five new and interesting things about my classroom.

Example: I noticed that there is a pencil holder on my teacher's desk. It is made of wood and has a smooth and shiny surface. It is light brown with streaky wood-grain lines on the surface. I also noticed that there is a small crack on its side.

1. _____

_____

_____

2. _____

_____

_____

3. _____

_____

_____

4. _____

_____

_____

5. _____

_____

_____

Handout 9.1   Touch

T o u c h

These fingers touch the world for me.
They know the feel of bark.

They know a tree from head to knee,
But cannot know a park.

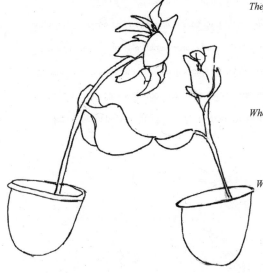

They communicate with leaves and grass
Within a six-foot reach

But great plains are truly strange
As is a glowing beach.

Whose parts like shells and sand and wet
Can nest into my palm.

Which tells me sharp or smooth or cold
But nothing about young or old,

Or when the sun has set.
For this they whisper in their night

For knowingness from brother
sight.

—Jan Sand

Handout 9.2   Session 9 Summary: Touching the World with Mindfulness

Throughout our lives, we each will encounter many different situations, events, and experiences. We will interact with many different people in many different ways. We often judge these experiences as being "good" or "bad" or "pleasant" or "unpleasant" without even being aware that we are judging. In this session, we practice *describing* our experiences. This may feel very different from *judging* the experience. As we practice mindfulness, we become more aware of *all* our experiences, including that automatic pilot habit we have of judging them.

With greater awareness, we may discover new opportunities or choice points. In a situation that normally makes us feel anxious, like taking a test, we may practice noting and describing whatever it is that we're experiencing rather than judging it. We might practice simply noting thoughts (*I think I'm going to fail*), feelings (*I'm worried and nervous*), and body sensations (*my face muscles are tense*). When we judge an experience as unpleasant, we often want to push it away. When we approach our experiences in a mindful way, we may feel as if we're seeing it differently. We may see new or different choice points. Seeing more choice points, we can discover that we have more freedom to choose how to respond to challenging events in our lives.

Handout 9.3   Session 9 Home Practices

- ***Three-Minute Breathing Space.*** Practice at least twice every day, or more if you wish.

- ***Mindfulness of the Body.*** Practice this activity four times (or more) this week. Begin by lying comfortably on your back on a flat surface. You may wish to put a pillow under your head. Rest your arms by your sides with your legs slightly apart. Stretch out so that your body is lying in a straight line. Maintain a half smile on your face, resting your attention with the breath. Bring attention to body sensations—practicing noting and describing them. Note also when thoughts might be judging ones. Practicing Mindfulness of the Body is simply a moment-by-moment awareness of what is happening. You may notice that thoughts and feelings keep coming and going even as you practice mindful awareness of body sensations. Each time the mind wanders, you have another opportunity to practice bringing attention back to the body sensations. Reminding yourself of what the body is doing can be helpful. Telling yourself, *Breathing in, I know that I am breathing in. Breathing out, I know that I am breathing out.* Practice observing and noting body sensations for ten to fifteen minutes each time.

- ***Mindful Touching.*** Find five small household objects to explore with your sense of touch. Practice focusing your attention on the sensations in your fingers, as best you can. Continue the practice of just noting the thoughts and feelings that arise while practicing mindful touching.

  Record your experiences on the Mindful Touching Record each time you do this practice.

Handout 9.4   Session 9 Mindful Touching Record

Name: _____   Week of: _____

Mindful Touching Record

I practice mindful touching and can discover things that I never knew or noticed before. As I explore objects with my sense of touch, I can make discoveries about the textures, shapes, sizes, temperatures, and weights of these objects—and perhaps discover something new about myself too. During this week, I have become more mindful of these five objects.

What Is the Object?	Description of Object	Thoughts	Feelings	Body Sensations
Example: A ball of cotton	*White, lightweight, fluffy, round, soft, squishy.*	*I never noticed that the edge glows when I hold the cotton up to a light.*	*I feel relaxed - and interested.*	*My fingers feel soft and dry against the cotton.*
1.				
2.				
3.				
4.				
5.				

TO BE OR NOT TO BE...

Two Approaches to Life

Being Mindful and Present with My Experiences

Judging and Fighting with My Experiences

The Plight of the Human Doing

- Wanting my experiences to be different.
- Wanting my experiences to be better.
- Wanting to change what is happening.
- Feeling that I should do it differently.
- Feeling that I should be better than I am.
- Judgments are all that I experience.
- I feel worried and unhappy.

The Art of the Human Being

- Being present with what is happening.
- Being aware of thoughts and feelings.
- Being aware of judging thoughts.
- Being touched by life.
- Seeing that this moment is okay just as it is.
- Knowing I can find my own choice points.
- I feel okay just the way I am.

Handout 10.2   Session 10 Summary: What the Nose Knows

All of our lives, we have experiences that we judge to be *pleasant, unpleasant,* or *neutral.* We often decide that many objects (and sometimes people) are either *good* or *bad.* This habit of judging became very clear when we practiced mindful smelling. We tend to very quickly judge the things we smell. We then often react from automatic pilot.

- Sometimes we judge experiences as being *pleasant.* Then we may want to hold onto them. We might want more of the good experience or even feel unhappy because we know the nice experience won't last. We look forward to enjoyable experiences and want to go back to them in our thoughts long after they have passed.

- Sometimes we judge experiences as being *unpleasant.* Then we may want them to go away. We might even become angry when we can't get rid of the bad experience. We may worry or feel anxious just anticipating a scary experience that hasn't even happened. We may feel sad thinking about an awful experience that happened last week.

- Sometimes we judge experiences as being *neutral.* Then we may not care about them. We may be bored, completely unaware of the situation, indifferent about what is happening, emotionally untouched, or unconcerned about the people involved. We are unmoved by the experience.

Judging our experiences can bring more stress to our lives, especially when we judge thoughts or feelings, because we then might want to push them away. We can't control many things that happen in our lives. We can, however, choose how we respond. Mindful awareness can sometimes help us discover more choice points. Choice points only occur in this moment. When we see them, we have more freedom to choose how to respond. We don't have to react on automatic pilot. Staying present with the breath can make it easier to respond as we *choose*—with mindful awareness.

Handout 10.3   Session 10 Home Practices

- *Three-Minute Breathing Space.* Practice this activity at least twice each day, or more if you wish. Bringing awareness to the breath may help us stay present as we continue to cultivate awareness of thoughts, feelings, and body sensations.

- *Mindful Yoga Movements.* Practice this activity at least three times during the week for about ten minutes each time. You may use the poses we have practiced (downward facing dog, cat and cow, butterfly, cobra, or tree) or invent some of your own. This is a practice of bringing greater awareness to the sensations and movements of your body. We also practice noting the thoughts that go through our heads and the feelings that arise while we move. How often do we judge how well we do the yoga movements? How does this affect the experience?

- *Mindful Smelling.* Choose two meals to practice smelling with mindful awareness. Describe the smells of two or three different foods on your plate (or the drink in your cup). Practice identifying the thoughts and feelings that arise when smelling each item. In what ways are judging and describing different? Can the thoughts be changing your experience in some way? Practice being mindful of the judging thoughts that might come up while smelling the different foods or drink. *Note your experiences on the Mindful Smelling Record each time you do this practice.*

Handout 10.4   **Session 10 Mindful Smelling Record**

Name: _____   Week of: _____

Mindful Smelling Record

Sometimes when I eat, I may not be aware of the different smells of the food on my plate or the drink in my cup. As I explore the scents and aromas of the foods I eat, I may discover new and interesting things. During this week, I am practicing bringing more awareness to smells.

Name of food	Description of smell	Thoughts	Feelings	What choice points do I have right now?	Might my experience be different if I were to make different choices?
Example: Peas with butter	The peas smell sweet and mushy. The butter smells salty but also a little sweet and creamy.	I don't like peas. I think they smell nasty.	I feel upset that I have to eat them.	I could explore all the smells on my plate like I had never smelled these things before.	Dinner is more interesting, and the peas don't really smell that bad. I'm okay with having to eat them.

Name of food	Description of smell	Thoughts	Feelings	What *choice points* do I have right now?	Might my experience be different if I were to make different choices?

Handout 10.5   Things We Can Learn from a Dog

Things We Can Learn from a Dog
Author unknown

- Never pass up the opportunity to go for a joyride.
- Allow the experience of fresh air and the wind in your face to be pure ecstasy.
- When loved ones come home, always run to greet them.
- When it's in your best interest, practice obedience.
- Let others know when they have invaded your territory.
- Take naps and stretch before rising.
- Run, romp, and play daily.
- Eat with gusto and enthusiasm.
- Be loyal.
- Never pretend to be something you're not.

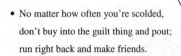

- If what you want lies buried, dig until you find it.
- When someone is having a bad day, be silent, sit close by, and nuzzle him or her gently.
- Thrive on attention and let people touch you.
- Avoid biting when a simple growl will do.
- On hot days, drink lots of water and lie under a shady tree.
- When you are happy, dance around and wag your entire body.

- No matter how often you're scolded, don't buy into the guilt thing and pout; run right back and make friends.
- Delight in the simple joys of a long walk.

Handout 11.1   Slow Dance

Slow Dance

Have you ever watched kids on a merry-go-round,
or listened to rain slapping the ground?
Ever followed a butterfly's erratic flight,
or gazed at the sun fading into the night?

You better slow down, don't dance so fast,
time is short, the music won't last.

Do you run through each day on the fly,
when you ask "How are you?"
do you hear the reply?

When the day is done, do you lie in your bed,
with the next hundred chores running through your head?

You better slow down, don't dance so fast,
time is short, the music won't last.
When you run so fast to get somewhere,
you miss half the fun of getting there.

When you worry and hurry through your day,
it's like an unopened gift thrown away.

Life isn't a race, so take it slower,
hear the music before your song is over.

—David L. Weatherford

Handout 11.2   Session 11 Summary: Life Is Not a Rehearsal

Many times every day we can choose to bring more awareness to our experiences. If we find our attention drawn to particular thoughts, feelings, or body sensations, we can choose to bring a gentle and friendly awareness to them. Choosing to bring greater awareness to our experiences is the cultivation of mindfulness in everyday life.

We can learn to become more aware of when we hold on to some thoughts or feelings and when we push others away. When we define some thoughts, feelings, or body sensations as *unpleasant,* we might want to push them away. When we define other experiences as *pleasant,* we might want to hold on to them. All this holding on and pushing away can make it very difficult to practice mindful acceptance. We may not need to struggle with thoughts like this. Instead, we might simply choose to accept them, because thoughts are *just thoughts.* Thoughts are not facts.

Accepting our experiences is less work than trying to create a completely different world with our thoughts. Practicing compassionate acceptance, we grow to become more aware and accepting of what is present. We learn to let an experience be what it is—and be more present with it—while deepening our understanding of and compassion for ourselves and others. Practicing mindful awareness is a path of discovery—learning to see all the remarkable details, variety, and fullness in every experience.

We choose to practice mindfulness in everyday life. We can always choose to bring more awareness to our lives with all our senses. In each new moment, we can choose to accept thoughts, feelings, body sensations, and all our experiences. Then we may see a variety of choice points in our everyday lives. To see choice points, we need only bring greater awareness to the moment—moment...by moment...by moment.

Handout 11.3   Session 11 Home Practices

- *Three-Minute Breathing Space.* Practice this activity at least twice each day, or more if you wish. This is one way to enhance awareness of thoughts, feelings, and body sensations.

- *Letter to My Self.* We are nearing the end of the program. We have done a lot of important work together. For this week's home practice, we would like you to think about your experiences over the past eleven weeks and write a letter to yourself about what you have learned. Allow enough time to write this important letter to yourself with mindful awareness. There are no right or wrong, or good or bad letters. Address the envelope to yourself. Bring the letter and envelope with you to the next session. If you wish, you can seal your letter in the addressed envelope. But, we will discuss the letters next week, so you may prefer not to seal it just yet. We promise we won't read your letter unless you want us to. We will mail your Letter to My Self back to you three months from now as a reminder of how practicing mindfulness has been helpful to you.

  You may wish to consider these questions before you write your letter:
  - What does mindfulness mean to me now?
  - How have my ideas about mindful awareness changed since I began the program?
  - Has mindfulness changed the way I interact with other people? If so, how?
  - Has mindful awareness helped me at home or school? If so, how?
  - What have I learned from this program?
  - What skills have I learned that might be helpful to me?
  - What was the most difficult part of the program for me?
  - Why did that part seem difficult?
  - Is it less difficult now than it was eleven weeks ago?
  - How would I describe my experience of being part of this group?
  - What does being a member of this group mean to me?
  - What did I learn from the other group members' experiences?
  - How would I like to continue cultivating mindful awareness in my everyday life?
  - In what ways might I practice mindfulness in the future?
  - What could I do that will help me remember to practice?
  - What do I most want to remember about being in this program?

Handout 11.4   Session 11 Letter to My Self

Date_____

Dear_____ ,

_____

_____

_____

_____

_____

_____

_____

_____

_____

_____

_____

_____

_____

_____

_____

_____

_____

_____

_____

_____

_____

_____

_____

_____

_____

_____

_____

_____

_____

_____

_____

_____

_____

_____

_____

_____

_____

Sincerely,

_____

Handout 12.1   **Little Gidding**

We shall not cease from exploration

And the end of all our exploring

Will be to arrive where we started

And know the place for the first time.

Through the unknown, remembered gate

When the last of earth left to discover

Is that which was the beginning;

At the source of the longest river

The voice of the hidden waterfall

And the children in the apple-tree

Not known, because not looked for

But heard, half-heard, in the stillness

Between two waves of the sea.

Quick now, here, now, always—

A condition of complete simplicity

(Costing not less than everything)

And all shall be well and

All manner of thing shall be well

When the tongues of flame are in-folded

Into the crowned knot of fire

And the fire and the rose are one.

T. S. Eliot
Four Quartets (1942)

Handout 12.2   Session 12 Summary: Living with Presence, Compassion, and Awareness

Living with Presence, Compassion, and Awareness

- Before you get out of bed in the morning, smile and practice bringing attention to the breath. You may choose to watch the rise and fall of your belly as you practice Taking Three Mindful Breaths.

- As you get ready for your day, bring your awareness to the body sensations of getting out of bed, brushing your teeth, combing your hair, or putting on your clothes.

- On your way to school, listen with awareness to sounds in your environment. You may notice a bird singing, a car honking, a door slamming, the subway rumbling, or a dog barking. Practice bringing awareness to thoughts, feelings, and body sensations as you listen to the sounds around you.

- Practicing the Three-Minute Breathing Space every day may heighten awareness of all your experiences.

- Practicing mindfulness of the breath can be helpful when you need to be grounded in this moment.

- You can choose how to respond to thoughts and feelings—or even choose not to respond at all.

- Whenever you experience anxiety or other strong feelings, simply breathe and practice noting the thoughts, feelings, and body sensations in the moment. Approach all your feelings with curiosity and kindness.

- From time to time, you might wish to remind yourself that noting, rather than judging, your experiences may allow you to discover more choice points as you respond to personal challenges.

- Getting up from a chair or walking across a classroom, you can choose to practice being mindful of the movements and sensations of the body as it shifts from sitting to standing to walking.

- On your way home from school, practice really looking at the things around you. When you attend to the world around you with intention and awareness, you are likely to discover new or different things.

- Practicing mindful yoga movements (like the cat and the cow) may help you to reconnect with the body and the breath. Practice being aware of whatever body sensations arise in each moment.

- As you eat dinner, practice bringing more awareness to the tastes and smells of the different foods on your plate. Are you delighting in each bite, savoring one bite at a time, moment by moment?

- When doing your schoolwork, start by becoming aware of your posture. Note any tightness you might have in your chest, neck, back, arms, or legs. Practice breathing into that tightness. Get to know it; perhaps become friends with it...and then let it go as best you can.

- As you get ready for bed, you may wish to practice bringing your awareness to the water on your face, the scrape of the toothbrush against your teeth, the feel of your pajamas or blanket against your skin.

- Perhaps you might remind yourself to check in with the breath before going to sleep. The breath has been with you all day. You might even say, "Thank you, breath," by practicing Taking Three Mindful Breaths.

- Never forget that the breath is always with you. The breath is an anchor that can help you stay clear, present, and aware throughout your day...moment by moment...day by day.

- I would like to continue this practice of bringing greater awareness into my life because _____

_____

_____

_____

Inspired by the work of Madeline Klyne, mindfulness instructor.

Handout 12.3   Session 12 Letter from Therapist to Child

Dear _____,

    You have worked really hard over the past twelve weeks, and we hope that you have gained a deeper understanding of mindfulness and how you can use this awareness to better manage the challenges that you may sometimes experience in life. Although the program is ending, we hope that you will continue to cultivate your daily mindfulness practice. Remember, your breath is always with you. Breathing with awareness can help you stay grounded in the present moment.

    We offer you this small gift as a symbol of your contribution to the group, of all your hard work over the past twelve weeks, and to remember the other children who have shared this journey with you. But above all, our gift is a reminder for you to continue the process you started, to discover with mindful awareness a new way of living and being, and to respond to your own experiences in a kinder and more caring way. We hope that you value this gift as much as we value your presence in the group.

    We enjoyed the time we spent with you, and we will remember you with fondness. We hope that you have enjoyed your experiences in this mindfulness program.

With our warmest wishes,

_____

Handout 12.4   **Session 12 Daily Practice Calendar**

DATE	MY DAILY MINDFULNESS PRACTICE	
1		
2		
3		
4		
5		
6		
7		
8		
9		
10		
11		
12		
13		
14		
15		
16		
17		
18		
19		
20		
21		
22		
23		
24		
25		
26		
27		
28		
29		
30		
31		

Handout F.1   **Three-Month Follow-up Letter from Therapist to Child**

Dear _____,

It's been three months since you graduated from the mindfulness program for children, and we hope that you are choosing to continue cultivating mindfulness in your everyday life. Remember that your breath is always with you and that you can use your breath to bring greater awareness to your life.

Enclosed is the letter that you wrote to yourself near the end of the program. This letter is a reminder of your experiences and some ways that you might continue living with greater presence, compassion, and awareness. With commitment, we can choose to respond to our experiences in gentle and caring ways. We hope that you will continue your discovery of this new way of living and being. To support your practice, we have enclosed another daily calendar.

We also want to say, "*Thank you very much!*" for your contributions to the group. You have touched our lives in many ways.

With our best wishes,

_____

Handout F.2   **Daily Practice Calendar**

DATE	MY DAILY MINDFULNESS PRACTICE	
1		
2		
3		
4		
5		
6		
7		
8		
9		
10		
11		
12		
13		
14		
15		
16		
17		
18		
19		
20		
21		
22		
23		
24		
25		
26		
27		
28		
29		
30		
31		

APPENDIX D

Program Evaluations

Mindfulness-Based Cognitive Therapy for Children
Parent Evaluation Questionnaire

Name (optional)_____ Date _____

Please circle the answer that best describes your experience.

1. Overall, how would you rate the Mindfulness-Based Cognitive Therapy for Children program?
   1   Very unhelpful
   2   Unhelpful
   3   Neutral / Not sure
   4   Helpful
   5   Very helpful

2. This program has been helpful to my child.
   1   Strongly disagree
   2   Disagree
   3   Neutral / Not sure
   4   Agree
   5   Strongly agree

3. I would recommend this program to the parents of other children.
   1   Strongly disagree
   2   Disagree
   3   Neutral / Not sure
   4   Agree
   5   Strongly agree

Please continue on the next page.

4. Since participating in this program, my child seems less anxious.

    1   Strongly disagree

    2   Disagree

    3   Neutral / Not sure

    4   Agree

    5   Strongly agree

Please explain. _____

_____

5. Since being in this program, my child is better able to manage his or her anger.

    1   Strongly disagree

    2   Disagree

    3   Neutral / Not sure

    4   Agree

    5   Strongly agree

Please explain. _____

_____

6. Since being in this program, my child has more positive interactions with other people.

    1   Strongly disagree

    2   Disagree

    3   Neutral / Not sure

    4   Agree

    5   Strongly agree

Please explain. _____

_____

Please continue on the next page.

7. Since being in this program, my child is more patient.
   1   Strongly disagree
   2   Disagree
   3   Neutral / Not sure
   4   Agree
   5   Strongly agree
Please explain. _____

_____

8. The program has helped my child in school.
   1   Strongly disagree
   2   Disagree
   3   Neutral / Not sure
   4   Agree
   5   Strongly agree
Please explain. _____

_____

9. The program has helped my child at home.
   1   Strongly disagree
   2   Disagree
   3   Neutral / Not sure
   4   Agree
   5   Strongly agree
Please explain. _____

_____

Please continue on the next page.

As best you can, please complete the following statements:

10. The most notable change I have seen in my child (if any) is

_____

_____

11. The most helpful aspect of the program is _____

_____

_____

12. The least helpful aspect of the program is _____

_____

_____

13. The most important thing my child has taken from the program is

_____

_____

14. In the future, I hope that my child _____

_____

_____

15. Please feel free to share any other thoughts or recommendations.

_____

_____

_____

_____

Thank you very much for taking the time to complete this evaluation!

Mindfulness-Based Cognitive Therapy for Children
Child Evaluation Questionnaire

Name (optional)_____ Date _____

Please circle the answer that best describes your experience.
There are no right or wrong answers.

1. Overall, how would you rate the Mindfulness-Based Cognitive
   Therapy for Children program?
   - 1   Very unhelpful
   - 2   Unhelpful
   - 3   Neutral / Not sure
   - 4   Helpful
   - 5   Very helpful

2. This program has been helpful to me.
   - 1   Strongly disagree
   - 2   Disagree
   - 3   Neutral / Not sure
   - 4   Agree
   - 5   Strongly agree

3. I would recommend this program to my friends.
   - 1   Strongly disagree
   - 2   Disagree
   - 3   Neutral / Not sure
   - 4   Agree
   - 5   Strongly agree

Please go on to next page.

4. Since being in this program, I feel less worried in my life.
    1   Strongly disagree
    2   Disagree
    3   Neutral / Not sure
    4   Agree
    5   Strongly agree

5. Since being in this program, I feel better able to manage my anger.
    1   Strongly disagree
    2   Disagree
    3   Neutral / Not sure
    4   Agree
    5   Strongly agree

6. Since being in this program, I have more positive interactions with others.
    1   Strongly disagree
    2   Disagree
    3   Neutral / Not sure
    4   Agree
    5   Strongly agree

7. Since being in this program, I am more patient in my life.
    1   Strongly disagree
    2   Disagree
    3   Neutral / Not sure
    4   Agree
    5   Strongly agree

Please go on to next page.

8. The program has helped me in school.
   1   Strongly disagree
   2   Disagree
   3   Neutral / Not sure
   4   Agree
   5   Strongly agree

9. The program has helped me at home.
   1   Strongly disagree
   2   Disagree
   3   Neutral / Not sure
   4   Agree
   5   Strongly agree

10. I will continue to practice mindful awareness in my life after the program is over.
    1   Strongly disagree
    2   Disagree
    3   Neutral / Not sure
    4   Agree
    5   Strongly agree

As best you can, please complete the following statements:

11. The most helpful part of the program is _____

_____

_____

_____

Please go on to next page.

12. The least helpful part of the program is _____

_____

_____

_____

_____

_____

13. The most helpful practice is _____

_____

_____

_____

_____

_____

14. The least helpful practice is _____

_____

_____

_____

_____

_____

15. When I look back on the past twelve weeks in the program, I feel

_____

_____

_____

_____

_____

Please go on to next page.

16. I will miss _____

_____

_____

_____

_____

_____

17. I will look forward to _____

_____

_____

_____

_____

_____

18. In the future, I hope that I will _____

_____

_____

_____

_____

_____

Please go on to next page.

Please rate these program activities:

Activity	Session	Very helpful	Helpful	Not sure	Not so helpful	Not at all helpful	I did not attend session
Taking Three Mindful Breaths	1–3	5	4	3	2	1	0
Mindfully Moooving Slooowly	2	5	4	3	2	1	0
Raisin Mindfulness (mindful tasting)	2, 11	5	4	3	2	1	0
Mindfulness of the Body	3, 5, 9	5	4	3	2	1	0
Opening to One Orange (mindful tasting)	4	5	4	3	2	1	0
Three-Minute Breathing Space	4–12	5	4	3	2	1	0
Mindful Yoga Movements (cat, cow, tree, cobra poses)	4, 6, 7, 10	5	4	3	2	1	0
Do You Hear What I Hear? (mindful hearing)	5	5	4	3	2	1	0
Sounding Out Emotions—Mindfully (mindful hearing)	6	5	4	3	2	1	0
Visualizing with Clarity (mindful seeing)	7	5	4	3	2	1	0
Seeing Through Illusions (mindful seeing)	8	5	4	3	2	1	0
Being in Touch (mindful touching)	9	5	4	3	2	1	0
Judging Stinks! (mindful smelling)	10	5	4	3	2	1	0

Thank you very much for taking the time to complete this evaluation!

References

Achenbach, T. M. (1991). *Manual for the Child Behavior Checklist: Ages 4–18 and 1991 profile*. University of Vermont, Department of Psychiatry, Burlington, VT.

Anderson, V. L., Levinson, E. M., Barker, W., & Kiewra, K. R. (1999). The effects of meditation on teacher perceived occupational stress, state and trait anxiety, and burnout. *School Psychology Quarterly, 14*, 3–25. doi:10.1037/h0088995

Baer, R. A. (2003). Mindfulness training as a clinical intervention: A conceptual and empirical review. *Clinical Psychology: Science and Practice, 10*, 125–143. doi:10.1093/clipsy/bpg015

Baer, R. A., Fischer, S., & Huss, D. B. (2005). Mindfulness-based cognitive therapy applied to binge eating: A case study. *Cognitive and Behavioral Practice, 12*, 351–358. doi:10.1016/S1077-7229(05)80057-4

Baer, R. A., Smith, G. T., & Allen, K. B. (2004). Assessment of mindfulness by self-report: The Kentucky Inventory of Mindfulness Skills. *Assessment, 11*, 191–206. doi:10.1177/1073191104268029

Baer, R. A., Smith, G. T., Hopkins, J., Krietemeyer, J., & Toney, L. (2006). Using self-report assessment methods to explore facets of mindfulness. *Assessment, 13*(1), 27–45. doi:10.1177/1073191105283504

Baer, R. A., Smith, G. T., Lykins, E., Button, D., Krietemeyer, J., Sauer, S., et al. (2008). Construct validity of the Five Facet Mindfulness Questionnaire in meditating and nonmeditating samples. *Assessment, 15*, 329–342. doi:10.1177/1073191107313003

Bailey, V. (2001). Cognitive-behavioural therapies for children and adolescents. *Advances in Psychiatric Treatment, 7*, 224–232. doi:10.1192/apt.7.3.224

Barlow, D. H. (2002). *Anxiety and its disorders: The nature and treatment of anxiety and panic* (2nd ed.). New York: Guilford Press.

Beck, A. T. (1976). *Cognitive therapy and the emotional disorders.* New York: International Universities Press.

Beck, A. T., & Emery, G. (1985). *Anxiety disorders and phobias: A cognitive perspective.* New York: Basic Books.

Bhikkhu Bodhi (Ed.). (1993). *A comprehensive manual of Abhidhamma.* Kandy, Sri Lanka: Buddhist Publication Society.

Birmaher, B., & Ollendick, T. H. (2004). Childhood-onset panic disorder. In T. H. Ollendick & J. S. March (Eds.), *Phobic and anxiety disorders in children and adolescents* (pp. 306–333). New York: Oxford University Press.

Bishop, S. R., Lau, M., Shapiro, S., Carlson, L., Anderson, N. D., Carmody, J., et al. (2004). Mindfulness: A proposed operational definition. *Clinical Psychology: Science and Practice, 11,* 230–241. doi:10.1093/clipsy/bph077

Bowen, S., Witkiewitz, K., Dillworth, T. M., Chawla, N., Simpson, T. L., Ostafin, B. D., et al. (2006). Mindfulness meditation and substance use in an incarcerated population. *Psychology of Addictive Behaviors, 20,* 343–347. doi:10.1037/0893-164X.20.3.343

Broadbent, D. E. (1971). *Decision and stress.* London: Academic Publishers.

Brown, K. W., & Ryan, R. M. (2003). The benefits of being present: Mindfulness and its role in psychological well-being. *Journal of Personality and Social Psychology, 84*(4), 822–848. doi:10.1037/0022-3514.84.4.822

Brown, K. W., West, A. M., Loverich, T. M., & Biegel, G. M. (in press). Assessing adolescent mindfulness: Validation of an adapted mindful attention awareness scale in adolescent normative and psychiatric populations. *Psychological Assessment.*

Brückl, T. M., Wittchen, H.-U., Höfler, M., Pfister, H., Schneider, S., & Lieb, R. (2006). Childhood separation anxiety and the risk of subsequent psychopathology: Results from a community study. *Psychotherapy and Psychosomatics, 76,* 47–56.

Cannon, W. B. (1929). *Bodily changes in pain, hunger, fear, and rage: An account of recent research into the function of emotional excitement* (2nd ed.). New York: Appleton-Century-Crofts.

Carlson, L. E., Ursuliak, Z., Goodey, E., Angen, M., & Speca, M. (2001). The effects of a mindfulness meditation–based stress reduction program on mood and symptoms of stress in cancer outpatients: Six month follow-up. *Supportive Care in Cancer, 9,* 112–123. doi:10.1007/s005200000206

Chambers, R., Lo, B. C. Y., & Allen, N. B. (2008). The impact of intensive mindfulness training on attentional control, cognitive style, and affect. *Cognitive Therapy and Research, 32,* 303–322. doi:10.1007/s10608-007-9119-0

Chavira, D. A., & Stein, M. B. (2005). Childhood social anxiety disorder: From understanding to treatment. *Child and Adolescent Psychiatric Clinics of North America, 14,* 797–818. doi:10.1016/j.chc.2005.05.003

Chiesa, A., & Serretti, A. (2009). Mindfulness-based stress reduction for stress management in healthy people: A review and meta-analysis. *The Journal of Alternative and Complementary Medicine, 15,* 593–600.

Clark, D. A., & Beck, A. T. (1990). Cognitive therapy of anxiety and depression. In R. E. Ingram (Ed.), *Contemporary psychological approaches to depression: Theory, research, and treatment* (pp. 155–167). New York: Plenum Publishing.

Cohen, J. A., Mannarino, A. P., & Deblinger, E. (2006). *Treating trauma and traumatic grief in children and adolescents.* New York: Guilford Press.

Crane, C., Barnhofer, T., Duggan, D. S., Hepburn, S., Fennell, M. V., & Williams, J. M. G. (2008). Mindfulness-based cognitive therapy and self-discrepancy in recovered depressed patients with a history of depression and suicidality. *Cognitive Therapy and Research, 32,* 775-787. doi:10.1007/s10608-008-9193-y

Creswell, J. D., Myers, H. F., Cole, S. W., & Irwin, M. R. (2009). Mindfulness meditation training effects on CD4+ T lymphocytes in HIV-1 infected adults: A small randomized controlled trial. *Brain, Behavior, and Immunity, 23,* 184–188. doi:10.1016/j.bbi.2008.07.004

Daleiden, E. L., & Vasey, M. W. (1997). An information-processing perspective on childhood anxiety. *Clinical Psychology Review, 17,* 407–429. doi:10.1016/S0272-7358(97)00010-X

Deikman, A. J. (1996). Intention, self, and spiritual experience: A functional model of consciousness. In S. R. Hameroff, A. W. Kaszniak, & A. C. Scott (Eds.), *Toward a science of consciousness: The first Tucson discussions and debates* (pp. 695–706). Cambridge, MA: MIT Press.

De Silva, P. (1985). Early Buddhist and modern behavioral strategies for the control of unwanted intrusive cognitions. *Psychological Record, 35,* 437–443.

Dhammananada, K. S. (1993). *What Buddhists believe.* Taipei, Taiwan: The Corporate Body of the Buddha Educational Foundation.

Doerfler, L. A., Connor, D. F., Volungis, A. M., & Toscano, P. F. (2007). Panic disorder in clinically referred children and adolescents. *Child Psychiatry and Human Development, 38,* 57–71. doi:10.1007/s10578-006-0042-5

Dumoulin, H. (1994). *Understanding Buddhism: Key themes* (J. S. O'Leary, Trans.). New York: Weatherhill.

Duncan, L. G., Coatsworth, J. D., & Greenberg, M. T. (2009). A model of mindful parenting: Implications for parent-child relationships and prevention research. *Clinical Child and Family Psychology Review, 12,* 255–270. doi:10.1007/s10567-009-0046-3

Eisendrath, S. J., Delucchi, K., Bitner, R., Fenimore, P., Smit, M., & McLane, M. (2008). Mindfulness-based cognitive therapy for treatment-resistant depression: A pilot study. *Psychotherapy and Psychosomatics, 77,* 319–320. doi:10.1159/000142525

Eldar, S., Ricon, T., & Bar-Haim, Y. (2008). Plasticity in attention: Implications for stress response in children. *Behaviour Research and Therapy, 46,* 450–461. doi:10.1016/j.brat.2008.01.012

Evans, S., Ferrando, S., Findler, M., Stowell, C., Smart, C., & Haglin, D. (2008). Mindfulness-based cognitive therapy for generalized anxiety disorder. *Journal of Anxiety Disorders, 22,* 716–721. doi:10.1016/j.janxdis.2007.07.005

Finucane, A., & Mercer, S. W. (2006). An exploratory mixed methods study of the acceptability and effectiveness of mindfulness-based cognitive therapy for patients with active depression and anxiety in primary care. *BMC Psychiatry, 6,* 14. doi:10.1186/1471-244X-6-14

Fleischman, P. R. (2005). *Karma and chaos.* Onalaska, WA: Vipassana Research Publications.

Foa, E. B., & Kozak, M. J. (1986). Emotional processing of fear: Exposure to corrective information. *Psychological Bulletin, 99,* 20–35. doi:10.1037/0033-2909.99.1.20

Freud, S. (1895). The psychotherapy of hysteria (J. Strachey, Trans.). In J. Breuer & S. Freud (Eds.), *Studies on Hysteria.* New York: Basic Books (reprinted 2000).

Galewitz, H. (Ed.). (2001). *Music: A book of quotations.* Mineola, NY: Dover Publications.

Greco, L., Smith, G. T., & Baer, R. A. (in press). Assessing mindfulness in children and adolescents: Development and validation of the Child and Adolescent Mindfulness Measure (CAMM). *Psychological Assessment.*

Greenberg, L. M., & Waldman, I. D. (1993). Developmental normative data on the test of variables of attention (T.O.V.A.). *Journal of Child Psychology and Psychiatry, 34,* 1019–1030. doi:10.1111/j.1469-7610.1993.tb01105.x

Greenland, S. K. (2010). *The mindful child: How to help your kid manage stress and become happier, kinder, and more compassionate.* New York: Free Press.

Gunaratana, H. (1993). *Mindfulness in plain English.* Boston: Wisdom Publications.

Hannesdottir, D. K., & Ollendick, T. H. (2007). The role of emotion regulation in the treatment of child anxiety disorders *Journal Clinical Child and Family Psychology 10,* 275–293.

Hayes, S. C. (2004). Acceptance and commitment therapy, relational frame theory, and the third wave of behavioral and cognitive therapies. *Behavior Therapy, 35,* 639–665. doi:10.1016/S0005-7894(04)80013-3

Heidenreich, T., Tuin, I., Pflug, B., Michal, M., & Michalak, J. (2006). Mindfulness-based cognitive therapy for persistent insomnia: A pilot study. *Psychotherapy and Psychosomatics, 75,* 188–189. doi:10.1159/000091778

Hendricks, C. G. (1975). Meditation as discrimination training: A theoretical note. *Journal of Transpersonal Psychology, 7,* 144–146.

Hettema, J. M., Neale, M. C., & Kendler, K. S. (2001). A review and meta-analysis of the genetic epidemiology of anxiety disorders. *American Journal of Psychiatry, 158,* 1568–1578. doi:10.1176/appi.ajp.158.10.1568

Hunt, C., Keogh, E., & French, C. C. (2007). Anxiety sensitivity, conscious awareness, and selective attentional biases in children. *Behaviour Research and Therapy, 45(3),* 497–509. doi:10.1016/j.brat.2006.04.001

In-Albon, T., & Schneider, S. (2007). Psychotherapy of childhood anxiety disorders: A meta-analysis. *Psychotherapy and Psychosomatics, 76,* 15–24. doi:10.1159/000096361

James A. A. C. J., Soler, A., & Weatherall, R. R. W. (2005). Cognitive behavioural therapy for anxiety disorders in children and adolescents. *Cochrane Database of Systematic Reviews, 19(4).* doi:10.1002/14651858.CD004690.pub2

James, W. (1890). *The principles of psychology.* New York: Dover Publications (reprinted 1950).

James, W. (1902). *The varieties of religious experience: A study in human nature.* New York: Random House (reprinted 1990).

Jha, A. P., Krompinger, J., & Baime, M. J. (2007). Mindfulness training modifies subsystems of attention. *Cognitive, Affective and Behavioral Neuroscience, 7,* 109–119. doi:10.3758/CABN.7.2.109

Kabat-Zinn, J. (1990). *Full catastrophe living.* New York: Bantam Doubleday Dell.

Kabat-Zinn, J. (1994). *Wherever you go, there you are: Mindfulness meditation for everyday life.* New York: Hyperion.

Kabat-Zinn, J. (2005). *Coming to our senses: Healing ourselves and the world through mindfulness.* New York: Hyperion.

Kabat-Zinn, J., Lipworth, L., & Burney, R. (1985). The clinical use of mindfulness meditation for the self-regulation of chronic pain. *Journal of Behavioral Medicine, 8,* 163–190. doi:10.1007/BF00845519

Kabat-Zinn, J., Massion, A. O., Kristeller, J., Peterson, L. G., Fletcher, K. E., Pbert, L., et al. (1992). Effectiveness of a meditation-based stress reduction program in the treatment of anxiety disorders. *American Journal of Psychiatry, 149,* 936–943.

Kabat-Zinn, M., & Kabat-Zinn, J. (1998). *Everyday blessings: The inner work of mindful parenting.* New York: Hyperion.

Kagan, J., & Snidman, N. (1999). Early childhood predictors of adult anxiety disorders. *Biological Psychiatry, 46,* 1536–1541. doi:10.1016/S0006-3223(99)00137-7

Kallen, V. L., Ferdinand, R. F., & Tulen, J. H. M. (2007). Early attention processes and anxiety in children. *Perceptual and Motor Skills, 104*(1), 221–235. doi:10.2466/PMS.104.1.221-235

Kearney, C. A., & Albano, A. M. (2000). *Therapist's guide for the prospective treatment of school refusal behavior.* San Antonio, TX: The Psychological Corporation.

Kenny, M. A., & Williams, J. M. G. (2007). Treatment-resistant depressed patients show a good response to mindfulness-based cognitive therapy. *Behaviour Research and Therapy, 45,* 617-625. doi:10.1016/j.brat.2006.04.008

Kessler, R. C., Berglund, P., Demler, O., Jin, R., & Walters, E. E. (2005). Lifetime prevalence and age-of-onset distributions of DSM–IV disorders in the National Comorbidity Survey Replication. *Archives of General Psychiatry, 62,* 593–602. doi:10.1001/archpsyc.62.6.593

Kessler, R. C., & Greenberg, P. E. (2002). The economic burden of anxiety and stress disorders. In K. L. Davis, D. Charney, J. T. Coyle, & C. Nemeroff (Eds.), *Neuropsychopharmacology: The fifth generation of progress* (pp. 981–992). Philadelphia: Lippincott Williams and Wilkins.

Kessler, R. C., Sonnega, A., Bromet, E., & Hughes, M. (1995). Posttraumatic stress disorder in the National Comorbidity Survey. *Archives of General Psychiatry, 52,* 1048–1060.

Khalid-Khan, S., Santibañez, M.-P., McMicken, C., & Rynn, M. A. (2007). Social anxiety disorder in children and adolescents: Epidemiology, diagnosis, and treatment. *Paediatric Drugs, 9,* 227–237. doi:10.2165/00148581-200709040-00004

Kierkegaard, S. (1844/1944). *The concept of dread* (W. Lowrie, Trans.). Princeton, NJ: Princeton University Press. (Original work published 1844).

Kingston, T., Dooley, B., Bates, A., Lawlor, E., & Malone, K. (2007). Mindfulness-based cognitive therapy for residual depressive symptoms. *Psychology and Psychotherapy: Theory, Research and Practice, 80,* 193–203.

Kuyken, W., Byford, S., Taylor, R. S., Holden, E., Barrett, B., Evans, A., et al. (2008). Mindfulness-based cognitive therapy to prevent relapse in recurrent depression. *Journal of Consulting and Clinical Psychology, 76,* 966–978. doi:10.1037/a0013786

Kwekkeboom, K. L. (2001). Pain management strategies used by patients with breast and gynecologic cancer with postoperative pain. *Cancer Nursing, 24,* 378–386. doi:10.1097/00002820-200110000-00009

Lantieri, L., & Goleman, D. (2008). *Building emotional intelligence: Techniques to cultivate inner strength in children.* Louisville, CO: Sounds True, Inc.

Lau, M. A., Bishop, S. R., Segal, Z. V., Buis, T., Anderson, N. D., Carlson, L., et al. (2006). The Toronto Mindfulness Scale: Development and validation. *Journal of Clinical Psychology, 62,* 1445–1467. doi:10.1002/jclp.20326

Lazarus, R. S., & Folkman, S. (1984). *Stress, appraisal, and coping.* New York: Springer.

Lee, J., Semple, R. J., Rosa, D., & Miller, L. (2008). Mindfulness-based cognitive therapy for children: Results of a pilot study. *Journal of Cognitive Psychotherapy, 22,* 15–28. doi:10.1891/0889.8391.22.1.15

Lewinsohn, P. M., Holm-Denoma, J. M., Small, J. W., Seeley, J. R., & Joiner Jr., T. E. (2008). Separation anxiety disorder in childhood as a risk factor for future mental illness. *Journal of the American Academy of Child and Adolescent Psychiatry, 47,* 548–555. doi:10.1097/CHI.0b013e31816765e7

Linehan, M. (1993). *Cognitive-behavioral treatment of borderline personality disorder.* New York: Guilford Press.

Lyubomirsky, S., Tucker, K. L., Caldwell, N. D., & Berg, K. (1999). Why ruminators are poor problem solvers: Clues from the phenomenology of dysphoric rumination. *Journal of Personality and Social Psychology, 77,* 1041–1060. doi:10.1037/0022-3514.77.5.1041

Ma, H. S., & Teasdale, J. D. (2004). Mindfulness-based cognitive therapy for depression: Replication and exploration of differential relapse prevention effects. *Journal of Consulting and Clinical Psychology, 72,* 31–40. doi:10.1037/0022-006X.72.1.31

Marks, I. M., & Gelder, M. G. (1966). Different ages of onset in varieties of phobia. *American Journal of Psychiatry, 123,* 218–221.

McEwen, B. (2002). *The end of stress as we know it.* Washington, DC: Joseph Henry Press.

McLeod, B. D., Wood, J. J., & Weisz, J. R. (2007). Examining the association between parenting and childhood anxiety: A meta-analysis. *Clinical Psychology Review, 27,* 155–172. doi:10.1016/j.cpr.2006.09.002

Merikangas, K. R., Avenevoli, S., Dierker, L., & Grillon, C. (1999). Vulnerability factors among children at risk for anxiety disorders. *Biological Psychiatry, 46,* 1523–1535. doi:10.1016/S0006-3223(99)00172-9

Merikangas, K. R., & Low, N. C. P. (2005). Genetic epidemiology of anxiety disorders. *Handbook of Experimental Pharmacology, 169,* 163–179.

Miller, J. J., Fletcher, K., & Kabat-Zinn, J. (1995). Three-year follow-up and clinical implications of a mindfulness meditation–based stress reduction intervention in the treatment of anxiety disorders. *General Hospital Psychiatry, 17,* 192–200. doi:10.1016/0163-8343(95)00025-M

Mowrer, O. H. (1960). *Learning theory and behavior.* New York: Wiley. doi:10.1037/10802-000

Muris, P., Mayer, B., Vermeulen, L., & Hiemstra, H. (2007). Theory-of-mind, cognitive development, and children's interpretation of anxiety-related physical symptoms. *Behaviour Research and Therapy, 45,* 2121–2132. doi:10.1016/j.brat.2007.02.014

Nolen-Hoeksema, S. (1998). Ruminative coping with depression. In J. Heckhausen & C. S. Dweck (Eds.), *Motivation and self-regulation across the life span* (pp. 237–256). New York: Cambridge University Press. doi:10.1017/CBO9780511527869.011

Ollendick, T. H., & Pincus, D. (2008). Panic disorder in adolescents. In R. G. Steele, T. D. Elkin, & M. C. Roberts (Eds.), *Handbook of evidence-based therapies for children and adolescents: Bridging science and practice. Issues in clinical child psychology* (pp. 83–102). New York Springer.

Orsillo, S. M., Roemer, L., & Barlow, D. H. (2003). Integrating acceptance and mindfulness into existing cognitive-behavioral treatment for GAD: A case study. *Cognitive and Behavioral Practice, 10,* 222–230. doi:10.1016/S1077-7229(03)80034-2

Piacentini, J., & Bergman, R. L. (2001). Developmental issues in cognitive therapy for childhood anxiety disorders. *Journal of Cognitive Psychotherapy, 15,* 165–182.

Piaget, J. (1962). The stages of the intellectual development of the child. *Bulletin of the Menninger Clinic, 26*(3), 120–128.

Pio, E. (1988). *Buddhist psychology: A modern perspective.* New Delhi, India: Abhinav Publications.

Proeve, M. J. (2001). *Remorse: Its description and its interpersonal effects.* Unpublished doctoral dissertation, University of South Australia, Adelaide.

Quirin, M., Pruessner, J. C., & Kuhl, J. (2008). HPA system regulation and adult attachment anxiety: Individual differences in reactive and awakening cortisol. *Psychoneuroendocrinology, 33,* 581–590. doi:10.1016/j.psyneuen.2008.01.013

Rapee, R. M., & Sanderson, W. C. (1998). *Social phobia: Clinical application of evidence-based psychotherapy.* Northvale, NJ: Jason Aronson.

Ree, M. J., & Craigie, M. A. (2007). Outcomes following mindfulness-based cognitive therapy in a heterogeneous sample of adult outpatients. *Behaviour Change, 24,* 70–86. doi:10.1375/bech.24.2.70

Ritchhart, R., & Perkins, D. N. (2000). Life in the mindful classroom: Nurturing the disposition of mindfulness. *Journal of Social Issues, 56,* 27–47. doi:10.1111/0022-4537.00150

Roemer, L., Salters-Pedneault, K., & Orsillo, S. M. (2006). Incorporating mindfulness- and acceptance-based strategies in the treatment of generalized anxiety disorder. In R. A. Baer (Ed.), *Mindfulness-based treatment approaches: Clinician's guide to evidence base and applications* (pp. xv, 424). Burlington, MA: Elsevier/Academic Press.

Ronan, K. R., & Kendall, P. C. (1997). Self-talk in distressed youth: States-of-mind and content specificity. *Journal of Clinical Child Psychology, 26*, 330–337. doi:10.1207/s15374424jccp2604_1

Roth, B., & Robbins, D. (2004). Mindfulness-based stress reduction and health-related quality of life: Findings from a bilingual inner-city patient population. *Psychosomatic Medicine, 66*, 113–123. doi:10.1097/01.PSY.0000097337.00754.09

Rousseau, J.-J. (1979). *Reveries of the solitary walker* (P. France, Trans.). London: Penguin. (Original work published 1782.)

Rueda, M., Fan, J., McCandliss, B. D., Halparin, J. D., Gruber, D. B., Lercari, L. P., et al. (2004). Development of attentional networks in childhood. *Neuropsychologia, 42*, 1029–1040. doi:10.1016/j.neuropsychologia.2003.12.012

Samuelson, M., Carmody, J., Kabat-Zinn, J., & Bratt, M. A. (2007). Mindfulness-based stress reduction in Massachusetts correctional facilities. *The Prison Journal, 87*, 254–268. doi:10.1177/0032885507303753

Sawyer Cohen, J. A., & Semple, R. J. (2009). Mindful parenting: A call for research. *Journal of Child and Family Studies.* doi:10.1007/s10826-009-9285-7

Schwartz, C. E., Snidman, N., & Kagan, J. (1999). Adolescent social anxiety as an outcome of inhibited temperament in childhood. *Journal of the American Academy of Child and Adolescent Psychiatry, 38*(8), 1008–1015.

Segal, Z. V., Bieling, P., Young, T., Macqueen, G., Cooke, R., Martin, L., et al. (2010). Antidepressant monotherapy vs sequential pharmacotherapy and Mindfulness-Based Cognitive Therapy, or placebo, for relapse prophylaxis in recurrent depression. *Archives of General Psychiatry, 67*, 1256–1264. PMID:21135325

Segal, Z. V., Williams, J. M. G., & Teasdale, J. D. (2002). *Mindfulness-based cognitive therapy for depression: A new approach to preventing relapse.* New York: Guilford Press.

Semple, R. J., & Lee, J. (2008). Treating anxiety with mindfulness: Mindfulness-based cognitive therapy for children. In L. A. Greco & S. C. Hayes (Eds.), *Acceptance and mindfulness interventions for children, adolescents, and families* (pp. 94–134). Oakland, CA: Context Press/New Harbinger Publications.

Semple, R. J., Lee, J., Rosa, D., & Miller, L. F. (2010). A randomized trial of mindfulness-based cognitive therapy for children: Promoting mindful attention to enhance social-emotional resiliency in children. *Journal of Child and Family Studies, 19*, 218–229. doi:10.1007/s10826-10009-19301-y

Semple, R. J., Reid, E. F. G, & Miller, L. (2005). Treating anxiety with mindfulness: An open trial of mindfulness training for anxious children. *Journal of Cognitive Psychotherapy, 19*, 379–392. doi:10.1891/jcop.2005.19.4.379

Shapiro, D. A. (1987). Implications of psychotherapy research for the study of meditation. In M. A. West (Ed.), *The psychology of meditation* (pp. 173–188). New York: Oxford University Press.

Shapiro, S. L., Bootzin, R. R., Figueredo, A. J., Lopez, A. M., & Schwartz, G. E. (2003). The efficacy of mindfulness-based stress reduction in the treatment of sleep disturbance in women with breast cancer: An exploratory study. *Journal of Psychosomatic Research, 54*(1), 85–91. doi:10.1016/S0022-3999(02)00546-9

Shapiro, S. L., Schwartz, G. E., & Bonner, G. (1998). Effects of mindfulness-based stress reduction on medical and premedical students. *Journal of Behavioral Medicine, 21,* 581–599. doi:10.1023/A:1018700829825

Shear, K., Jin, R., Ruscio, A. M., Walters, E. E., & Kessler, R. C. (2006). Prevalence and correlates of estimated DSM–IV child and adult separation anxiety disorder in the National Comorbidity Survey Replication. *American Journal of Psychiatry, 163,* 1074–1083. doi:10.1176/appi.ajp.163.6.1074

Sheehan, D. V., Sheehan, K. E., & Minichiello, W. E. (1981). Age of onset of phobic disorders: A reevaluation. *Comprehensive Psychiatry, 22,* 544–553. doi: 10.1016/0010-440X(81)90002-X

Sibinga, E. M. S., Stewart, M., Magyari, T., Welsh, C. K., Hutton, N., & Ellen, J. M. (2008). Mindfulness-based stress reduction for HIV-infected youth: A pilot study. *Explore: The Journal of Science and Healing, 4,* 36–37. doi:10.1016/j.explore.2007.10.002

Siegel, D. J. (2007). *The mindful brain: Reflection and attunement in the cultivation of well-being.* New York: Norton.

Silverman, W. K., Pina, A. A., & Viswesvaran, C. (2008). Evidence-based psychosocial treatments for phobic and anxiety disorders in children and adolescents. *Journal of Clinical Child and Adolescent Psychology, 37,* 105–130. doi:10.1080/15374410701817907

Southam-Gerow, M. A., & Kendall, P. C. (2000). A preliminary study of the emotion understanding of youths referred for treatment of anxiety disorders. *Journal of Clinical Child Psychology, 29,* 319–327. doi:10.1207/S15374424JCCP2903_3

Spielberger, C. D., & Sarason, I. G. (Eds.). (1978). *Stress and anxiety.* Washington, DC: Hemisphere.

Suttie, J. (2007). Mindful kids, peaceful schools. *Greater Good, 4,* 28–31.

Tang, Y.-Y., Ma, Y., Wang, J., Fan, Y., Feng, S., Lu, Q., et al. (2007). Short-term meditation training improves attention and self-regulation. *Proceedings of the National Academy of Sciences, 104,* 17152–17156. doi:10.1073/pnas.0707678104

Teasdale, J. D. (1999). Metacognition, mindfulness, and the modification of mood disorders. *Clinical Psychology and Psychotherapy, 6,* 146–155. doi:10.1002/(SICI)1099-0879(199905)6:2<146::AID-CPP195>3.0.CO;2-E

Teasdale, J. D., Segal, Z., & Williams, J. M. G. (1995). How does cognitive therapy prevent depressive relapse and why should attentional control (mindfulness) training help? *Behaviour Research and Therapy, 33,* 25–39. doi:10.1016/0005-7967(94)E0011-7

Teasdale, J. D., Segal, Z. V., Williams, J. M. G., Ridgeway, V. A., Soulsby, J. M., & Lau, M. A. (2000). Prevention of relapse/recurrence in major depression by mindfulness-based cognitive therapy. *Journal of Consulting and Clinical Psychology, 68,* 615–623. doi:10.1037/0022-006X.68.4.615

Twenge, J. M. (2000). The age of anxiety? Birth cohort change in anxiety and neuroticism, 1952–1993. *Journal of Personality and Social Psychology, 79,* 1007–1021. doi:10.1037/0022-3514.79.6.1007

Vogel, J. M., & Vernberg, E. M. (1993). Psychological responses of children to natural and human-made disasters: I. Children's psychological responses to disasters. *Journal of Clinical Child Psychology, 22,* 464–484. doi:10.1207/s15374424jccp2204_7

Walach, H., Buchheld, N., Buttenmüller, V., Kleinknecht, N., & Schmidt, S. (2006). Measuring mindfulness: The Freiburg Mindfulness Inventory (FMI). *Personality and Individual Differences, 40*, 1543–1555. doi:10.1016/j.paid.2005.11.025

Washburn, M. C. (1978). Observations relevant to a unified theory of meditation. *Journal of Transpersonal Psychology, 10*, 45–65.

Watson, D., Mineka, S., Clark, L. A., & Starcevic, V. (1999). Dimensions underlying the anxiety disorders: A hierarchical perspective. *Current Opinion in Psychiatry, 12*, 181–186. doi:10.1097/00001504-199903000-00007

Watts, A. (1961). *Psychotherapy east and west.* New York: Random House.

Wells, A. (2002). GAD, metacognition, and mindfulness: An information processing analysis. *Clinical Psychology: Science and Practice, 9*, 95–100. doi:10.1093/clipsy/9.1.95

Wenk-Sormaz, H. (2005). Meditation can reduce habitual responding. *Advances in Mind-Body Medicine, 21*, 33–49.

Williams, J. M. G., Alatiq, Y., Crane, C., Barnhofer, T., Fennell, M. J. V., Duggan, D. S., et al. (2008). Mindfulness-based cognitive therapy (MBCT) in bipolar disorder: Preliminary evaluation of immediate effects on between-episode functioning. *Journal of Affective Disorders, 107*, 275–279. doi:10.1016/j.jad.2007.08.022

Williams, J. M. G., Duggan, D. S., Crane, C., & Fennell, M. J. V. (2006). Mindfulness-based cognitive therapy for prevention of recurrence of suicidal behavior. *Journal of Clinical Psychology, 62*, 201–210. doi:10.1002/jclp.20223

Williams, J. M. G., Teasdale, J. D., Segal, Z. V., & Soulsby, J. (2000). Mindfulness-based cognitive therapy reduces overgeneral autobiographical memory in formerly depressed patients. *Journal of Abnormal Psychology, 109*, 150–155. doi:10.1037/0021-843X.109.1.150

Wisner, B. L., Jones, B., & Gwin, D. (2010). School-based meditation practices for adolescents: A resource for strengthening self-regulation, emotional coping, and self-esteem. *Children and Schools, 32*, 150–159.

Witkiewitz, K., Marlatt, G. A., & Walker, D. (2005). Mindfulness-based relapse prevention for alcohol and substance use disorders. *Journal of Cognitive Psychotherapy, 19*, 211-228. doi:10.1891/jcop.2005.19.3.211

Woody, S. R., Chambless, D. L., & Glass, C. R. (1997). Self-focused attention in the treatment of social phobia. *Behaviour Research and Therapy, 35*, 117–129. doi:10.1016/S0005-7967(96)00084-8

Yalom, I. D. (2005). *The theory and practice of group psychotherapy* (5th ed.). New York: Basic Books.

Yook, K., Lee, S.-H., Ryu, M., Kim, K.-H., Choi, T. K., Suh, S. Y., et al. (2008). Usefulness of mindfulness-based cognitive therapy for treating insomnia in patients with anxiety disorders: A pilot study. *Journal of Nervous and Mental Disease, 196*, 501–503. doi:10.1097/NMD.0b013e31817762ac

Zylowska, L., Ackerman, D. L., Yang, M. H., Futrell, J. L., Horton, N. L., Hale, T. S., et al. (2008). Mindfulness meditation training in adults and adolescents with ADHD: A feasibility study. *Journal of Attention Disorders, 11*, 737–746. doi:10.1177/1087054707308502

Randye J. Semple, PhD, is assistant professor in the department of psychiatry and behavioral sciences at the University of Southern California, where she teaches and provides clinical supervision to psychiatry residents and graduate students. Her research and clinical interests focus on the development and integration of mindfulness-based interventions for children in psychiatric clinical care.

Jennifer Lee, PhD, is a clinical psychologist in private practice and at the Children's Home of Poughkeepsie, a residential treatment center, where she provides clinical consultation and direct care for at-risk children and their families. She holds an adjunct faculty appointment at Marist College teaching graduate students in the field of mental health counseling.

Illustrator Denise McMorrow Mahone, MFA, is an artist pursuing a doctorate in clinical psychology at Duquesne University in Pittsburgh, PA. Her writing, sculpture, drawing, and photography explore our spiritual, ecological, and poetic aspects as human beings. She lives with her husband, Paco, and young sons, Eamonn and Gabriel.

Index

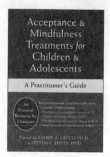
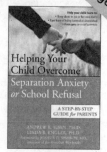

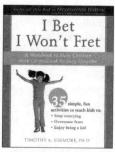
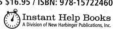